Cases and Readings
in
Quantitative Analysis
for
Management

Barry Render
University of New Orleans

Ralph M. Stair, Jr.
Florida State University

Cases and Readings
in
Quantitative Analysis
for
Management

Allyn and Bacon, Inc.

BOSTON   **LONDON**   **SYDNEY**   **TORONTO**

Library of Congress Cataloging in Publication Data

Render, Barry.
    Cases and readings in quantitative analysis for management.

    1. Management science—Case studies.   2. Operations research—Case studies.   I. Stair, Ralph M.
II. Title.
T56.R543   658.4'03   81-20498
ISBN 0-205-07754-4 (pbk.)   AACR2

Printed in the United States of America.
10 9 8 7 6 5 4 3 2 1   87 86 85 84 83 82

To

Pnina and Gershon

Randy and Judy

Contents

PART TWO

Readings

Topical Table of Contents

Linear Programming

Transportation Modeling

Assignment Modeling

Goal Programming

Queuing Theory

Simulation

Network Analysis

Markov Analysis

Implementation

Preface

While the standard lecture used in most courses is an adequate method of teaching students the fundamentals of quantitative analysis, it does not always bridge the gap between theory and application. Furthermore, much of the difficulty in using quantitative techniques has not been with the theory, but with the actual application of these techniques to real problems. The purpose of *Cases and Readings in Quantitative Analysis for Management* is to help bridge that gap.

This book contains cases and readings which cover all the major management science techniques. It is an important part of our comprehensive and up-to-date learning package in quantitative analysis. This package includes an easy-to-understand text, *Quantitative Analysis for Management* (Allyn and Bacon, 1982), on the fundamentals of quantitative analysis; a study guide for students; this book; and an instructor's manual to aid in presenting the importance and use of quantitative analysis techniques. This case/reader, however, can be used to accompany any standard management science textbook. It can also be used with our book, *Management Science: A Self-Correcting Approach* (Allyn and Bacon, 1978).

A topical listing at the beginning of this book will help you find the cases and readings appropriate to the quantitative technique you are covering. "How to Analyze and Present a Case," at the beginning of the "Cases" section, provides guidelines for students who understand quantitative models but have difficulty presenting the results of their study. All of the cases and readings are followed by discussion questions.

Part One contains thirty-six nontheoretical cases describing real situations and companies (some of the names have been changed). The cases use various quantitative analysis techniques and address problems related to marketing, finance, management, accounting, and production. Each major area of management science is covered. Students will be able to apply their knowledge of quantitative techniques by developing, step-by-step, solutions to realistic problems. Most of the cases are short (fewer than four pages), allowing students time to analyze and present the case thoroughly. This helps students start at a reasonable pace, and provides them with positive reinforcement in using quantitative techniques.

Part Two of this book contains readings in quantitative analysis. Some of these readings explore complex and difficult problems that have taken a team of people a year or more to complete. Time limitations would make it difficult to investigate these broader problems through the case method. Most students do not have the time during their academic year to undertake such a detailed analysis. The readings provide an excellent opportunity to see how complex problems can be solved using quantitative techniques.

The readings present applications of quantitative analysis in business, industry, and government. They include a wide mix of quantitative techniques, problem length and complexity, and functional areas. All recent publications, they use a minimum of mathematics while describing real applications to problems as diverse as college admissions, hospital surgery scheduling, and drive-in banking.

Quantitative analysis is a dynamic and exciting management tool. Today's world offers numerous opportunities to use quantitative analysis in solving difficult problems. *Cases and Readings in Quantitative Analysis for Management,* as part of our learning package in quantitative analysis, will enable you to use logic and rationality instead of whim and emotion in making intelligent choices.

These cases should be used for educational purposes only. They are designed for classroom purposes and not for purposes of research nor to illustrate either effective or ineffective handling of administrative problems.

Cases and Readings
in
Quantitative Analysis
for
Management

PART ONE

Cases

How to Analyze and Present a Case

While quantitative analysis techniques have been successfully implemented many times, numerous projects have also ended in partial or complete failure. Several recurring problems that prevent success are: (1) the inability to recognize the important problems, (2) difficulty in formulating the central problem, (3) the inability to actually visualize or understand the situation, (4) the inability to communicate with other managers and decision makers, (5) not meeting the assumptions of the quantitative techniques being used, (6) a lack of experience in working with "messy" data, and (7) a lack of experience in working in a complex organizational environment.

The case approach offers an excellent opportunity for students to employ quantitative analysis in realistic situations. It also provides a number of advantages that are either impossible or difficult to realize using standard lectures alone. A few of the advantages of the case method are:

1. The chance to identify and isolate the real problem from symptoms and from trivial problems.
2. Experience in developing one or more models that embody the essential elements of a particular situation or problem.
3. Increased awareness of the organization and how it really functions.
4. The ability to understand the impact of various environmental concerns, such as political, social, and legal systems, on the organization and the application of quantitative analysis techniques.
5. The opportunity to ask the appropriate questions when formulating the problem and gathering relevant information.
6. Experience in applying quantitative analysis techniques.
7. The ability to understand barriers that have blocked the successful application of quantitative techniques.

8. The opportunity to identify and isolate *qualitative* factors that will have a significant impact on the application of quantitative analysis methods.
9. The ability to think clearly in ambiguous and complex situations.
10. The chance to develop recommendations and action plans that are consistent with the organization's goals and creative in their problem-solving strategy.
11. The opportunity to determine what information is required in applying one or more quantitative analysis techniques in an actual setting.
12. Practice in making verbal presentations and in discussing quantitative analysis techniques in groups.
13. Practice in writing formal reports that use quantitative analysis to solve problems.

How to Analyze a Case

There is no one best approach to analyze a quantitative analysis case. However, a number of general steps and guidelines can be followed to ensure better case analysis. While the following steps are presented sequentially, it may be necessary during a specific case analysis to reorder or modify them, for they are intended to provide a general framework.

1. Preview the Case.   The purpose of the first step is to give you an overview of the case and the existing situation. You may wish to read rapidly or to skim through the case, taking notes and jotting down important ideas, key problems, and critical factors. You may even wish to write down ideas relating to the main problems or issues in the case at this point.

2. Read the Case.   Once you have previewed the case, read it in detail, taking careful notes on important facts, problems, and issues found within the case. While you are reading the case in detail, you should be looking for major problems, subproblems, controllable and uncontrollable variables, constraints and limitations, alternatives available to the organization, and possible quantitative analysis techniques that might be used in solving the problems facing the organization. All of these factors should be listed and then summarized in writing.

3. Formulate the Problem.   If you have done a good job with the first two steps, problem formulation will be greatly simplified. The purpose of this step is to specify the major problem or issue at hand. At this point, you should not be concerned with what quantitative analysis techniques will be used. Instead, you should strive to isolate the major issues and the central problems facing the organization. To formulate the problem, it may be necessary to reread certain parts of the case. After the problem has been formulated, it should be summarized and recorded in writing.

4. Identify Important Variables.   Once the problem has been identified, the next step is to identify important variables. These variables could be the number of people in a maintenance department, the number of items to produce in a manufacturing operation, the return from an investment, the state of the economy in six months, the outcome of future legislation or a political race, and so on. The variables that are identified in this step should be related to the problem. Only those variables that could have an impact on the problem should be identified. Furthermore, it is important to distinguish between controllable and uncontrollable variables. A controllable variable is one over which the manager or decision maker has total control, while an uncontrollable variable is one over which the manager or decision maker has little or no control.

5. Determine Organizational Objectives.   Before any problem can be solved, it is necessary to specify the goals and objectives of the organization. For most situations, this will be profit maximization or cost minimization. However, other organizational goals or objectives may be important. For example, a company may wish to avoid stockouts, or a hospital may desire a specific patient-to-doctor ratio. It is desirable to specify mathematically the objectives of the organization. For example, it may be possible to develop a mathematical expression for the organization's profit. This could be similar or identical to the objective function of a linear programming problem. If it is impossible to write a mathematical expression for the organization's objectives, a concise written statement of the organization's objectives should be prepared.

6. Determine Organizational Restrictions or Constraints.   Typically, companies and organizations have a number of limitations or constraints over which they have little or no control, for example, short run restriction of plant capacity, or legal restraints on trade and business interactions. Whenever possible, mathematically specify these restrictions and constraints. When such specification is not possible, a concise word statement should be written.

7. List the Alternatives.   The next step is to list the alternatives available to management in solving the problem. A common mistake is not developing a complete list. Creativity and imagination are useful talents to use in developing viable alternatives. If an alternative is not listed, it likely will not be considered during later stages of analysis. As a result, many viable alternatives may be totally overlooked. Don't forget that you will always have the alternative of doing nothing.

8. Analyze the Assumption. The eighth step is to discover and specify assumptions that must be made in analyzing the case. You may have to assume, for example, that demand for a particular product over a specified time period is constant; or that the only relevant inventory costs are holding costs and carrying costs; or that the arrival of individuals at a hospital is Poisson distributed. All relevant assumptions must be concisely formulated and listed.

9. Select a Quantitative Technique. If a good job has been done in the previous steps, it will be easy to select the appropriate quantitative analysis technique. This technique will allow you to solve the problem and obtain the organizational objectives without violating the inherent restrictions and constraints, while operating within the assumptions of the situation.

10. Acquire Input Data. Once a quantitative analysis technique has been selected, the next step is to acquire the necessary input data. To do this you simply identify what inputs are necessary and locate these data in the case. In some cases, however, the necessary input data for one or more quantitative techniques will not be presented in the case. For these situations, it may be feasible to make assumptions about the input data. If such assumptions are made, don't forget to list them in Step 8.

11. Develop the Solution. This usually involves the application of one or more quantitative analysis techniques, e.g., a linear programming problem, a transportation problem, an inventory problem, etc. Many times the solution should also embody important qualitative and judgmental factors that cannot be quantified. Your solution should be both *quantitative* and *qualitative*. People solve problems, models do not. If the assumptions made in applying the quantitative analysis technique are not consistent with the situation, the quantitative analysis technique should not be used, or it should be used as an input factor along with other judgmental factors in making a sound decision.

12. Test the Solution.   When quantitative analysis techniques are used, the solution should be tested for both internal and external validity. Internal validity checks the extent to which the model and quantitative analysis technique are internally consistent and accurate. External validity investigates the extent to which the solution and the model accurately represent the actual situation under investigation. All quantitative analysis techniques can undergo sensitivity analysis. Sensitivity analysis tests to see how sensitive the final solution is to changes in the input data or in the model itself. Solutions that are highly sensitive should be analyzed with care. If the input data could be inaccurate or if the model could be incorrectly specified, great care should be taken in interpreting the solution.

13. Analyze the Results.   The solution of the quantitative analysis technique may represent only one of many inputs a decision maker uses in solving the stated problem. Moreover, the model results may have to be tempered with information about the environment, the assumptions of the model, and the quality of the input data. Analyzing the results involves incorporating the quantitative analysis solution with the judgmental factors that have an important bearing on the possible alternative actions. At this stage, it may become apparent that you have incorrectly formulated the problem, and thus it will be necessary to return to an earlier step to incorporate considerations not previously included. The result of this step is a written statement that integrates the quantitative analysis with all other factors deemed important to the solution of the stated problem.

14. Formulate the Action Plan. The formulation of the action plan is an extension of the analysis of results (the previous step). Here you must make specific recommendations aimed at solving all of the problems and subproblems. The action plan should attempt to solve both present and future problems. Undesirable situations that may occur in the future should also be addressed during this stage. In addition, the action plan should also embody the rationale you used in selecting alternatives for inclusion in the action plan.

15. Present the Action Plan. The action plan or recommendations can be presented either in writing or verbally during class discussion. Because of the importance of this presentation, the following section will be devoted to presenting the results of case analysis, and therefore this topic will not be discussed at any length at this point.

16. Implement, Evaluate, and Maintain the Action Plan. Unfortunately, many quantitative analysis personnel believe their job is over after the action plan has been formulated. However, for an action plan to be useful, it must be carefully implemented and periodically evaluated and maintained. Implementation is the process of placing the plan into action; it requires that you develop written procedures for making the action plan operational. Procedures should also be established that will force the periodic evaluation and maintenance of the action plan. Since we live in a dynamic environment, it becomes necessary to evaluate the action plan periodically and modify it as necessary. This modification is called action plan maintenance.

How to Present a Case
After you analyze a case, you may be asked to present the case in a written report or verbally to the class. During your presentation, you have two overall

objectives. First, you should inform your instructor and classmates, either in writing or through the verbal presentation, of the results of your case analysis. Here you will discuss the steps you completed during case analysis, including the formulation of the problem and the subproblems, the identification of important variables, the objectives and the goals of the organization, constraints and restrictions to be considered, alternatives facing the organization, important assumptions, the quantitative technique or techniques employed, the input data for and solution from the quantitative techniques, how the solution was tested and analyzed, how the action plan was formulated, and suggestions for action plan implementation evaluation and maintenance. Your second objective is to convince your instructor and classmates that your approach and action plan are the best. Here you will be marketing and selling your ideas to others. You need to note other action plans you considered, and reveal why yours is better and will help the organization discussed in the case obtain its goals and objectives while solving its inherent problems.

If you are preparing a written case, you should have a well organized report. While there is no one best way of organizing the written report, the following outline may be used as a model in preparing major sections for your written report:

   I.   Table of Contents
  II.   Summary of Findings
 III.   Background Information
  IV.   Problem Statement
   V.   Analysis of Alternatives
  VI.   Detailed Recommendations
 VII.   Implementation and Evaluation
VIII.   Appendices

In developing the written report you should develop a draft and then revise the draft in producing the final written report. Before you write the draft you should consider the level and needs of the reader, carefully organize and outline the report, and determine what you plan to say and how you will be persuading others to accept your action plan. When writing the *draft*, do the following: write quickly and without hesitation, not worrying about spelling or grammar; use paragraphs that contain only one or two major ideas; use familiar and simple words; support all statements with fact; and use forceful and convincing arguments. In *revising* the draft you need to check the organization of the paper to make sure it is logical and clear, correct and accurate, and free from grammatical errors and problems.

The same outline employed with the written report can be used for an oral presentation. When making an oral presentation, you should keep a number of points in mind. These are briefly outlined.

1. Adequately prepare the case before class.
2. Keep an open mind.
3. Market and sell your ideas.
4. Incorporate outside experiences.
5. Listen to others.
6. Be brief.
7. Take an offensive position instead of a defensive position.
8. Listen to and learn from other students.
9. Be courteous and constructive.
10. Don't repeat yourself.
11. Don't repeat others.
12. Don't overemphasize one particular idea.
13. Avoid changing the topic suddenly.

Abjar Transport Company

1

In 1980, Samir Khaldoun, after receiving an MBA degree from a leading university in the United States, returned to Jeddah, Saudi Arabia, where his family has extensive business holdings. Samir's first assignment was to stabilize and develop a newly formed, family-owned transport company—Abjar Transport.

An immediate problem facing Samir was the determination of the number of trucks needed to handle the forecasted freight volume. Heretofore, trucks were added to the fleet on an "as needed" basis without comprehensive capacity planning. This approach created problems of driver recruitment, truck service and maintenance, and excessive demurrage because of delays at unloading docks and retention of cargo containers.

Demurrage penalties are quite high for the Jeddah Islamic port. The following is a demurrage schedule for unloaded freight:

1. A 10-day "free period" is allowed to clear the dock of freight.
2. After the "free period," a penalty of one riyal[1] will be levied per cargo ton for the

By Amr Salaam and Professor Joe Iverstine, Southeastern Louisiana State University. Used by permission.

1. Approximately three riyals equal one U.S. dollar.

first 24 hours. A penalty of two riyals per cargo ton will be assessed for the second 24 hours; a penalty of three riyals per cargo ton will be levied for the third 24 hours, and so forth.

As one can see from this schedule, high demurrage penalties will be assessed if freight is unduly delayed at the Jeddah dock.

Samir forecasts that Abjar's freight volume should average 160,000 tons per month with a standard deviation of 30,000 tons. Freight is unloaded on a uniform basis throughout the month. A schedule of freight volume and corresponding probabilities are included in Table 1.

Table 1.

Less than (tons)	Probability
100,000	0.02
130,000	0.16
160,000	0.50
190,000	0.84
220,000	0.98

After extensive investigation, Samir concluded that the fleet should be standardized to 40-foot Mercedes 2624 6×4 tractor-trailer rigs, which are suitable for carrying two 20-foot containers, one 30-foot container, or one 40-foot container. Cargo capacity is approximately 60 tons per rig. Each tractor-trailer unit is estimated to cost 240,000 riyals. Moreover, they must meet Saudi Arabian specifications—double cooling fans, oversized radiators, and special high-temperature tires. Historical evidence suggests that these Mercedes rigs will operate 96 percent of the time.

Approximately 25 percent of the freight handled by these tractor-trailer rigs is containerized in container lengths of 20, 30, and 40 feet. (The balance of the freight—75 percent—is not containerized.) The 20-foot containers hold approximately 20 tons of cargo; the 30-foot containers hold 45 tons; and the 40-foot containers

hold 60 tons of freight. Approximately 60 percent of the containerized freight is shipped in 40-foot units; 20 percent is shipped in 30-foot units; and 20 percent is transported in 20-foot units. The demurrage schedule for containers is as follows:

1. A five-day "free period" is allowed to return containers to the port.
2. After the "free period" a penalty of 1,000 riyals is levied per container for the first 24 hours. A penalty of 2,000 riyals is assessed per container for the second 24 hours. A penalty of 3,000 riyals per container is assessed for the third 24 hours, and so forth.

Abjar Transport picks up freight at the dock and delivers it directly to customers, or warehouses it for later delivery. Based on his study of truck routing and scheduling patterns, Samir concluded that each rig should pick up freight at the dock three times each day.

An analysis of financial statements reveals that the profit and overhead contribution of each ton of freight handled is 2.25 riyals. The Khaldoun family has estimated that its opportunity cost for invested capital is 20 percent.

DISCUSSION QUESTION

How many tractor-trailer rigs should makeup the Abjar Transport fleet?

Agri-Chem Corporation

2

In June, 1980, Harry Sinclair, General Manager of the Texas Division of Agri-Chem Corporation, received notification from Ben Elliot of Enerco that natural gas supplies were being rapidly depleted. In the event of a shortage, Enerco, the main producer and distributor of natural gas in the Gulf South region, would allocate gas to its customers under the following provisions established by the Federal Power Commission:

First Priority: Residential and commercial heating and cooling

Second Priority: Commercial and industrial firms that use natural gas as a source of raw material

Third Priority: Industrial firms that use natural gas as a boiler fuel

Elliot related to Sinclair that most of Agri-Chem's uses were in the second and third priority classifications. Hence, Agri-Chem would probably be subjected to "rolling brownouts"— temporary and periodic curtailments of natural gas supplies. Enerco planned to monitor its pipeline pressures and order reductions to maintain minimum levels. Elliot preferred that Enerco's customers initiate the reduction process to minimize the effect on their industrial processes.

By Professors Jerry Kinard and Joe Iverstine, Southeastern Louisiana State University. Used by permission.

Enerco was authorized, however, to curtail supplies unilaterally if pipeline pressure fell below minimum levels.

The natural gas shortage was created by the unprecedented heat wave of the summer of 1980. Electrical generating plants were operating at capacity to supply electricity to operate air conditioning and refrigeration units. Although long-range plans called for these utility companies to convert to coal, oil, or nuclear fuel, natural gas remained the dominant boiler fuel.

CURTAILMENT PLAN

Agri-Chem's problem was to determine which of its complexes would be least affected by a gas curtailment. Its Texas Division is located in the greater Houston area; plants are located in the suburbs of Dear Park and Battleground. Both of these areas would be included in the curtailment region in the event of a brownout. Except for Agri-Chem's ammonia operations, all gas purchased was used as boiler fuel. In its am-

Table 1. *Contribution to Profit and Overhead*

Product	$/ton
ammonia	80
ammonium phosphate	120
ammonium nitrate	140
urea	140
hydrofluoric acid	90
chlorine	70
caustic soda	60
vinyl chloride monomer	90

monia plant, gas was used as a source of raw materials. (The manufacture of ammonia uses natural gas in the steam reforming process.)

In a detailed discussion with Elliot, Sinclair learned that Enerco would not specify the products to be curtailed. The curtailment procedure would be based primarily on a customer's usage pattern. Hence, Agri-Chem had the flexibility to absorb curtailments where they would have minimum impact on profits.

On this information, Sinclair called a staff meeting to discuss a contingency plan for allocation of natural gas among the firm's products if curtailments became a reality. The specific objective was to minimize the impact on profits/ overhead contribution. After a week of study, the information in Tables 1 and 2 was presented to Sinclair.

Agri-Chem's contract with Enerco specified a maximum of 90,000 cu.ft. $\times 10^3$ per day for its complexes. However, curtailments are projected to be based on current usage, not on contractual maximums. Enerco projects curtailments in the range of 20 to 40 percent.

DISCUSSION QUESTIONS

1. Given the information presented above, develop a curtailment plan with a 20-percent reduction in natural gas.

2. Develop a second curtailment plan with a 40-percent reduction in natural gas.

Table 2. *Operational Data*

Product	Capacity (tons/day)	Production Rate (% of capacity)	Natural Gas Consumption (1000 cu.ft./ton)
ammonia	1500	80	8.0
ammonium phosphate	600	90	10.0
ammonium nitrate	700	70	12.0
urea	200	80	12.0
hydrofluoric acid	800	70	7.0
chlorine	1500	80	18.0
caustic soda	1600	80	20.0
vinyl chlorine monomer	1400	60	14.0

The Alpha Beta Gamma Record

3

Evan Hart is the managing editor of the monthly magazine for the collegiate members of Alpha Beta Gamma ($\alpha\beta\gamma$) National Fraternity. The $\alpha\beta\gamma$ *Record* is a 16-page two-color magazine with a circulation of 2,400.

There are two large phases of publishing the magazine. The first phase encompasses those tasks which the editor, Evan, performs himself. Evan is responsible for all facets of the magazine's production, from conception to preparation for the printer. His tasks, the most likely times for completion, and each task's predecessor(s) are delineated in Table 1.

The second phase includes those activities that the printer performs. The editor, of course, checks the printer's work for accuracy, but the primary responsibility for the completion of these tasks falls on the printer.

For the past few months, Evan has been faced with delays in completing the final product. Despite his efforts to produce a quality magazine at peak efficiencies, the delays recurred. These repeated delays naturally cause delays in mailing the subscriptions. Since the $\alpha\beta\gamma$ *Record* is the only source of information on upcoming regional events for collegiate members, it is important that the publication be released on time

By Michael Reiner and Professor Barry Render, Universit of New Orleans.

Table 1. *Evan's Tasks*

Activity	Predecessor(s)	Description	Time in Days
A	—	Greek happenings and correspondence	2
B	—	Conceptualizing the current issue	2
C	A	Applying happenings to current issue	1
D	C, B	Research or resource review	1
E	C, B	Interview with national officer	2
F	C, B	Photograph subjects	1
G	E	Photograph interviewee	2
H	F, G	Developing photograph	1
I	H	Printing photograph	3
J	E	Interview notes converted into copy (text)	3
K	D	Research notes converted into copy	2
L	K, J	Copy rewrite, corrections, and accurate typing	2
M	L	Copy submitted for review	2
N	M	Correction of reviewed copy	1
O	N	Copy folder compiled	0.5
P	I	Photo folder compiled	0.5
Q	O, P	Thumbnail layout sketch	1
R	Q	Submission of photos for galleys*	0
S	O, P	Manuscript to printer	1

*Galleys are typeset columns of submitted manuscript copy that is camera-ready.

so that the members have ample time to register for these functions. Most of these regional activities are not parties. Although they are designed to be enjoyable, the national organization has long emphasized the development of individual qualities, such as leadership, over party-ing. Since many $\alpha\beta\gamma$ alumni attend these functions, the collegians like to attend in order to make contacts with people with whom they might seek employment in a few years. Therefore, it is crucial that the issues be completed on time.

Table 2. *Printer's Tasks*

Act.	Pred.	Description	Thrift Print Time	Kwik Print Time
T	S	Galleys typeset	3	5
U	T	Galleys to editor and corrected	1	1
V	U	Galleys returned to printer	1	1
W	R,V	Paste-up	3	3
X	W	Pages* to editor for correction	1	0.5
Y	X	Pages to printer	1	1
Z	Y	Blueline† sent to editor	4	1
AA	Z	Blueline returned to printer	1	1
BB	AA	Customer copies	4	3

* Pages are xeroxed copies of the galleys pasted up into magazine format. They do not include photographs.
† Blueline is a one-color final product that includes photographs ready for final review. This is the last opportunity to make corrections before the final printing.

Since he cannot control the operations of his present printer, Thrift Print, Evan decided to investigate the possibility of changing printers in order to meet his deadlines for the magazine. He found another printer, Kwik Print, for a comparable price. The description of the second phase's activities, each activity's predecessor(s), and the most likely times for their completions for the respective printers is found in Table 2.

DISCUSSION QUESTIONS

1. Draw a PERT diagram of the production of the magazine from conception to completion.

2. Should Evan change printers? Why?

3. Evan has just learned that the owner of Thrift Print is an alumnus of $\alpha\beta\gamma$. What should he do in light of this fact?

Bartlett Nurseries, Inc.

4

In 1960, Harry Bartlett, a mechanical engineer for Mid-West Pump and Supply Company of Cleveland, Ohio, was transferred to Arlington, Texas, when the firm expanded its manufacturing operations to the Southwest. The proceeds from the sale of their Cleveland residence enabled the Bartlett family to purchase a five-acre tract of land just outside Arlington in the greater Dallas–Ft. Worth area. Except for the family dwelling on the property, the land was virtually barren. To improve the appearance of the homesite, the Bartletts planted fruit trees of various types, shrubbery, and a few small hardwood species. In addition, they continued to enjoy a hobby that they first experienced in Cleveland—the potting of small delicate plants. To accommodate and protect the growing volume of potted plants, a greenhouse was constructed, complete with heating and a sprinkler system.

The Bartlett home became the focal point for neighboring gardeners seeking vegetable plants, ferns, and various potted plants. At the suggestion of a neighbor Jenny Bartlett, Harry's wife, began selling these items to help defray some of their gardening expenses. Soon, the revenue generated from Jenny's sales required

By Professors Jerry Kinard and Joe Iverstine, Southeastern Louisiana State Univesity. Used by permission.

Harry Bartlett to obtain business licenses required by the state.

From 1960 through 1964, the Bartlett's oldest son, Mitchell, pursued a degree in landscape architecture at a nearby university. After graduation, he contemplated several job offers, but finally decided to open a family-owned nursery, thereby combining his knowledge and resources with those of his father. Bartlett Nurseries, Inc. was immediately successful. Mitchell received several landscaping contracts from banks, shopping centers, and fast food chains. In addition to providing plants and shrubbery for these projects, the nursery was awarded maintenance contracts as well.

FERTILIZER BLENDING

From the beginning, Harry Bartlett worked closely with the local agricultural extension service in order to recommend fertilizers to his customers. After extensive soil analyses, he discovered that standard fertilizer blends did not quite match the requirements of the north Texas soil conditions. Upon the recommendation of area soil chemists, and on the belief that significant profits could be made from selling fertilizer, Bartlett began mixing his own blends for sale to local customers. He was fully aware that

he would need to minimize his costs in order to compete with commercial fertilizers.

Harry's favorite blend was Nitrogrow-X. (Nitrogrow was the brand name adopted by Bartlett for his packaged fertilizer.) This fertilizer combined the following chemical compounds containing nitrogen: NG-100, NG-250, NG-350, and NG-500. The cost per pound for each compound is listed below.

Compound	Cost per pound
NG-100	$0.04
NG-250	0.05
NG-350	0.06
NG-500	0.08

Specifications for the Nitrogrow-X blend follow:

1. Fertilizer is packaged and sold in 100-pound bags.
2. NG-100 and NG-250 can constitute no more than 40 percent of the blend.
3. NG-350 and NG-500 must constitute at least 50 percent of the blend.
4. NG-500 must constitute at least 10 percent of the blend.

DISCUSSION QUESTION

What blend of the compounds will enable Bartlett to minimize the cost of a 100-pound bag of fertilizer?

Bay Area Bakery Company

5

PROPOSAL TO BUILD A NEW BAKERY

Bay Area Bakery Company[1] was a regional baker and distributor of bread and operated six bakeries, shown on the map in Figure 1. The manager of transportation and customer service for Bay Area Bakery Company was asked to prepare a report outlining the effect of the proposed San Jose, California, baking facility on the company's physical distribution system. The problem centered around the fact that marketing territories served by the Santa Cruz and Stockton bakeries had increased rapidly in population, necessitating consideration for locating and equipping a new baking plant at San Jose.

Varying costs of labor, ingredients, and operation affected the total cost of baking a standard quantity of bread at each of the locations. This average cost for each of the bakeries is shown in Table 1, along with the daily capacity at each location. The full line of the company's goods was baked at each of the six locations.

Bay Area sold its products at an average delivered price of $3.00 per cwt. and main-

James L. Heskett, Lewis M. Schneider, Robert M. Ivie, and Nicholas A. Glaskowsky, Jr., *Case Problems in Business Logistics.* Copyright © 1973 by the Ronald Press Company, New York. Reprinted by permission of John Wiley & Sons, Inc.

1. Names have been disguised.

over-the-road units. It was the transportation and customer service manager's job to minimize transportation costs from each of the baking plants to market areas. Within the limitations of the company's operations, he had achieved levels of costs shown in Table 2. He had also prepared an analysis of projected delivery costs between all company baking facilities and market areas, as shown in Table 3. Included in this projection were those costs of delivery which could be expected between the proposed plant at San Jose and other market areas.

A major reason for the suggested new baking plant at San Jose was the especially rapidly growing market which the area represented. It was expected that this market would double in the next 5 years, compared to an expected 10-percent increase in other markets (except less than 10 percent in San Francisco) during the same period. Also, the inefficiencies involved in serving San Jose from the Santa Cruz bakery could be relieved by the construction of a more efficient bakery in the growing San Jose market.

A bakery with daily capacity of 1,200 cwt. was planned. It was estimated that a facility of this size would cost $4 million fully equipped, and would be able to turn out bakery products at an average cost of $17 per hundred pounds. With the expected 5-year increase in demand, the supply pattern shown in Table 4 was projected for 5 years into the future.

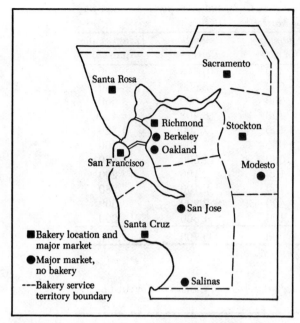

Figure 1. *Map of Bakeries and Marketing Territories Served by Each Bay Area Bakery*

tained uniform delivered prices on comparable quantity orders throughout its marketing territory. Average daily sales from each bakery for each major center of consumption are shown in Table 2.

To control physical distributing costs closely and to maintain tight control over the freshness of baked items, Bay Area operated its own fleet of privately owned local delivery trucks and

Table 1. *Baking Costs and Capacities, Bay Area Bakery Company Bakeries*

Location	Baking Cost (per cwt)	Daily Baking Capacity (in cwt)*
Santa Rosa	$19	500
Sacramento	$17	1,000
Richmond	$16	2,700
San Francisco	$17	2,000
Stockton	$18	500
Santa Cruz	$21	800

*Current value of each plant was roughly estimated at $300 per unit of daily capacity (cwt).

Table 2. *Current Average Daily Sales, Production Costs, and Transportation Costs, Bay Area Bakery Company (by Bakery and Major Market)**

Major Market	Bakery of Origin	Quantity (in cwt)	Production Costs ($)	Transportation Costs ($)
Santa Rosa	Santa Rosa	300	5,700	600
Sacramento	Sacramento	500	8,500	750
Richmond	Richmond	600	9,600	600
Berkeley	Richmond	400	6,400	400
Oakland	Richmond	1,100	17,600	1,320
San Francisco	San Francisco	1,300	22,100	1,300
San Jose	Santa Cruz	600	12,600	1,260
Santa Cruz	Santa Cruz	100	2,100	200
Salinas	Santa Cruz	100	2,100	280
Stockton	Stockton	400	7,200	600
Modesto	Stockton	100	1,800	260
	Total	5,500	95,700	7,570

*Bakeries operated approximately 300 days per year.

Table 3. *Estimated Delivery Costs* ($) Between Bakeries and Customers, Bay Area Bakery Company (per cwt)*

	Plants						
	Santa Rosa	Sacramento	Richmond	San Francisco	Stockton	Santa Cruz	San Jose†
Santa Rosa	2.00	4.40	3.20	3.20	4.20	4.80	4.20
Sacramento	3.90	1.50	2.90	3.60	2.50	4.50	3.90
Richmond	2.00	2.40	1.00	1.40	2.60	2.60	2.00
Berkeley	2.00	2.40	1.00	1.40	2.60	2.60	2.00
Oakland	2.20	2.60	1.20	1.20	2.60	2.40	1.80
San Francisco	2.20	2.80	1.40	1.00	2.80	2.60	2.00
San Jose	3.70	3.90	2.50	2.50	2.90	2.10	1.50
Santa Cruz	4.80	5.00	3.60	3.60	4.00	2.00	2.60
Salinas	5.60	5.60	4.20	4.40	4.60	2.80	3.20
Stockton	3.70	2.50	3.10	3.10	1.50	3.50	2.90
Modesto	4.80	3.60	4.00	4.00	2.60	4.20	3.60

*Delivery costs are influenced primarily by (1) the distance of the market area from the bakery, and (2) the distance between deliveries in the market area.
†Proposed plant.

Table 4. *Five-year Projected Supply Pattern, Bay Area Bakery Company*

Major Market	Bakery of Origin	Daily Quantity (in cwt)
Santa Rosa	Sant Rosa	330
Sacramento	Sacramento	500
Richmond	Richmond	660
Berkeley	Richmond	440
Oakland	Richmond	1,210
San Francisco	San Francisco	1,300
San Jose	San Jose	1,200
Santa Cruz	Santa Cruz	110
Salinas	Santa Cruz	110
Stockton	Stockton	290
Stockton	Sacramento	50
Modesto	Stockton	110

DISCUSSION QUESTIONS

1. As manager of transportation and customer service for Bay Area Bakery Company, would you agree with the proposal to build a new baking facility in San Jose? In order to support your opinion, assume that you have a computer code at your disposal that will optimize transportation problems. What method of financial analysis would you use? Make any necessary assumptions regarding inflation and future building and production costs.

2. If you do not agree with the proposal, what action would you recommend for consideration by other members of the company's top management group? Is the current distribution pattern optimal?

3. If we project similar market growth for 10 years, what effect will this have on the decisions about whether and when to build a new plant?

4. What additonal factors would have to be taken into consideration before reaching a final decision in this matter?

Blake Electronics

6

In 1947, Steve Blake founded Blake Electronics in Long Beach, California, to manufacture resistors, capacitors, inductors, and other electronic components. During World War II, Steve was a radio operator, and it was during this time that he became proficient at repairing radios and other communications equipment. Steve viewed his four-year experience with the army with mixed feelings. He hated army life, but this experience gave him the confidence and the initiative to start his own electronics firm.

Over the years, Steve kept the business relatively unchanged. By 1960, total annual sales were in excess of two million dollars. In 1964, Steve's son, Jim, joined the company after finishing high school and two years of courses in electronics at Long Beach Community College. Jim was always aggressive in high school athletics, and he became even more aggressive as general sales manager of Blake Electronics. This aggressiveness bothered Steve, who was more conservative. Jim would make deals to supply companies with electronic components before he bothered to find out if Blake Electronics had the ability or capacity to produce the components. On several occasions this behavior caused the company some embarrassing moments when

By Professor Ralph M. Stair, Jr., Florida State University.

Blake Electronics was unable to produce the electronic components for companies with which Jim had made deals.

In 1968, Jim started to go after government contracts for electronic components. By 1970, total annual sales had increased to over ten million dollars, and the number of employees exceeded two hundred. Many of these employees were electronic specialists and graduates of electrical engineering programs from top colleges and universities. But Jim's tendency to stretch Blake Electronics to contracts continued as well, and by 1975, Blake Electronics had a reputation with government agencies as a company that could not deliver what it promised. Almost overnight, government contracts stopped, and Blake Electronics was left with an idle work force and unused manufacturing equipment. This high overhead started to melt away profits, and in 1977, Blake Electronics was faced with the possibility of sustaining a loss for the first time in its history.

In 1978, Steve decided to look at the possibility of manufacturing electronic components for home use. Although this was a totally new market for Blake Electronics, Steve was convinced that this was the only way to keep Blake Electronics from dipping into the red. The research team of Blake Electronics was given the task of developing new electronic devices for home use. The first idea from the research team was the Master Control Center. The basic components for this system are shown in Figure 1.

The heart of the system is the master control box. This unit, which would have a retail price of $250, has two rows of five buttons. Each button controls one light or appliance, and can either be set as a switch or as a rheostat. When set as a switch, a light finger touch on the bottom either turns a light or appliance on or off. When set as a rheostat, a finger touching the bottom controls the intensity of the light. Leaving your finger on the bottom makes the light go through a complete cycle ranging from off to bright and back to off again.

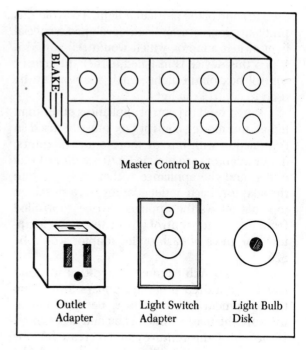

Figure 1. *Master Control Center*

In order to allow for maximum flexibility, each master control box is powered by two D-sized batteries that can last up to a year, depending on usage. In addition, the research team has developed three versions of the master control box—versions A, B, and C. If a family wants to control more than ten lights or appliances, another master control box can be purchased.

The light bulb disk, which would have a retail price of $2.50, is controlled by the master control box and is used to control the intensity of any light. A different disk is available for each button position for all three master control boxes. By inserting the light bulb disk between the light bulb and the socket, the appropriate button on the master control box can completely control the intensity of the light. If a standard light switch is used, it must be on at all times for the master control box to work.

One disadvantage of using a standard light switch is that only the master control box can be used to control the particular light. To avoid this problem, the research team developed a special light switch adaptor which would sell for $15. When this device is installed, either the master control box or the light switch adaptor can be used to control the light.

When used to control appliances other than lights, the master control box must be used in conjunction with one or more outlet adaptors. These adaptors are plugged into a standard wall outlet, and the appliance is then plugged into the adaptor. Each outlet adaptor has a switch on top that allows the appliance to be controlled from the master control box or the outlet adaptor. The price of each outlet adaptor would be $25.

The research team estimated that it would cost five hundred thousand dollars to develop the equipment and procedures needed to manufacture the master control box and accessories. If successful, this venture could increase sales by approximately two million dollars. But will the master control boxes be a successful venture? With a 60-percent chance of success estimated by the research team, Steve had serious doubts about trying to market the master control boxes even though he liked the basic idea. Because of his reservations, Steve decided to send requests for proposals (RFPs) for additional marketing research to 30 marketing research companies in southern California.

The first RFP to come back was from a small company called Marketing Associates, Inc. (MAI), which would charge $100,000 for the survey. According to their proposal, MAI has been in business for about three years, and has conducted about one hundred marketing research projects. MAI's major strengths appeared to be individual attention to each account, experienced staff, and fast work. Steve was particularly interested in one part of the proposal, which revealed MAI's success record with previous accounts. This is shown in Figure 2.

The only other proposal to be returned was by a branch office of Iverstine and Kinard, one

	Survey Results		
Outcome	Favorable	Unfavorable	Totals
Successful Venture	35	20	55
Unsuccessful Venture	15	30	45

Figure 2. *Success Figures for MAI*

of the largest marketing research firms in the country. The cost for a complete survey would be $300,000. While the proposal did not contain the same success record as MAI, the proposal from Iverstine and Kinard did contain some interesting information. The chance of getting a favorable survey result, given a successful venture, was 90 percent. On the other hand, the chance of getting an unfavorable survey result, given an unsuccessful venture, was 80 percent. Thus, it appeared to Steve that Iverstine and Kinard would be able to predict the success or failure of the master control boxes with a great amount of certainty.

Steve pondered the situation. Unfortunately, both marketing research teams gave different types of information in their proposals. Steve concluded that there would be no way that the two proposals could be compared unless he got additional information from Iverstine and Kinard. Furthermore, Steve wasn't sure what he would do with the information, and if it would be worth the expense of hiring one of the marketing research firms.

DISCUSSION QUESTIONS

1. Does Steve need additional information from Iverstine and Kinard?

2. What would you recommend?

Buffalo Alkali and Plastics

7

Buffalo Alkali and Plastics, a prominent producer of soda ash, began operations in the United States in 1880 using the Solvay Process.[1] Buffalo, New York, was selected as the site for the soda ash operation because of the close proximity of both brine wells (permitting solution mining of salt) and limestone deposits. The initial complex was later expanded for the production of chlorine, caustic soda, chlorinated solvents, industrial detergents, and polyvinyl chloride. Having experienced considerable success in this initial operation, Buffalo Alkali and Plastics built eight additional plants in the central and southern regions of the United States during the first half of the twentieth century.

Even with this diversification and expansion, Buffalo Alkali and Plastics' principal product continues to be soda ash. Until the 1960s, soda ash was almost exclusively produced by the Solvay Process. However, huge deposits of trona, or natural soda ash, have been discovered in Wyoming. (Trona ore is mined directly and is

By Professors Jerry Kinard and Joe Iverstine, Southeastern Louisiana State University. Used by permission.

1. The Solvay Process for producing soda ash involves exposing sodium bicarbonate (soda) to intense heat. Soda is initially formed through the carbonation of ammoniated brine. (Ammonia gas is absorbed in brine; then the ammonia-brine solution is saturated with carbon dioxide gas from the burning of limestone in kilns.)

purified by dissolution, evaporation, and re-crystallization. Production costs for natural soda ash are much lower than those for synthetic soda ash produced by the Solvay Process.) Thus, Buffalo Alkali and Plastics' plants remain competitive only because of their close proximity to markets. Freight charges incurred in shipping soda ash from Wyoming to markets served by the synthetic plants tend to offset the lower production costs of mining/purification operations. (Principally, soda ash is used in the manufacture of glass by combining certain ratios of sand and soda ash and fusing the mixture under high temperature.)

THE CALCINERS

Even when freight charges are considered, synthetic soda ash producers remain competitive with trona producers only if their plants maintain high volume operations. Synthetic plants have large investments in fixed costs and must sustain high production rates to remain above the break-even point. Area markets support these high rates. Glass manufacturers and other users of soda ash consume the entire output of local synthetic plants and supplement this source of supply by purchasing higher priced trona ash.

Production rates for the synthetic plants are usually dependent on the number of calciners (pronounced cal-cī-ners) available for operation.[2] The Buffalo, New York, complex has 32 calciners, each with a daily capacity of 100 tons

of soda ash. The plant capacity is 3,000 tons per day; hence, 30 of the 32 calciners must be available for service to maintain maximum output.

THE PROBLEM

Because of the intense heat in the fire zone, the one-inch thick steel shell eventually is oxidized and cracks. When this occurs, the shell is pulled from the brick housing and the burned-cracked section (approximately 15 feet) is cut out and a new section is welded into place. The repaired shell is reinstalled in the brick housing; drive mechanisms are attached; and the calciner is returned to service. (Heat resistant alloys are judged to be impractical for this operation because of the enormous cost and prolonged delivery dates for such alloy shells.)

The central problem for this operation is the determination of appropriate maintenance forces to effect calciner repairs. A large number of recent shell failures has reduced the number of calciners available for service to 25. A check of maintenance logs for the past ten years revealed 180 shell failures. Upon further examination of these logs, monthly failure probabilities were developed. These are included in Table 1. Repair procedures involve laying 100 feet of railroad track at the end of a failed calciner on which a crane rides to remove the cracked shell. The repair procedure averages three weeks (15 working days) with a standard deviation of three days. A schedule of repair

---

2. A calciner is comprised of a steel pipe, 60 feet in length and six feet in diameter. This pipe, or shell, is fitted with a drive sprocket at one end and is supported by tines (steel rollers) at both ends. Through a gear drive mechanism, the shell is rotated about 30 rpm on fixed rollers. The shell lies horizontal in a fire brick housing. Approximately 30 feet of the shell are included in a fire-box or gas-fired furnace. Sodium bicarbonate (soda) is fed into one end of the shell and is conveyed to the other end by internal flights. When the soda passes through the fire zone, it is converted into sodium carbonate or soda ash. This process is called calcination.

Table I. *Monthly Shell Failure Probabilities*

Failures	Probability
0	0.22
1 or less	0.55
2 or less	0.80
3 or less	0.92
4 or less	0.96
5 or less	0.97
6 or less	0.98

Table 2. *Repair Time Probabilities Utilizing Normal Repair Procedures (Crane Track)*

Time	Probability
6 days or less	0.001
9 days or less	0.02
12 days or less	0.16
15 days or less	0.50
18 days or less	0.84
21 days or less	0.98
24 days or less	0.999

Table 3. *Repair Time Probabilities Utilizing Accelerated Procedures (Rental Crane)*

Time	Probability
4 days or less	0.001
6 days or less	0.02
8 days or less	0.16
10 days or less	0.50
12 days or less	0.84
14 days or less	0.98
16 days or less	0.999

time vs. cumulative probability is in Table 2. (The dispersion is usually a result of working overtime.) The crane track cannot be permanently installed at each calciner because of obstruction of other equipment repairs.

Repairs may be expedited, however, by renting a large mobile crane. The rental cost of this crane is $1,500 per day with a minimum charge of $12,000 per rental. With the rented crane, two calciners may be repaired simultaneously. Moreover, the average time for repairs using the rented crane is reduced from three weeks to two weeks (ten working days) with a standard deviation of two days. A schedule of repair times vs. cumulative probability is included in Table 3. Other maintenance material and labor costs for these two repair approaches (rented crane and installed crane) are estimated to be equal. Profit and overhead contribution from a ton of soda ash is estimated to be $12.00

DISCUSSION QUESTION

As a maintenance manager, develop a plan of action for the restoration of the failed calciners and present a policy that will be implemented in the future.

Century Chemical Company

8

Century Chemical Company, formed in 1955 as a result of the merger of three smaller firms, produces chlorine and caustic soda through the electrolysis of brine. Century's largest plant, located in St. Gabriel, Louisiana, produces approximately 1,500 tons of chlorine and 1,700 tons of caustic soda annually. The St. Gabriel plant operates at capacity; its entire output is sold.

A major problem confronting Century Chemical Corporation is associated with its chlorine collection and handling system. The system incorporates headers that collect chlorine gas from the electrolytic cells. The gas then passes through heat exchangers for cooling and condensation of water entrained in the chlorine. Residual water in the chlorine gas is removed by "scrubbing" with concentrated sulfuric acid. Thereafter, the dry chlorine gas is chilled by being bubbled through liquid chlorine before being fed to the chlorine compressor. The chlorine compressor is the "heart" of the handling system. It pulls the gas from the cells through the cooling and drying system. Then it compresses the gas for liquefaction and storage as liquid chlorine.

By Professors Jerry Kinard and Joe Iverstine, Southeastern Louisiana State University. Used by permission.

A major problem for the production manager of Century Chemical is the gradual deterioration of the plant's compressor capacity because of the fouling of component parts. The reliability of Century's centrifugal compressor at its St. Gabriel complex is 0.92. The eight-percent downtime includes cleaning and restoration of capacity as well as other mechanical/electrical failures. Heretofore, management at Century has chosen to incur the downtime and lost sales associated with compressor failures. However, from time to time, management considers the installation of a spare compressor. Currently, the cost of such an installation is estimated to total $800,000. The spare compressor is also projected to have a 0.92 reliability factor.

Approximately 12 hours of downtime are required to change over to an installed spare compressor. Profit and overhead contribution for chlorine is estimated at $50/ton; the profit and overhead contribution for caustic soda is $40/ton. Century's cost of capital or opportunity cost is estimated to equal 20 percent. Useful life of the compressor installation is estimated to be ten years. Salvage is assumed to be zero. The effective tax rate is 40 percent.

DISCUSSION QUESTION

Should management of Century Chemical install the spare compressor? Why or why not?

Cranston Construction Company

9

The Cranston Construction Company is a small Mississippi construction company that undertakes building projects of a medium- to large-scale nature based on local and statewide needs. Although the company is capable of operating outside of its native state, it usually does not bid on out-of-state business. It maintains an office with a small staff and usually has several construction projects going on at the same time. Cranston has just received the contract for construction of a new humanities building on the campus of Northern Mississippi State University.

Although the university and the State Building Commission are pleased to have completed negotiations for the new building, a significant task lies ahead for Mr. Daniel Cranston, the president of Cranston Construction Company. He must select a project manager and arrange for allocation of necessary resources for construction. He must then work with the project manager to develop a schedule for constructing the building in order to assist in the timely decision making that involves financial needs and shifting of equipment from other job sites.

Following the development sequence for a construction project, as shown by Figure 1, Mr. Cranston decides that the detailed planning, lay-

Although various elements of this case have been fictionalized, it is based on an actual experience of its author, Dr. Gerald L. Pauler, Pittsburgh State University. Used by permission.

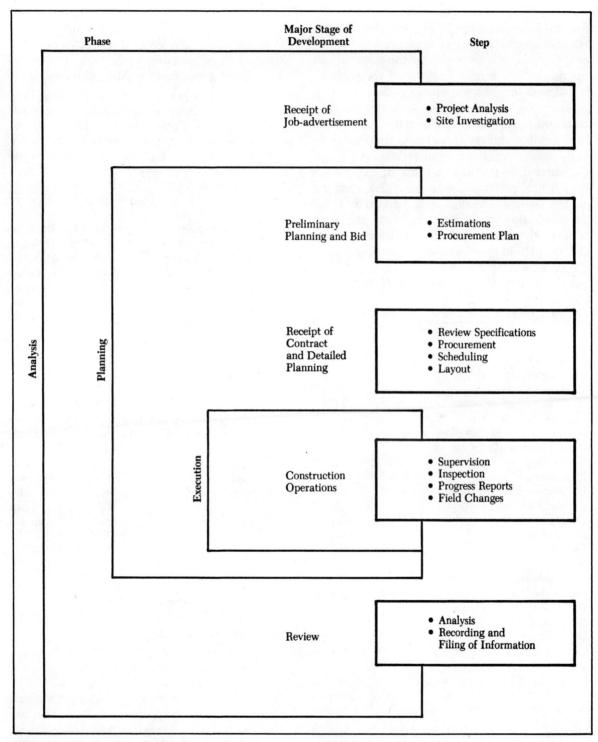

Figure 1. *Development of a Construction Project*

out and scheduling can be provided by his project manager. The project manager will further be delegated total authority for the construction operations, the execution phase of the project.

Based on past experience, Mr. Cranston makes up a job breakdown with approximate costs (shown in Table 1). Since the bid was for over a million dollars, these costs represent company targets and are confidential. Although Cranston does not have significant experience with critical path analysis, he also makes up the activity list and time allowances (shown in Table 2). These time allowances represent the span between the earliest date he thinks each activity can begin and the latest date by which each should end.

With these initial efforts Mr. Cranston calls in Mr. Henry Nolton to discuss his appointment as project manager. After a lengthy discussion Mr. Nolton accepts the appointment but makes the following statement to Mr. Cranston:

> Your cost targets are probably reasonable; however, your time estimates and activity list do not really provide believable information. According to your figures, the project will be finished in less than 370 days and, therefore, you will not incur any penalty costs. However, if most of your time estimates are close to being correct, then I believe that the project will take longer than 370 days.
>
> As an example, let me point out that your duration times look like total time allowances rather than activity times. Take the activity of "architectural and miscellaneous metals." I'd say that this would take about two weeks to complete and could be one of the last items accomplished, probably following completion of all the stairwells.
>
> Another major problem with your listing is that we'll be using reinforcing steel with all of the concrete work and, since it's a three story building with a penthouse, we'll be doing concrete activities floor by floor. Thus, in order to schedule and control this job, I need to decide on an activity list which is based on the actual sequence of construction, floor by floor.
>
> Further, I need some accurate time estimates for each activity. Give me a few days for planning and I will show you a list of activities that will serve as a plan for this project. I can also have a critical path network drawn up which will show the most important set of activities requiring management attention.

In conference later that week with some of his subcontractors, Mr. Nolton decides on the set of activities shown in Table 3. Having spent a great deal of time with the time estimates, he feels that they are very realistic. In reviewing the contract he notes that if the project takes longer than 370 days, the company will incur a penalty cost for each day over 370; specifically, $500 a day for each day late will be subtracted from final construction payments received from the State Building Commission. He designates an

Table 1. *Job Breakdown Humanities Building*

1.	Sales tax, bond, and insurance	$ 22,000
2.	General conditions	25,000
3.	Site work	8,000
4.	Reinforcing steel	57,000
5.	Concrete footings	17,000
6.	Concrete grade beams	14,000
7.	Structural concrete	115,000
8.	Structural and miscellaneous steel	21,000
9.	Masonry (includes stone)	125,000
10.	Roofing and sheet metal and insulation	16,000
11.	Doors and frames	2,000
12.	Architectural and miscellaneous metal and accessories	5,000
13.	Metal windows	2,000
14.	Lath and plaster	24,000
15.	Ceramic and marble	5,000
16.	Millwork	34,000
17.	Hardware	9,000
18.	Resilient floor	10,000
19.	Glazing and store front	20,000
20.	Acoustic ceiling	10,000
21.	Painting	10,000
22.	Elevator	19,000
23.	Carpet	8,000
24.	Finish grade and site work	10,000
25.	Clean-up and move-out	4,000
26.	Miscellaneous labor and materials	20,000
	Total Contract Price	$612,000

Table 2. *Project Activities and Duration*

Number	Activity	Time Allowed (Days)
1	Sales Tax, Bond, Insurance	35
2	Move In, Tool House General Conditions	35
3	Clean, Clear, Excavate, and Grade	28
4	Reinforcing Steel	217
5	Concrete Footings	35
6	Concrete Grade Beams	35
7	Structural Concrete Framing and Slabs	35
8	Structural and Miscellaneous Steel	210
9	Masonry and Stone	231
10	Roofing and Sheet Metal	80
11	Metal Doors and Frames	203
12	Architectural and Miscellaneous Metals	266
13	Metal Windows	231
14	Lath and Plaster	154
15	Ceramic Tile and Marble	30
16	Millwork	234
17	Finish Hardware	133
18	Resilient Floor	161
19	Glazing and Store Front	203
20	Acoustic Ceiling	35
21	Painting	161
22	Elevator	119
23	Carpet	35
24	Finish Grade and Sitework	28
25	Clean Up and Move Out	49

administrative assistant to develop a critical path based on his more realistic set of activities.

The sequence of activities begins with activities 1, 2, and 3 (from Table 3), which can begin immediately. As soon as the layout and excavation are complete, grade beams and foundation work can begin. Lower-floor concrete work can then be completed so that columns and then framing may be undertaken in sequence. Once the lower-floor concrete framing is complete, glazing, exterior doors, lower-floor door frames, middle-floor concrete and stairwell activities can begin. Following the middle-floor concrete, the middle-floor columns and then the middle-floor concrete framing may be completed similar to the first-floor logic. After framing is complete, middle-floor door frames, upper-floor concrete and lath and plaster activities can start. Lower-floor masonry and middle-floor door frames must be complete before middle-floor masonry can begin. Following lath and plaster, ceramic tile and marble can be placed. After the stairwells are complete, hardware, architectural, and miscellaneous metals can be installed.

As with the first two floors, upper-floor columns are emplaced following the upper-floor concrete work. Next, upper-floor concrete framing can be completed. At this juncture, upper-floor door frames, roofing, and elevator activities can begin. Once these three activities are completed, plus completion of middle-floor masonry, the upper-floor masonry, penthouse work, and ceiling work can be started. Following ceiling work, painting can begin and must be finished before tiling and carpeting which follow millwork. The millwork and finish grading start after upper-floor masonry and penthouse activities.

Cranston Construction Company

Table 3. *New Activity List*

Number	Activity	Duration (days)
1	Sales tax, bond, insurance	21
2	Layout and excavation	28
3	Move in, general conditions	7
4	Grade beams	11
5	Foundation, concrete footings	11
6	Lower-floor concrete	10
7	Lower-floor columns	21
8	Lower-floor concrete framing	35
9	Glazing and store front	35
10	Exterior doors	21
11	Lower-floor door frames	14
12	Middle-floor concrete	14
13	Stairwells	35
14	Middle-floor columns	23
15	Middle-floor concrete framing	37
16	Lower-floor masonry and interior doors	35
17	Middle-floor door frames	14
18	Upper-floor concrete	14
19	Lath and plaster	21
20	Upper-floor columns	23
21	Upper-floor concrete framing	37
22	Upper-floor door frames	14
23	Elevator	21
24	Roof slab, beams, and sheet metal	21
25	Penthouse steel, concrete, and masonry	21
26	Ceilings	42
27	Millwork	42
28	Paint	42
29	Middle-floor masonry and interior doors	35
30	Upper-floor masonry and interior doors	21
31	Ceramic tile and marble	14
32	Hardware, arch., and miscellaneous metals	14
33	Tile floors and carpet	21
34	Finish grade and sitework	28
35	Clean up, inspect, and move out	2

DISCUSSION QUESTIONS

1. Acting as Mr. Nolton's administrative assistant, draw up a critical path network in final form. The network must show activities from Table 3, their durations, and relationships in order to provide construction personnel with expected project time, critical tasks, the points in time when tasks should begin and end, tasks that may be expedited if it is desired to reduce overall time, and the leeway (float) available for scheduling tasks, e.g., subcontracts.

2. Write a report to Mr. Nolton addressing the problems of project duration and specifying which activities may require the closest management attention. If it appears that the project will not be finished on time, which activities would you recommend be investigated for crashing?

Drake Radio

10

Drake Radio got its start during World War I by manufacturing radio communications equipment for the military. By the start of World War II, Drake was one of the largest suppliers of military communications equipment. After World War II, Drake diversified into the following three market areas:

1. Military Communications Equipment
2. Amateur Radio Equipment
3. CB Radios and Equipment

Using its technology and experience gained from manufacturing military communications equipment, Drake became known as one of the best producers of amateur radio equipment. Drake especially excelled with its single sideband radios and its two-meter radios for amateur use. Although these radios were expensive, they were of the finest quality and always in demand.

In developing CB radios, however, Drake decided to mass produce cheap units that would have a wide appeal and a low price. To help protect its good name in military communications equipment and amateur (ham) radios, these inexpensive CB radios were marketed under the brand name of Hustler.

By Professor Ralph M. Stair, Jr., Florida State University.

In 1975, George Populas, the president of Drake Electronics, decided to investigate the possibilities of entering into the market of home stereo systems. These stereo systems would be high quality, highly priced, and marketed with the Drake name.

The most remarkable stereo system that Drake manufactured was the DR-2000, which was a sophisticated stereo receiver. The demand for the DR-2000 was fairly constant from month to month. (See Figure 1.)

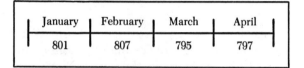

January	February	March	April
801	807	795	797

Figure 1. *Demand for DR-2000's in Units*

The DR-2000 had all the features of a stereo receiver that carried a price tag of $765. Some of these features included the ability to connect four different speaker systems, loudness control, flatness control, blend control, and completely digital read out. Of course, it could be connected to one or more receivers, tape units, turntables, etc. Instead of having a base control to regulate the low frequencies and a treble control to regulate the high frequencies, the DR-2000 had five separate controls that regulated five frequency ranges. One control regulated frequencies from 0 to 500 Hz; another control regulated frequencies from 500 to 5,000 Hz; a third regulated the frequencies between 5,000 to 10,000 Hz; a fourth regulated frequencies between 10,000 to 15,000 Hz; and a fifth, the frequencies between 15,000 and 50,000 Hz.

One of the biggest selling features of the DR-2000 was its ability to use the DR-2000 RC, the remote control device for the stereo receiver. Because all of the switching and components were solid state, the engineers of Drake Electronics were able to develop a complete remote control station that was no bigger than a cigarette pack. The basic idea for the remote control device was borrowed from that of television, and Drake engineers were able to control *all* functions by the DR-2000 RC. Each remote control box cost $75, and many people purchased more than one unit. The ability to control the stereo system from literally anywhere in a house was one of the system's biggest selling features, but it also caused some problems in homes with children. As a result, Drake developed a master control unit that parents could keep and that would override all other remote control units and the controls on the stereo receiver.

Another outstanding feature of the DR-2000 was its completely modular design, shown in Figure 2. Each module was contained in a completely separate, color-coded box. By unlatching four hidden slides, the top of the cabinet could be removed, giving access to all of the modules.

The control module contained a microprocessor chip that monitored the operations of all of the other modules. If one of the modules stopped functioning correctly, the control module would activate a warning light on the front panel that indicated which module was not working properly. The owner could pull out the appropriate module and replace it with a new module from a nearby Drake dealership. If a Drake dealership was not close, Drake promised two-day, COD delivery. The malfunctioning module could even be sent to Drake or given to a Drake dealership to be repaired or for a refund.

All of the modules, except the FM tuner, were manufactured by Drake and stored until they were needed. Annual carrying cost was estimated to be 25 percent for all modules. The FM tuner modules were supplied by Collins Electronics, which also adjusted and sealed them. The cost to place an order was estimated at $50 per order, and the time to receive an order from Collins was approximately two weeks. Collins also offered quantity discounts on its FM tuners. (See Table 1.)

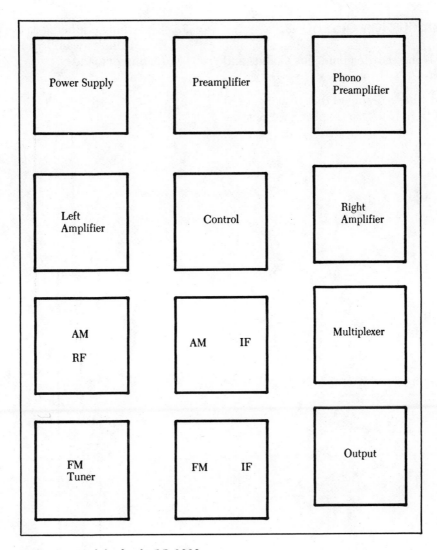

Figure 2. *Modules for the DR-2000*

Nitobitso Electronics also manufactured FM tuners compatible with the DR-2000. Because of its location in Japan, the time to receive an order was about two months, and the ordering cost was $100 because of the additional required paperwork. (See Table 2.)

Table 1. *Quantity Discount from Collins on FM Tuners*

Quantity	Price
0–100	$25
101–500	24
501 and over	22

Table 2. *Quantity Discount from Nitobitso on FM Tuners*

Quantity	Price
0–200	$25
201–800	23
801–2,000	22
2,001 or more	21

DISCUSSION QUESTIONS

1. What is the reorder point for Collins and Nitobitso?

2. . Would you recommend that Drake get FM tuners from Nitobitso? Explain your answer.

3. Everything else being equal, which supplier of FM tuners would you want with a fluctuating demand?

Kwik Lube (A)

11

Dick Johnson received his Ph.D. in the early 1950s from the University of Southern California when he was 25 years old. He accepted a teaching position as an Assistant Professor of English with the University of Washington, and in 1962 wrote one of the leading text books in basic English principles. At the age of 45, Dick retired from the University of Washington with a net worth of approximately a half-million dollars.

Although Dick enjoyed traveling, he found retirement somewhat boring, and in 1969, during one of his trips to Los Angeles, he came across a very interesting type of new business. It was a very small gas station that specialized only in oil changes and lubrication jobs. The old gas station had been remodeled, the gas pumps had been removed, and the large sign above the small building read "OIL AND LUBE—$10 and 10 MINUTES." For two hours, Dick observed the converted gas station from a restaurant across the street, and although the mechanics were never able to do a complete oil and lubrication job in ten minutes, they were fast and had plenty of business.

The next day, Dick talked with one of the mechanics and found that the owner, George Day, at one time ran the old gas station. During

By Professor Ralph M. Stair, Jr., Florida State University.

the next month, Dick made three trips to Los Angeles to talk to George about how he got into the business and how the business worked. Dick paid George $1,000 for his advice and information and promised never to compete directly with George or ever to open or operate a similar type of business in the Los Angeles area.

After talking to his lawyer and accountant, Dick started to organize a new business—"KWIK LUBE." The first Kwik Lube station was designed to be very similar to the small converted gas station in Los Angeles. The building was new and very attractive, and the equipment was of the best quality and very expensive. In March 1971, Dick had built his first Kwik Lube, and he purchased options to buy two other commercial lots for two additional Kwik Lube stations. In May 1971, Dick decided to exercise his options, and by the end of 1971, he had completed two additional Kwik Lubes in the Seattle area. The total gross revenues in 1971 from all three stations was $26,000.

Between 1971 and 1975, business picked up rapidly. Total gross sales in 1972 and 1973 were $68,000 and $75,000 respectively. In 1974, total gross sales for the three Kwik Lube stations was $75,000, and in 1975, total gross sales was $78,000. Dick was convinced that this sales increase was due to his not significantly increasing the cost of his basic service, which was to change the oil, change the filter, and do a lube job. In 1971, the total cost was $9.95. In 1974, the total cost per job was $10.50, and by 1975, the total cost was only $10.95. Dick was pleased with the operation of Kwik Lube, especially when he considered the consequences of the recession in 1974, which in his opinion reduced his potential sales for 1974 and 1975. But Dick was still not satisfied with this success.

A number of franchised service stations, transmission shops, brake and shock stores, and muffler shops were doing extremely well. The type of products and services offered by Kwik Lube were similar to these franchise operations. In addition to running his three Kwik Lube stations in Seattle, Dick desired to franchise his idea in other cities in Washington and in other states such as Oregon, Idaho, and Montana. During the last three years, Dick had acquired considerable knowledge about this type of business. He was able to obtain the best possible prices for oil, lubricants, and filters. If he franchised Kwik Lube, he would even be able to make a profit from selling oil, filters, and lubricants.

Dick invested over $5,000 in lawyers' fees and another $2,000 in talking to other companies in the franchise business. He decided to set his franchise fee at $8,000, plus six percent of the gross sales of the stations. In addition, each new Kwik Lube station had to conform to exacting standards for the building and all of the equipment. Depending on the location, Dick could build and equip a Kwik Lube station for under $100,000. Like his own Kwik Lube stations, these new stations would have two-car or vehicle bays. In 1976, Dick sold his first franchise to T. A. Williams and another franchise to an investor in Eugene, Oregon. By 1979, Dick had sold a total of 11 franchises in Spokane, Washington; Eugene, Oregon; Portland, Oregon; Butte, Montana; and Boise, Idaho. In addition, Dick experienced a substantial growth rate for total gross sales for his three Kwik Lube stations in Seattle. In 1976, total gross sales were $99,000. In 1977, total gross sales were $104,000; in 1978, $120,000; and in 1979, $133,000.

Dick knew that it would only be a matter of time before someone else would start to compete directly with his Kwik Lube stations, but he never believed that the first competition would be in Seattle. Construction on the first two Speedy Lube stations started in 1979, and both stations were in operation in early 1980. The two stores were almost identical to the Kwik Lube stations, but Speedy Lube was priced two dollars less than Kwik Lube's current price, which was now $14.95. Dick never dreamed that this new competition would cut so deeply into his total gross sales. Total gross sales for the three Kwik Lube stations in Seattle dropped to $111,000 for 1980, and the situation did not look any better for 1981. (Indeed, when 1981 figures became available, sales were again only $111,000.)

Soon after the total gross sales figures came in for 1980, Dick got some startling information from one of his friends in Spokane. Over 50 percent of the stock in Speedy Lube, Inc. was owned by Richland, Inc., a holding company owned by T. A. Williams. Dick was outraged that one of the people that purchased a franchise from him was directly competing with his Kwik Lube stores and in direct violation of the franchise contract, which contained a non-competition clause in fine print.

Dick had only two goals for the coming year: 1) to shut down the two Speedy Lube stations, and 2) to regain his lost sales for the two years from T. A. Williams. Both objectives were to be accomplished with a lawsuit.

DISCUSSION QUESTIONS

1. What factors would you discuss in the lawsuit?

2. Determine the total loss in gross sales for Dick's Kwik Lube stations over the two-year period. Use regression analysis.

Kwik Lube (B)

12

Dick Johnson's lawyer strongly suggested that Dick employ an expert witness to testify on his behalf against Speedy Lube. While there seemed to be no question about who would win the case, Dick's lawyer believed that an expert witness could more accurately determine the damages. In addition, most juries place more importance on expert testimony. As a result, Dick decided to employ the services of Dr. Warren Gunn.

Dr. Gunn was a professor of marketing at Eastern Washington University, which was very close to Spokane. He had more than ten years experience as an expert witness, and his specialty was determining damages for antitrust and franchise cases. His basic strategy was to find data about the same industry or a similar one in a location resembling the area in which the original problem occurred. In this case, Dr. Gunn needed data about the fast oil and lubrication business in a location similar to Seattle. Because Dick originally obtained his idea from a small station in Los Angeles and because Los Angeles had hundreds of these types of businesses by 1980, Dr. Gunn decided to collect data in the Los Angeles area. This would require the development and pilot testing of a questionnaire that could determine the total gross number of cars serviced for fast oil and lubrication busi-

By Professor Ralph M. Stair, Jr., Florida State University.

nesses in the Los Angeles area between 1973 and 1981.

Table 1. *Analysis of Average Fast Oil and Lubrication Total Gross Number of Cars Serviced at Los Angeles Stations (Using two bays as a basis for comparison)*

Year	Average Total Sales
1971	$19,000
1972	22,000
1973	25,000
1974	24,000
1975	26,000
1976	33,000
1977	35,000
1978	39,000
1979	44,000
1980	47,000
1981	52,000

Although the questionnaire study would cost $2,000 to perform, Dr. Gunn and Dick both believed that it was the best approach. The data were collected in two weeks, and are summarized in Table 1. Both Dr. Gunn and Dick knew that if the results of the questionnaire were not favorable, they would not use it during the case.

DISCUSSION QUESTIONS

1. Using the data in Table 1, compute the loss for Kwik Lube stations during the last two years using regression.

2. Was it worth $2,000 to perform the marketing research?

LaPlace Power and Light

13

The Southeastern Division of LaPlace Power and Light Company is responsible for providing dependable electric service to customers in and around the areas of Metairie, Kenner, Destrehan, LaPlace, Lutcher, Hammond, Pontchatoula, Amite, and Bogalusa, Louisiana. One material used extensively to provide this service is the ⅙ AWG aluminum triplex cable, which delivers the electricity from the distribution pole to the meter loop on the house.

The Southeastern Division Storeroom purchases the cable that this division will use. For the coming year, this division will need 499,500 feet of this service cable. Since this cable is only used on routine service work, practically all of it is installed during the five normal work days. The current cost of this cable is 41.4 cents per foot. Under the present arrangement with the supplier, the Southeastern Storeroom must take one-twelfth of its annual need every month. This agreement was reached in order to reduce lead time by assuring LaPlace a regular spot in the supplier's production schedule. Without this agreement, the lead time would be about twelve weeks. No quantity discounts are offered on this cable; however, the supplier requires that a minimum of 15,000 feet be on an order. The Southeastern Storeroom has the space to store a

By Professor Barry Render, University of New Orleans.

maximum of 300,000 feet of ⅙ AWG aluminum service cable.

Associated with each cable shipment are ordering costs of $50 which include all the costs from making the purchase requisition to issuing a check for payment. In addition, inventory carrying costs (including taxes) on all items in stores are considered to be ten percent of the purchase price per unit per year.

Being a government-regulated, investor-owned utility, both the Louisiana Public Service Commission and its stockholders watch closely how effectively the company, including inventory management, is managed.

DISCUSSION QUESTION

Evalute the effectiveness of the current ordering system. Can it be improved?

Mid-Continent Pipeline Construction Company

14

The construction of 30-inch-diameter pipelines required to transmit natural gas from the intercoastal waterways of southeast Texas and southern Louisiana to the heavily populated, highly industrialized regions of the midwest requires the coordinated efforts of hundreds of people employed by several firms, each with its own responsibilities and problems. Quite often, such gas lines are constructed in geographic areas never before crossed by such pipelines; in other instances, new lines are laid parallel to existing lines which can no longer carry the volume of gas required by the industrial and residential consumers located in regions of the country that do not provide enough energy to sustain their respective economies.

Since 1960, a leading firm in constructing gas transmission networks from the gas producing regions of the country to areas in the north and midwest is Minnesota–Michigan Transmission Company, which has total ownership of its pipelines and which exercises ultimate authority over all phases of each pipeline's construction. Typically, three other firms are directly accountable to Minnesota–Michigan Transmission Company with regard to the physical operation

By Professors Jerry Kinard and Joe Iverstine, Southeastern Louisiana State University. Used by permission.

of pipeline construction. On its present construction project, Minnesota–Michigan Transmission Company has subcontracted the following operations:

Mid-Continent Pipeline Construction Company, a subcontractor experienced in natural gas pipeline construction, provides personnel and equipment necessary to perform all physical activities on all segments of the network in south Texas and Louisiana. Such activities include the clearing of right-of-ways (after they have been secured from land owners by Minnesota–Michigan Transmission Company); stringing the pipe along the right-of-way and bending it to conform to the contour of the terrain; digging the trench; welding; coating and wrapping the pipe, testing it for "geeps," and laying it in the trenches (including the crossing of rivers and highways); testing for "geeps" after the pipe is covered (and repaired if bare spaces are detected in the coating); clean-up, including the planting of grass seed over the right-of-way; final tie-in with other segments of the line; and final testing.

International Inspectors, Inc., a firm that has assigned inspectors to all phases of construction, assures that all activities performed by Mid-Continent Pipeline Construction Company conform to accepted construction standards and that all satisfy the safety requirements imposed by the Interstate Commerce Commission and other regulatory agencies. All inspectors employed by International Inspectors, Inc. are seasoned veterans of pipeline construction; they have earned their livelihoods performing the tasks they are presently inspecting. All inspectors have absolute authority to accept or reject any work performed under their jurisdiction. Thus, special effort is given to employing persons who not only have considerable experience but who demonstrate high personal integrity. Usually, the inspector who assumes the greatest responsibility for maintaining quality in pipeline construction (excluding the Chief Inspector who has responsibility for all inspections) is the Welding Inspector.

Dixie Gamma-Ray Company systematically x-rays all welds made by Mid-Continent Pipeline Construction Company and presents the x-ray results to the Welding Inspector for approval or rejection. X-ray equipment is mounted on pick-up trucks which are driven down the line as construction progress is made.

THE PROBLEM

Raymond Richards, the construction superintendent in charge of all construction activities for Mid-Continent Pipeline Construction Company, is responsible for the logistics involved in getting ample supplies of pipe and support equipment to the various construction sites. Currently, the problem facing Richards is a determination of when an area pipe-yard should be established. Procuring pipe, supplies, and equipment long before they are needed ties up huge sums of money and creates the need for maintaining security over the equipment and supplies until they are needed. However, a delay in setting up the pipe-yard from which pipe is trucked to the right-of-way results in idle workers and a slowdown of the entire project. To pinpoint bottlenecks in construction, thereby minimizing construction time, Richards utilizes PERT (Program Evaluation and Review Technique), a management tool that allows him to calculate the probability of completing a segment of pipeline construction on a given day. Consequently, he can then determine the date on which construction of a new segment can begin (and, hence, the day that pipe, supplies, and equipment must be available).

Pipeline construction is directly affected by both weather conditions and the terrain. For example, rainy weather causes considerable delays, as do river and road crossings. Based on the prevailing and expected weather, Richards

Mid-Continent Pipeline Construction Company

Activities	a	m	b
AB	5	7	9
BC	3	5	7
BD	8	10	12
CE	4	6	8
DE	1	2	7
DF	3	4	6
EG	6	10	12
FG	8	9	10
GH	5	6	7

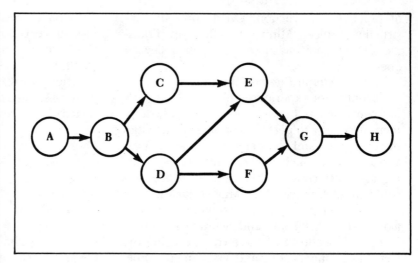

has estimated optimistic (a), most likely (m), and pessimistic (b) time estimates for all major activities remaining to be completed on the segment currently under construction. The following network shows these activities and events in parallel and sequential format. Time estimates (in days) appear in the table (above).

DISCUSSION QUESTIONS

1. Calculate the slack time for events not on the critical path.

2. What is the probability of completing this segment of pipeline in 35 days (scheduled time)?

MSA Shipping Lines, Inc.

15

MSA Shipping Lines, Inc. operates a fleet of five oceangoing steamship vessels on the commercial trade route from the Gulf Coast to Europe. Each of MSA's vessels averages three completed voyages per year, for an overall company terminated voyage rate of fifteen per year. These vessels call on Gulf Coast ports such as New Orleans, Houston, Tampa, Mobile, Baton Rouge, and Biloxi-Gulfport, and various ports in Europe such as Rotterdam, Livorno, Pireaus, and Lisbon. Dale Crossman, MSA's finance director is considering dropping Mobile as a port of call. Since manufacturers in the Mobile area are the primary source of cargo for the firm, the size and value of their cargo shipped on MSA Lines will determine if it will be profitable to continue to call on Mobile.

Freight-forwarders in the Mobile area advise the smaller manufacturers to combine cargo and ship them together for more attractive shipping rates. Thus, the shipment of some cargo depends on other cargo being shipped. Crossman decides that if he were to run a simulation for the next year, he might be able to determine if it will be profitable to continue to call on Mobile. He would like to run the simulation based on fifteen voyages. From past information, he

By Professor Barry Render, University of New Orleans.

has set up a frequency table on tons carried per voyage, and revenue per ton carried per voyage.

Tons	No. of Voyages	Revenue per Ton	No. of Voyages
700	5	$50	1
800	11	60	10
900	6	70	11
1,000	4	80	5
1,100	4	90	3
	30		30

Crossman also estimates that general port costs for each vessel are about $5,000 per voyage; tug boat hire runs $5,000 per voyage; pilotage is $2,000 per voyage; and other costs, including cargo handling, are $38,000 per voyage. It also costs $150,000 to operate the Mobile office every year. This includes salaries and indirect overhead costs allocated from the main office in New Orleans.

DISCUSSION QUESTION

Because of fine customer loyalty over the years, MSA will continue to call Mobile, even if it only breaks even in doing so. Will the calls at Mobile generate enough revenue to cover MSA's costs there during the next year?

MSA Shipping Lines, Inc.

NASA's Space Shuttle: Background

"I didn't have to worry about the profit motive on Gemini or Apollo."
(*Former astronaut Captain James Lovell, Jr.*)

The National Aeronautics and Space Administration (NASA) was established by an Act of Congress in 1958, in part to conduct activities required for space exploration, research, and applications, including the development and operation of vehicles carrying instruments, equipment, supplies, or living organisms through space. Its most visible program was the Apollo landing. But even as this "development" phase of NASA progressed into the launching of Skylab and later with the Apollo-Soyuz flight, intensive planning was already underway for the next generation of space vehicles which would represent the space agency's "operational" phase. (See Exhibit I for a summary of space "firsts.")

The rush of the "space race" during the 'sixties had required the use of enormously expensive rockets that could only be launched once since they fell into the ocean or were left in space after they served their purpose. Needless to say, throwing away most of the launch equipment was quite expensive. Because of budget cutbacks as public sentiment waned after the Apollo flights, the potential of space would be realized only if cargo (known as "payloads" in space jargon) could be transported back and forth economically. The reduced costs of operations from these future space vehicles would be the only way NASA could retain a meaningful space program.

The idea of developing and building a staffed and reusable "Space Shuttle" that will permit the exploration of space is recognized as an essential

This background note and accompanying series of cases, prepared by Professor Paul Miesing of the State University of New York, Albany, and Professor Barry Render, of the University of New Orleans, are intended to serve as a basis for class discussion rather than to illustrate either effective or ineffective handling of an administrative situation. Some of the data have been modified for the sake of simplification and clarity and need not completely represent the current shuttle system.

Exhibit I.   *Major Milestones in Space*

Launch Date	Mission	Event
Oct. 4, 1957	Sputnik 1	Manufactured earth satellite
Jan. 2, 1959	Luna 1	Escape from earth's gravity
Sep. 12, 1959	Luna 2	Lunar impact
Apr. 1, 1960	Tiros 1	Global weather photograph
Apr. 30, 1960	Transit 1B	Navigation satellite
Aug. 12, 1960	ECHO 1	Communications satellite
Apr. 12, 1961	Vostod 1	Manned flight and recovery
Aug. 26, 1962	Mariner 2	Interplanetary probe
Oct. 12, 1964	Voshkod 1	Multi-manned spacecraft
Mar. 18, 1965	Voshkod 2	Space walk
Jan. 31, 1966	Luna 9	Lunar soft landing
Dec. 21, 1968	Apollo 8	Manned lunar orbit
July 16, 1969	Apollo 11	Manned lunar landing
Apr. 19, 1971	Salyut 1	Space station
July 23, 1972	ERTS 1	Earth resources satellite
July 15, 1975	Apollo-Soyuz	Manned international cooperative mission
Apr. 12, 1981	Space Shuttle	Manned shuttle flight

part of the nation's future in space. The Space Shuttle is clearly NASA's major program of the 1980s, and moves the country from the age of space "exploration" to one of space "exploitation."

On March 27, 1979—seventy-five years after the Wright Brothers achieved the first sustained flight of a powered aircraft; just two decades after mankind entered the space age; and only ten years after the high point of the United States' space adventure when an American was the first man to walk on the moon—President Jimmy Carter acknowledged a new national dedication to space by telling the U.S. Congress, "We are entering a new era. The Space Shuttle—our national space transportation system for the coming decades—will increase the flexibility of space operations, reduce costs, improve national security, and make possible new cooperative activities with other nations. . . . It is important that we maintain our world leadership in space."

The Shuttle's first customers will be satellites for communications and for observing the earth's weather, natural resources, agricultural crops, and industrial pollution. Other satellites will leave the earth in hopes of sensing and recording data from distant planets and stars. By the mid-eighties, however, vast numbers of new users (foreign governments, commercial firms, universities) will be able to take advantage of the unique characteristics of space by processing materials in weightlessness to produce perfectly round ball bearings, pure glass, and large silicon crystals. Later on in the decade, biological processes, life sciences, and other medical applications may give us new wonder drugs. By the end of this century, as today's space transportation system becomes replaced by the next generation of space vehicles, large space structures and stations will complete the transition to the next industrial revolution. Full commercialization of space is estimated to reach sales as high as twenty billion dollars annually by then.

But that's admittedly in the far distant future. For now, the primary objective of the Shuttle is to deliver payloads economically to and from near-earth orbit. This will be made possible because the vehicle will be vertically launched into orbit at a speed slow enough to open up true space travel to anyone of reasonable health. It will also be capable of hauling as much as 65,000 pounds to and from earth orbit like a truck, carrying all sorts of satellites, experimental equipment, or materials at one time. By landing horizontally like a glider when it returns to earth for its runway landing, the Shuttle will eliminate the expensive sea recoveries that were necessary in our space infancy. This craft will also be used again and again, moving its people and freight from one location to another as it brings the evolution of transportation to a new plateau.

The cornerstone of this new space transportation system will be a fleet of five reusable Shuttle Orbiters, each the size of a commercial DC-9 jetliner. Besides an Orbiter, the Space Shuttle configuration also consists of the Orbiter's three Main Engines; the fuel drum that the Orbiter is mounted on—known as the External Tank—which will hold and mix the Main Engines' propellants; and the two Solid Rocket Boosters on each side of the External Tank to assist lift-off by being fired simultaneously with the Main Engines. After two minutes, these Solid Rocket Boosters will be jettisoned and will fall into the ocean where they will be recovered by tugboats and towed to shore to be refurbished for later use. Just before the Shuttle goes into near-earth orbit, the External Tank will run out of fuel and will also be released, burning up as it tumbles back to earth. The Orbiter will then be on its own for a day, a week, or a month, until it completes its mission and is ready to be flown back to earth for landing. After about two weeks on the ground for refueling, refurbishment, and reloading, each Orbiter will be ready for another mission.

These frequently scheduled flights will turn previously difficult and expensive space travel into routine and reliable operations by cutting in half what today's largest rockets typically cost. Besides the greater weight capability, the Shuttle will also remove restrictions on payload shape to permit flexibility in designing less complex spacecraft; astronauts will now be able to launch satellites from their mobile space platform, or check out, repair, and even return older ones if needed; the gentle cargo bay interior will eliminate the need for payloads to be able to withstand the sort of traumatic launch shocks and vibrations that they would be subject to when perched on top of a missile; instruments mounted on the ribs of the cargo bay can be carried wherever and whenever desired and even operated manually if desired; experiments may be conducted which would be difficult, if not impossible, to duplicate on earth; and multiple payloads can be carried for users who will share the launch costs by paying only for the portion of the capacity they require.

Many unresolved problems still remain. Not only must operations reliability be demonstrated so that customers will decide to fly, but there are also numerous economic and political uncertainties. Yet one thing is clear: the Space Shuttle will take NASA into new and uncharted realms of management. Typically, real world situations are much more complex than can possibly be described in several pages. But finding a solution to any problem requires reducing it to a size that can be handled without losing the flavor of the decision maker's day-to-day pursuit of unbiased data sources, accurate interpretation of the results, and the ability to implement the recommended solutions.

NASA's Space Shuttle (A): Likelihood of Satisfying the Anticipated Demand

16

One of the most significant breakthroughs of the Space Age was NASA's ability to fulfill President John F. Kennedy's 1961 pledge to land a man on the moon and safely return him to earth before the end of that decade. The completion of that national desire was seen as the culmination of the United States space program. Although highly successful, it did not come about without its share of problems and failures. (See Exhibit 1 for a history of manned space flight performance.)

All of NASA's space vehicles have been nonreturnable, except of course for the modules that the astronauts landed in. This will change as the remainder of this century becomes the era of a national "Space Transportation System." The initial program will take twelve years at a cost of 12.5 billion dollars and will utilize a fleet of five orbiters, each of which could be used approximately 100 times. (The breakdown of

Exhibit 1. *Total NASA Performance for Manned Space Flights (1959–1973)*

Program	Success/ Attempts	Percent Success
Mercury (1959–63)	20/23	87
Gemini (1964–66)	17/19	89
Apollo (1961–75)	28/30	93
Skylab (1973)	4/4	100
Totals	69/76	91

Exhibit 2. *Anticipated Demand for STS Launches*

Customer	'81	'82	'83	'84	'85	'86	'87	'88	'89	'90	'91	'92	Totals
NASA	1	8	11	11	19	21	16	20	18	20	20	12	177
Department of Defense	0	2	3	11	12	14	18	15	15	14	17	13	134
Other U.S. Government	1	1	0	2	1	2	2	5	2	5	3	4	28
U.S. Commercial	4	2	3	3	4	6	5	9	8	8	5	3	60
Foreign	1	2	5	3	3	5	8	6	7	7	7	8	62
Totals	7	15	22	30	39	48	49	55	50	54	52	40	461

anticipated flights to meet demand is shown in Exhibit 2.)

NASA planners are concerned with the number of scheduled flights that may fail. These failures can occur during takeoff, or because of a mechanical error in outer space that requires an early return to earth, an unforeseen problem preventing the experiment or research project from taking place, or not placing a satellite into orbit as planned. Whenever this occurs, another launch must be made to replace the original flight. Should the number of failures exceed the ability of the system to meet demand for any reason whatsoever, then the planned launch schedules would be jeopardized. The resulting bottleneck would increase costs to NASA and ill will from Shuttle users. If too many flight failures occur, then the anticipated demand cannot be satisfied within the total 500 flight capacity of the shuttle fleet.

DISCUSSION QUESTIONS

1. Based on prior NASA performance, what is the probability of having one unsuccess-

ful launch in 1982? The probability of two unsuccessful launches in 1982? Of three unsuccessful launches in 1982? What are the comparable probability figures for 1983?

2. The Director of the program states that there must be less than a 45-percent chance of having even one failure per year in any program year. What change in the failure rate would have to occur in order for this to be accomplished?

3. Considering the total 12-year anticipated demand, explain how NASA could compute the chance that it will not have to exceed the 500 flight capacity. Describe how to estimate the failure rate that could occur without jeopardizing this anticipated demand. What additional information should the director of the program have?

4. Analyze the use of data such as Exhibit 1 in projecting failure rates for future missions. What changes might you suggest?

NASA's Space Shuttle (B): Forecasting Customer Billings

17

The operation of the Space Transportation System is being developed and built by the National Aeronautics and Space Administration (NASA) to be paid for by its users. These paying customers include U.S. government agencies such as the Department of Defense, commercial firms such as Western Union, and foreign governments or organizations such as Messerschmitt Aircraft of West Germany. The price that each user is charged is fixed at the time the contract is negotiated with NASA. The Shuttle rental fees are expensive, sometimes costing tens of millions of dollars for each customer. Because of this large fee for a service that will be delivered several years in the future, the customer is expected to make a series of progress payments beginning at the time the launch is agreed upon.

NASA's pricing system is set so as to protect the Shuttle operations from inflationary spirals that might make the costs of a 1983, 1986, or 1990 launch quite a bit higher than prices agreed to in the 1970s. All user prices are therefore stated in the value of the dollar at the end of 1974, but escalator adjustments are built into each progress bill. Hence, NASA's billings include the projected value of payments to the due date.

Escalation adjustments are estimated for each quarter of the year in which a progress bill is issued. It is to the advantage of both NASA

Exhibit 1. *Index of Compensation per Hour[1] (Seasonally Adjusted)*

Quarter	1967	1974	1975	1976	1977	1978
Q1	—	—	176.2	190.5	207.5	225.2
Q2	—	—	179.2	194.5	210.5	229.6
Q3	—	—	181.1	198.6	215.3	235.8
Q4	—	172.0	184.6	202.7	218.8	—
Annual	100.0	—	180.2	196.5	213.0	232.9

[1] These indices represent the average increase in hourly pay for the American worker employed by private business firms and are expressed with 1967 as the reference year (1967 = 100.0).

and the paying customer to have a reliable index to determine these price adjustments. After a lengthy study, an index called the "Hourly Compensation" was selected which reflects the change in hourly pay for the average American worker in the private business sector. (See Exhibit 1.) NASA chose this particular index because it is published quarterly by the Bureau of Labor Statistics, making it public and easily accessible to Space Shuttle customers. If NASA had developed its own index, it might have been accused of using one that suited its own needs—and of using data that might not be easily verified by outsiders. It decided not to use a common index, such as the Consumer Price Index (CPI), because that series heavily weighs food, clothing, and medical items that have little to do with actual aerospace costs. NASA economists have determined to their satisfaction that "Hourly Compensation" tracks fairly well with cost increases in the aerospace field.

To illustrate NASA's billing procedure, a payment due on February 1, 1979, would be mailed to the customer sometime during the fourth quarter of 1978. (See Exhibit 2, page 62.) But since the latest available Hourly Compensation Index by the Bureau of Labor Statistics at that time is from the third quarter of 1978, NASA needs to project the compensation index for two quarters into the future before the bill can be issued; the current quarter in which a statement is prepared does not have an index; plus the following quarter that is being billed.

The escalation adjustment is then simply computed as the forecast index value divided by the value for the 1974 base year, which happens to be 172.0. The change in value between these two periods is also applied to the amount due. In this example, the final amount billed turns out to be $621,990.

DISCUSSION QUESTIONS

1. The bill shown in Exhibit 2 is an example of a Space Shuttle customer billing. On that bill is the forecasted index NASA uses to determine the estimated escalation adjustment. Develop your own method to help determine billings through escalation adjustment. Use the new index to recompute NASA's bill. Defend your choice of forecasting methods.

2. NASA's own method for forecasting the index shown in Exhibit 2 is probably one you would not have considered. It simply plots the most recently published hourly compensation index and the index for the corresponding quarter of the prior year, draws a straight line between them, and extrapolates the appropriate number of months (in this case, four months) into the future. Comment on this approach. What other factors should NASA take into account?

NASA's Space Shuttle (B)

Stock Form 1114
October 1967
Title 7, GAO Manual
1114-106

BILL FOR COLLECTION

Bill No. ___C/A 347___

National Aeronautics and Space Administration

(Department of Establishment and Bureau or Office)

Date ___12/4/78___

Washington, DC 20546

(Address)

PAYER:

Messerschmitt-Bokow-Blohm GmbH
Postfach 801-169
8000 Muchen 80
Federal Republic of Germany

This bill should be returned by the payer with his remittance.
SEE INSTRUCTIONS BELOW.

Date	DESCRIPTION	Quantity	Unit Price Cost	Per	Amount
12/4/78	Progress Payment No. 1 for Shuttle Launch Services				$ 621, 990
	Charges per Preliminary Payment Schedule:				
	Services subject to Escalation— $439,000				
	Services not subject to Escalation— 103,000				
	Total charges per payment schedule $542,000				
	Add: Est. Escalation charge for 1/1/78–2/1/79 179,990				
	Total Progress Payment No. 1 $721,990				
	Less: Earnest money on hand 100,000				
	Net Amount Due $621,990				
	Base Year Index Value 172.0				
	Forecast Index Value 242.6				
	Est. Escalation Adjustment 41.0%				
	Payable 2/1/79	AMOUNT DUE THIS BILL,			$ 621, 990

This is not a receipt

INSTRUCTIONS

Tender of payment of the above bill may be made in cash, United States postal money order, express money order, bank draft, or check to the office indicated. Such tender, when in any other form than cash, should be drawn to the order of the Department or Establishment and Bureau or Office indicated above.

Receipts will be issued in all cases where "cash" is received, and only upon request when remittance is in any other form. If tender of payment of this bill is other than cash or United States postal money order, the receipt shall not become an acquittance until such tender has been cleared and the amount received by the Department or Establishment and Bureau or Office indicated above.

Failure to receive a receipt for a cash payment should be promptly reported by the payer to the chief administrative officer of the bureau or agency mentioned above.

U.S. GOVERNMENT PRINTING OFFICE: 1974 0-552-200

Exhibit 2. *Example of Customer Billing*

NASA's Space Shuttle (C):
Astronaut Candidates for the Space Shuttle

18

On January 16, 1978, the Administrator of the National Aeronautics and Space Administration (NASA) announced that 35 astronaut candidates had been selected for the Space Shuttle program from over eight thousand that had applied. The culmination of a year-long recruiting period, which ended on June 30, 1977, resulted in 14 civilians and 21 military officers making the final group. Women were included as astronaut candidates for the first time, with six in this group.

In making the announcement, the Administrator said: "The long and difficult task of selecting the most qualified candidates for the Space Shuttle program has been concluded and we are very pleased with the results. We have selected an outstanding group of women and men who represent the most competent, talented, and experienced people available to us today."

The candidates reported to NASA's Johnson Space Center (JSC) in Houston, Texas, on July 1, 1978, to begin a two-year training and evaluation program. Successful candidates will become astronauts and enter the Shuttle training program leading to eventual selection of a flight crew. The crew for each Shuttle launch will consist of one flight "Commander," who is in charge of overall Shuttle operations; one "Pilot," who will operate the Shuttle Orbiter, maneuvering it in near-earth orbit and flying it to its runway landing; and at least one "Mission Specialist," who will have overall responsibility for successful satellite launch and retrieval, monitoring space working conditions, managing supplies and facilities on the mission, and who might even participate in space walks. (In addition to these crew members, some flights may also have several "Payload Specialists" who work on a specific experiment in space; candidates for this job have not yet been selected.)

The current group of candidates consists of 15 pilots and 20 mission specialists. Although those in the latter group run the gamut in experience and education from physician to physicist to engineer to astronomer to computer technician, each mission specialist candidate will be trained to contribute productively to the orbital mission within his or her own area of expertise.

An Astronaut Candidate Assessment Board—made up of the training program manager and individuals from the astronaut office—

Exhibit 1. *Biographies for Selected Mission Specialist Candidates*

NAME: Guion S. Bluford, Jr., MAJ, USAF (PhD)—Mission Specialist
BIRTH: November 22, 1942, Philadelphia, PA
EDUCATION: Overbrook Senior High School, Philadelphia, PA; BS, Aerospace Engineering, Pennsylvania State University, 1964; MS, Aerospace Engineering, Air Force Institute of Technology, 1974; PhD, Aerospace Engineering, Air Force Institute of Technology, 1977
MARITAL STATUS: Married to the former Linda M. Tull of Philadelphia, PA
CHILDREN: Two
PRESELECTION POSITION: Chief, Aerodynamics and Airframe Branch, Aeromechanics Division, Air Force Dynamics Laboratory, Wright-Patterson AFB, OH

NAME: John M. Fabian, MAJ, USAF (PhD)—Mission Specialist
BIRTH: January 28, 1939, Goosecreek, TX
EDUCATION: Pullman High School, Pullman, WA; BS, Mechanical Engineering, Washington State University, 1962; MS, Aerospace Engineering, Air Force Institute of Technology, 1964; PhD, Aeronautics/Astronautics, University of Washington, 1974
MARITAL STATUS: Married to the former Donna K. Buboltz of Lewiston, ID
CHILDREN: Two
PRESELECTION POSITION: Assistant Professor of Aeronautics, USAF Academy, CO

NAME: Anna L. Fisher, MD—Mission Specialist
BIRTH: August 24, 1949, Albany, NY
EDUCATION: San Pedro High School, San Pedro, CA; BS, Chemistry, University of California, Los Angeles, 1971; MD, University of California, Los Angeles, School of Medicine, 1976
MARITAL STATUS: Married to Dr. William F. Fisher of Dallas, TX
PRESELECTION POSITION: Physician, Los Angeles, CA

NAME: Steven A. Hawley, PhD—Mission Specialist
BIRTH: December 12, 1951, Ottawa, KS
EDUCATION: Salina Central High School, Salina, KS; BA, Astronomy and Physics, University of Kansas, 1973; PhD, Astronomy, University of California, Santa Cruz, 1977
MARITAL STATUS: Unmarried
PRESELECTION POSITION: Postdoctoral Research Associate, Cerro Tololo Inter-American Observatory, La Serena, Chile

NAME: Jeffrey A. Hoffman, PhD—Mission Specialist
BIRTH: November 2, 1944, New York, NY
EDUCATION: Scarsdale High School, Scarsdale, NY; BA, Astronomy, Amherst College, 1966; PhD, Astrophysics, Harvard University, 1971
MARITAL STATUS: Married to the former Barbara C. Attridge of London, England
CHILDREN: One
PRESELECTION POSITION: Astrophysics Research Staff, Massachusetts Institute of Technology, Center for Space Research, Cambridge, MA

will assign the mission specialists to flights. The selected astronauts then begin intensified training for their specific mission. After each flight, the astronaut is recycled into a pool of qualified astronauts to await a new assignment. Between flights, astronauts are assigned other duties relevant to the Space Shuttle.

Usually only one mission specialist is required to meet the needs of any one mission. However, in planning for its first two years of operations, the assessment board identified four flights that will require one specialist in each of the two following areas: 1) a life scientist with a degree in either medicine (M.D.) or biochemistry (Ph.D.); and 2) an earth or physical scientist with a Ph.D. in physics, astronomy, aeronautics, or engineering. (A short biographical description of the dozen candidates meeting the requirements for either group is presented in Exhibit 1.)

To have an objective selection process based on the background, training, and qualifications of the candidates, each board member individually looked at straight-forward criteria for ev-

Exhibit 1. (*Continued*)

NAME: Shannon W. Lucid, PhD—Mission Specialist
BIRTH: January 14, 1943, Shanghai, China
EDUCATION: Bethany High School, Bethany, OK; BS, Chemistry, University of Oklahoma, 1963; MS, Biochemistry, University of Oklahoma, 1970; PhD, Biochemistry, University of Oklahoma, 1973
MARITAL STATUS: Married to Michael F. Lucid of Indianapolis, IN
CHILDREN: Three
PRESELECTION POSITION: Postdoctoral Fellow, Oklahoma Medical Research Foundation, Oklahoma City, OK

NAME: Ronald E. McNair, PhD—Mission Specialist
BIRTH: October 21, 1950, Lake City, SC
EDUCATION: Carver High School, Lake City, SC; BS, Physics, North Carolina A & T University, 1971; PhD, Physics, Massachusetts Institute of Technology, 1977
MARITAL STATUS: Married to the former Cheryl B. Moore of Brooklyn, NY
PRESELECTION POSITION: Member of the Technical Staff, Optical Physics Department, Hughes Research Laboratories, Malibu, CA

NAME: George D. Nelson, PhD—Mission Specialist
BIRTH: July 13, 1950, Charles City, IA
EDUCATION: Willmar Senior High School, Willmar, MN; BS, Physics, Harvey Mudd University, 1972; MS, Astronomy, University of Washington, 1974; PhD, Astronomy, University of Washington, 1977
MARITAL STATUS: Married to the former Susan L. Howard of Alhambra, CA
CHILDREN: Two
PRESELECTION POSITION: Research Associate, Astronomy Department, University of Washington, Seattle, WA

NAME: Judith A. Resnik, PhD—Mission Specialist
BIRTH: April 5, 1949, Akron, OH
EDUCATION: Firestone High School, Akron, OH; BS, Electrical Engineering, Carnegie-Mellon University, 1970; PhD, Electrical Engineering, University of Maryland, 1977
MARITAL STATUS: Unmarried
PRESELECTION POSITION: Engineering Staff, Product Development, Xerox Corporation, El Segundo, CA

(Continued)

ery candidate, such as grades, courses taken, experience, and professional accomplishments, and later interviewed the candidates one at a time to determine their motivation and depth of knowledge. (Exhibit 2 summarizes one board member's independent ratings for each qualified mission specialist candidate on each of the four flights.) The independent evaluations made by all of the board members will later be combined to make the final flight assignments. For the sake of morale, the board decided that no one selected from either of these two groups will fly a second time until all other members of that group have also flown. Besides, it was not yet known how long it would take for astronauts to prepare for their next flight.

Exhibit 1. (*Continued*)

NAME: Margaret R. Seddon, MD—Mission Specialist
BIRTH: November 8, 1947, Murfreesboro, TN
EDUCATION: Central High School, Murfreesboro, TN; BA, Physiology, University of California, Berkeley, 1970; MD, University of Tennessee College of Medicine, 1973
MARITAL STATUS: Unmarried
PRESELECTION POSITION: Resident Physician, Department of Surgery, City of Memphis Hospital, Memphis, TN

NAME: Norman E. Thagard, MD—Mission Specialist
BIRTH: July 3, 1943, Marianna, FL
EDUCATION: Paxon High School, Jacksonville, FL; BS, Engineering Science, Florida State University, 1965; MS, Engineering Science, Florida State University, 1966; MD, University of Texas Southwestern Medical School, 1977
MARITAL STATUS: Married to the former Rex K. Johnson of Atlanta, GA
CHILDREN: Two
PRESELECTION POSITION: Intern, Department of Internal Medicine, Medical University of South Carolina, Charleston, SC

NAME: James D. van Hoften, PhD—Mission Specialist
BIRTH: June 11, 1944, Fresno, CA
EDUCATION: Mills High School, Millbrae, CA; BS, Civil Engineering, University of California, Berkeley, 1966; MS, Hydraulic Engineering, Colorado State University, 1968; PhD, Fluid Mechanics, Colorado State University, 1976
MARITAL STATUS: Married to the former Vallarie Davis of Pasadena, CA
CHILDREN: Two
PRESELECTION POSITION: Assistant Professor of Civil Engineering, University of Houston, Houston, TX

Exhibit 2. *Candidate Assessment Ratings[1] for Four Space Shuttle Flights*

	Flight			
Astronaut	A	B	C	D
Bluford	85	73	95	51
Fabian	80	81	91	63
Fisher	76	40	88	56
Hawley	22	96	70	43
Hoffman	82	96	70	43
Lucid	37	91	60	50
McNair	56	67	83	89
Nelson	18	93	59	40
Resnik	88	80	85	45
Seddon	86	56	79	90
Thagard	82	75	33	91
van Hoften	51	21	94	76

[1] Higher ratings indicate greater proficiency for that flight's mission.

DISCUSSION QUESTIONS

1. Based solely on the preliminary candidate ratings available from one board member, which two mission specialists should be assigned to each of the four Shuttle flights?

2. What sort of assessment procedure would you recommend to assure complete objectivity and avoid bias?

3. As a board member, what reservations might you have regarding this selection process? What questions would you raise?

NASA's Space Shuttle (D): Ordering the External Tanks

19

The Space Shuttle will provide routine and inexpensive access to space because each of the five planned Orbiters will be used about 100 times. Launched like a missile and returned like a glider, the Orbiters will have two Solid Rocket Boosters to assist the lift-off. These will then separate and deploy parachutes, allowing them to float into the ocean where they can be recovered by tugboats, towed to land, refurbished, and reused about 20 times each. The only non-reusable element of this "system" is the External Tank that provides the liquid fuel mixture to the Orbiter's three Main Engines. Just before the Shuttle attains orbit, the External Tank will be jettisoned in a manner causing it to tumble away from the Orbiter and either burn up in the earth's atmosphere or fall harmlessly into a remote ocean area.

Since one tank must be used for each flight, it is important to schedule its purchases and control the inventory to coincide with the launch schedule. The flight plan for the heavily scheduled years 1987 through 1989 is shown in Exhibit 1. Should a flight not occur within a month of its planned launch date, then the customer(s) may receive a full refund of the 18 million dollars per flight cost (see Exhibit 2), or a proportionate share of the Orbiter capacity that was leased.

The logistics staff is budgeted for three-year cycles and hence would like to place an order

Exhibit 1. *Anticipated Flight Schedule for Space Shuttle Flights*

Year	Number of Shuttle Launches
1987	49
1988	55
1989	50

for the three years shown at one time. On the other hand, the procurement department is interested in devising a logical yet rapid purchasing strategy that would meet the requirements for the three-year period. Demand will be stable enough within the budget cycle to allow the use of traditional inventory models, with variations approximating a normal distribution.

To meet this anticipated flight schedule at as low a cost as possible, the procurement department has tentatively decided to purchase ten tanks at a time. The reasons for the decision to purchase lot-sized is to have a buffer against demand fluctuations as well as to take advantage of the discount purchase price (as given in Exhibit 2). If fewer than ten units were purchased, the price would be compounded by ten-percent increments for each unit less than ten.

The procurement department is now worried about several major factors that it thinks

Exhibit 2. *Cost per Space Shuttle Flight*

Item	Cost per Flight
Orbiter	$ 534,000
Crew Equipment	193,000
Main Engines	283,000
Solid Rocket Boosters	3,459,000
External Tank[1]	3,393,000
Propellants	717,000
Ground Support Equipment	310,000
Contract Administration	140,000
Operations Support	3,296,000
Launch Operations	4,407,000
Contingency	1,268,000
Total Flight Price	$18,000,000

[1] Estimate based on lot-size purchase for ten units.

should be considered. For example, it recognizes that its own time commitment is a major cost in placing an order. Since several staff members would, of necessity, spend a significant amount of labor-hours in preparing each tank order to be placed, such departmental overhead expenses would generally be built into the procurement cost. In addition, inspection costs upon delivery are very high. The department estimates that these fixed order placement costs add up to ten thousand dollars.

The logistics staff is concerned about many unknowns that currently exist regarding tank obsolescence, defects, and storage costs. For an estimate of the costs of holding each tank, a comparison with other large-dollar aerospace items ordered in the past was made. It appears that it costs about 20 percent of the actual price of a part to hold it for one year. The cost of capital tie-up is included in this figure.

The logistics staff and procurement department are aware that there is an 18-month lead-time to order and receive these tanks, and the storage warehouse can hold no more than 20 tanks at any given time.

DISCUSSION QUESTIONS

1. Develop an order policy for the External Tanks, assuming that demand is constant during each yearly ordering cycle.

2. NASA also wishes to consider the possibility of uneven or probabilistic demand during each reorder cycle. Procurement specialists estimate that the standard deviation of demand at any time is six tanks. If NASA is willing to tolerate one stockout in eight orders, what safety stock level should be maintained?

3. What other factors do you think should be accounted for in determining an ordering policy for the External Tanks? Under what circumstances should a three-year inventory purchase be made?

New England Castings

20

For over 75 years, New England Castings, Inc. has manufactured wood stoves for home use. In recent years, with increasing energy prices, George Mathison, president of New England Castings, has seen sales triple. This dramatic increase in sales has made it even more difficult for George to maintain quality in all of the wood stoves and related products.

Unlike other companies manufacturing wood stoves, New England Castings is *only* in the business of making stoves and stove-related products. Their major products are the Warmglo I, the Warmglo II, the Warmglo III, and the Warmglo IV. The Warmglo I is the smallest wood stove, with a heat output of 30,000 BTUs, while the Warmglo IV is the largest, with a heat output of 60,000 BTUs. In addition, New England Castings, Inc. produces a large array of products that have been designed to be used with one of their four stoves. These products include warming shelves, surface thermometers, stovepipes, adaptors, stove gloves, trivets, mittenracks, andirons, chimneys, and heat shields. New England Castings also publishes a newsletter and several paperback books on stove installation, stove operation, stove maintenance, and wood sources and cutting. It was George's belief that their wide assortment of products was a major contributor to the sales increases.

By Professor Ralph M. Stair, Jr., Florida State University.

The Warmglo III outsold all of the other stoves by a wide margin. The heat output and available accessories were ideal for the typical home. The Warmglo also had a number of outstanding features that made it one of the most attractive and heat efficient stoves on the market. Each Warmglo had a thermostatically controlled primary air intake valve that allowed the stove to adjust itself automatically to produce the correct heat output for varying weather conditions. A secondary air opening was used to increase the heat output in case of very cold weather. The internal stove parts produced a horizontal flame path for more efficient burning, and the output gases were forced to take an S-shaped path through the stove. The S-shaped path allowed more complete combustion of the gases and better heat transfer from the fire and gases through the cast iron to the area to be heated. These features, along with the accessories, resulted in expanding sales and prompted George to build a new factory to manufacture Warmglo III stoves. An overview diagram of the factory is shown in Figure 1.

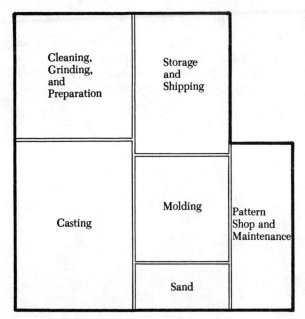

Figure 1. *Overview of Factory*

The new foundry used the latest equipment, including a new Disamatic that helped in manufacturing stove parts. Regardless of new equipment or procedures, casting operations have remained basically unchanged for hundreds of years. To begin with, a wooden pattern is made for every cast iron piece in the stove. The wooden pattern is an exact duplication of the cast iron piece that is to be manufactured. New England Castings has all of its patterns made by Precision Patterns, Inc., and these patterns are stored in the pattern shop and maintenance room. Then, a specially formulated sand is molded around the wooden pattern. There can be two or more sand molds for each pattern. Mixing the sand and making the molds is done in the molding room. When the wooden pattern is removed, the resulting sand molds form a negative image of the desired casting. Next, the molds are transported to the casting room, where molten iron is poured into the molds and allowed to cool. When the iron has solidified, the molds are moved into the cleaning, grinding, and preparation room. The molds are dumped into large vibrators that shake most of the sand from the casting. The rough castings are then subjected to both sandblasting to remove the rest of the sand and grinding to finish some of the surfaces of the castings. The castings are then painted with a special heat-resistant paint, assembled into workable stoves, and inspected for manufacturing defects that may have gone undetected thus far. Finally, the finished stoves are moved to storage and shipping, where they are packaged and shipped to the appropriate locations.

At present, the pattern shop and the maintenance department are located in the same room. One large counter is used by both maintenance personnel to get tools and parts, and by sand molders that need various patterns for the molding operation. Pete Nawler and Bob Bryan, who work behind the counter, are able to service ten people per hour. On the average, four people from maintenance and three people from the molding department arrive at the counter per hour. People from the molding department and from maintenance arrive randomly, and to be served they form a single line. Pete and Bob have always had a policy of first come, first served. Because of the location of the pattern shop and maintenance department, it takes about three minutes for an individual from the maintenance department to walk to the pattern and maintenance room, and it takes about one minute for an individual to walk from the molding department to the pattern and maintenance room.

After observing the operation of the pattern shop and maintenance room for several weeks, George decided to make some changes to the layout of the factory. An overview of these changes appears in Figure 2.

Separating the maintenance shop from the pattern shop had a number of advantages. It would take people from the maintenance department only one minute instead of three to get to the new maintenance department. Using time and motion studies, George was also able to determine that improving the layout of the maintenance department would allow Bob to serve six people from the maintenance department per hour, and improving the layout of the pattern department would allow Pete to serve seven people from the molding shop per hour.

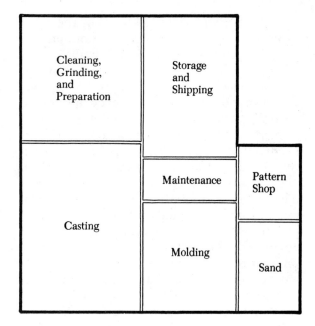

Figure 2. *Overview of Factory after Changes*

DISCUSSION QUESTIONS

1. How much time would the new layout save?

2. If maintenance personnel were paid $9.50 per hour and molding personnel were paid $11.75 per hour, how much could be saved with the new factory layout?

The Old Oregon Wood Store (A)

21

In 1975, George Brown started The Old Oregon Wood Store to manufacture "Old Oregon" tables. Each table was carefully constructed by hand, using the highest quality oak. Old Oregon tables could support over 500 pounds, and since the start of The Old Oregon Wood Store, not one table has been returned because of faulty workmanship or structural problems. In addition to being rugged, each table was beautifully finished using a urethane varnish that George developed over 20 years of working with wood-finishing materials.

The manufacturing process consists of four steps: preparation, assembly, finishing, and packaging. Each step is performed by one person. In addition to overseeing the entire operation, George does all of the finishing. Tom Surowski performs the preparation step, which involves cutting and forming the basic components of the tables. Leon Davis is in charge of the assembly, and Cathy Stark performs the packaging.

While each person is responsible for only one step in the manufacturing process, everyone can perform any one of the steps. It is George's policy that occasionally everyone should complete several tables on his or her own without

By Professor Ralph M. Stair, Florida State University.

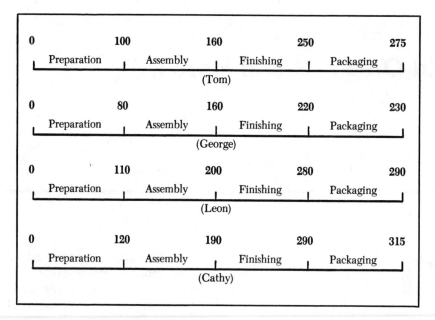

Figure 1. *Manufacturing Time in Minutes*

any help or assistance. A small competition is used to see who can complete an entire table in the least amount of time. George maintains average total and intermediate completion times. The results are shown in Figure 1.

It took Cathy longer than the other employees to construct an Old Oregon Table. In addition to being slower than the other employees, Cathy was also unhappy about her current responsibility of packaging. Her first preference was finishing, and her second preference was preparation.

DISCUSSION QUESTIONS

1. Is there a faster way to manufacture Old Oregon tables?

2. What would be the consequences if Cathy performed finishing instead of packaging?

3. What would be the consequences if Cathy performed preparation?

The Old Oregon Wood Store (B)

22

In addition to quality, George was very concerned with costs and efficiency. When one of the employees missed a day, it caused major scheduling problems. In some cases, George would assign another employee overtime to complete the necessary work. At other times, George would simply wait until the employee returned to work to complete his or her step in the manufacturing process. Both solutions caused problems. Overtime was expensive, and waiting caused delays and sometimes stopped the entire manufacturing process.

To overcome some of these problems, Randy Lane was hired. Randy's major duties were to perform miscellaneous jobs and to help out if one of the employees were absent. George had given Randy training in all phases of the manufacturing process, and he was pleased with the speed at which Randy was able to learn how to completely assemble Old Oregon tables. Total and intermediate completion times for Randy are given in Figure 1.

By Professor Ralph M. Stair, Jr., Florida State University.

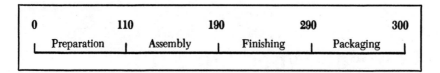

Figure 1. *Manufacturing Times in Minutes for Randy Lane*

DISCUSSION QUESTIONS

1. What do you think of George's policy to let Randy step in and perform the job of an absent employee?

2. Do you think that Randy will eventually become good enough to perform one of the manufacturing steps on a full-time basis?

Red Brand Canners

23

On Monday, September 13, 1965, Mr. Mitchell Gordon, Vice President of Operations, asked the Controller, the Sales Manager, and the Production Manager to meet with him to discuss the amount of tomato products to pack that season. The tomato crop, which had been purchased at planting, was beginning to arrive at the cannery, and packing operations would have to be started by the following Monday. Red Brand Canners was a medium-sized company which canned and distributed a variety of fruit and vegetable products under private brands in the western states.

Mr. William Cooper, the Controller, and Mr. Charles Myers, the Sales Manager, were the first to arrive in Mr. Gordon's office. Dan Tucker, the Production Manager, came in a few minutes later and said that he had picked up Produce Inspection's latest estimate of the quality of the incoming tomatoes. According to their report, about 20 percent of the crop was Grade A quality and the remaining portion of the 3-million pound crop was Grade B.

Gordon asked Myers about the demand for tomato products for the coming year. Myers replied that they could sell all of the whole canned tomatoes they could produce. The expected de-

Reprinted from *Stanford Business Cases 1965, 1977* with permission of the Publishers, Stanford University Graduate School of Business, © 1965 and 1977 by the Board of Trustees of the Leland Stanford Junior University.

Exhibit 1. *Demand Forecasts*

Product	Selling Price per Case	Demand Forecast (Cases)
24—2½ whole tomatoes	$4.00	800,000
24—2½ choice peach halves	5.40	10,000
24—2½ peach nectar	4.60	5,000
24—2½ tomato juice	4.50	50,000
24—2½ cooking apples	4.90	15,000
24—2½ tomato paste	3.80	80,000

mand for tomato juice and tomato paste, on the other hand, was limited. The Sales Manager then passed around the latest demand forecast, which is shown in Exhibit 1. He reminded the group that the selling prices had been set in light of the long-term marketing strategy of the company and that the potential sales had been forecast at these prices.

Bill Cooper, after looking at Myers' estimates of demand, said that it looked like the company "should do quite well [on the tomato crop] this year." With the new accounting system that had been set up, he had been able to compute the contribution for each product, and according to his analysis the incremental profit on whole tomatoes was greater than the incremental profit on any other tomato product. In May, after Red Brand had signed contracts agreeing to purchase the grower's production at an average delivered price of 6 cents per pound, Cooper had computed the tomato products' contributions (see Exhibit 2).

Exhibit 2. *Product Item Profitability*

Product	24—2½ whole tomatoes	24—2½ choice peach halves	24—2½ peach nectar	24—2½ tomato juice	24—2½ cooking apples	24—2½ tomato paste
Selling price	$4.00	$5.40	$4.60	$4.50	$4.90	$3.80
Variable costs:						
Direct labor	1.18	1.40	1.27	1.32	0.70	0.54
Variable overhead	0.24	0.32	0.23	0.36	0.22	0.26
Variable selling	0.40	0.30	0.40	0.85	0.28	0.38
Packaging material	0.70	0.56	0.60	0.65	0.70	0.77
Fruit*	1.08	1.80	1.70	1.20	0.90	1.50
Total variable costs	3.60	4.38	4.20	4.38	2.80	3.45
Contribution	0.40	1.02	0.40	0.12	1.10	0.35
Less allocated overhead	0.28	0.70	0.52	0.21	0.75	0.23
Net profit	0.12	0.32	(0.12)	(0.09)	0.35	0.12

*Product usage is as given below:

Product	Pounds Per Case
Whole tomatoes	18
Peach halves	18
Peach nectar	17
Tomato juice	20
Cooking apples	27
Tomato paste	25

Red Brand Canners

Exhibit 3. *Marginal Analysis of Tomato Products*

Z = Cost per pound of Grade A tomatoes in cents.
Y = Cost per pound of Grade B tomatoes in cents.

$$(600{,}000 \text{ lb} \times Z) + (2{,}400{,}000 \text{ lb} \times Y) = (3{,}000{,}000 \text{ lb} \times 6) \quad (1)$$

$$\frac{Z}{9} = \frac{Y}{5} \quad (2)$$

Z = 9.32 cents per pound
Y = 5.18 cents per pound

Product	Canned whole tomatoes	Tomato juice	Tomato paste
Selling price	$4.00	$4.50	$3.80
Variable cost (excluding tomato cost)	2.52	3.18	1.95
	$1.48	$1.32	$1.85
Tomato cost	1.49	1.24	1.30
Marginal profit	($0.01)	$0.08	$0.55

Dan Tucker brought to Cooper's attention that although there was ample production capacity, it was impossible to produce all whole tomatoes since too small a portion of the tomato crop was "A" quality. Red Brand used a numerical scale to record the quality of both raw produce and prepared products. This scale ran from zero to ten, the higher number representing better quality. According to this scale, "A" tomatoes averaged nine points per pound and "B" tomatoes averaged five points per pound. Tucker noted that the minimum average input quality was eight points per pound for canned whole tomatoes and six points per pound for juice. Paste could be made entirely from "B"-grade tomatoes. This meant that whole tomato production was limited to 800,000 pounds.

Gordon stated that this was not a real limitation. He had been recently solicited to purchase 80,000 pounds of Grade A tomatoes at 8½ cents per pound and at that time had turned down the offer. He felt, however, that the tomatoes were still available.

Myers, who had been doing some calculations, said that although he agreed that the company "should do quite well this year," it would not be by canning whole tomatoes. It seemed to him that the tomato cost should be allocated on the basis of quality and quantity rather than by quantity only, as Cooper had done. Therefore, he had recomputed the marginal profit on this basis (see Exhibit 3), and from his results had concluded that Red Brand should use 2,000,000 pounds of the "B" tomatoes for paste, and the remaining 400,000 pounds of "B" tomatoes and all of the "A" tomatoes for juice. If the demand expectations were realized, a contribution of $48,000 would be made on this year's tomato crop.

DISCUSSION QUESTIONS

1. Structure this problem verbally, including a written description of the constraints and objective. What are the decision variables?

2. Develop a *mathematical* formulation for Red Brand's objective function and constraints.

Rentall Trucks (A)

24

Jim Fox, an executive for Rentall Trucks, could not believe it. He had hired one of the town's best law firms, Folley, Smith, and Christensen. Their fee for drawing up the legal contracts was over 50 thousand dollars. Folley, Smith, and Christensen had made one important omission from the contracts, and this blunder would more than likely cost Rentall Trucks millions of dollars. For the hundredth time, Jim carefully reconstructed the situation and pondered the inevitable.

Rentall Trucks was started by Robert (Bob) Renton over ten years ago. It specialized in renting trucks to businesses and private individuals. The company prospered, and Bob increased his net worth by millions of dollars. Bob was a legend in the rental business and was known all over the world for his keen business abilities.

Only a year and a half ago some of the executives of Rentall and some additional outside investors offered to buy Rentall from Bob. Bob was close to retirement, and the offer was unbelievable. His children and their children would be able to live in high style off the proceeds of the sale. Folley, Smith, and Christensen developed the contracts for the executives of Rentall and other investors, and the sale was made.

By Professor Ralph M. Stair, Jr., Florida State University.

Being a perfectionist, it was only a matter of time until Bob was marching down to the Rentall headquarters, telling everyone the mistakes that Rentall was making and how to solve some of their problems. Pete Rosen, president of Rentall, became extremely angry about Bob's constant interference, and in a brief ten-minute meeting, Pete told Bob never to enter the Rentall offices again. It was at this time that Bob decided to reread the contracts, and it was also at this time that Bob and his lawyer discovered that there was no clause in the contracts that prevented Bob from competing directly with Rentall.

The brief ten-minute meeting with Pete Rosen was the beginning of Rentran. In less than six months, Bob Renton had lured some of the key executives away from Rentall and into his new business, Rentran, which would compete directly with Rentall Trucks in every way. After a few months of operation, Bob estimated that Rentran had about five percent of the total national market for truck rentals. Rentall had about 80 percent of the market, and another company, National Rentals, had the remaining 15 percent of the market.

Rentall's Jim Fox was in total shock. In a few months, Rentran had already captured five percent of the total market. At this rate, Rentran might completely dominate the market in a few short years. Pete Rosen even wondered if Rentall could maintain 50 percent of the market in the long run. As a result of these concerns, Pete hired a marketing research firm that analyzed a random sample of truck rental customers. The sample consisted of 1,000 existing or potential customers. The marketing research firm was very careful to make sure that the sample represented the true market conditions. The sample was taken in August. There were 800 customers of Rentall, 60 customers of Rentran, and the remainder were National customers. The same sample was then analyzed the next month concerning the customers' propensity to switch companies. Of the original Rentall customers, 200 switched to Rentran, and 80 switched to National. Rentran was able to retain 51 of their original customers. Three customers switched to Rentall, and six customers switched to National. Finally, 14 customers switched from National to Rentall, and 35 customers switched from National to Rentran.

DISCUSSION QUESTIONS

1. What will the market shares be in one month?

2. What will the market shares be in three months?

3. If market conditions remain the same, could Rentall end up with under 50 percent of the market?

Rentall Trucks (A)

Rentall Trucks (B)

By Professor Ralph M. Stair, Jr., Florida State University.

25

The board of directors meeting was only two weeks away, and there would be some difficult questions to answer—what happened and what can be done about Rentran. In Jim Fox's opinion, nothing could be done about the costly omission made by Folley, Smith, and Christensen. The only solution was to take immediate corrective action that would curb Rentran's ability to lure customers away from Rentall.

After a careful analysis of Rentran, Rentall, and the truck rental business in general, Jim concluded that immediate changes would be needed in three areas: rental policy, advertising, and product line. In regards to rental policy, a number of changes were needed to make truck rental both easier and faster. Rentall could implement many of the techniques used by Hertz and other car rental agencies. In addition, changes in the product line were needed. Rentall's smaller trucks had to be more comfortable and easier to drive. Automatic transmission, comfortable bucket seats, air conditioners, quality radio and tape stereo systems, and cruise control should be included. Although expensive and difficult to maintain, these items could make a significant difference in market shares. Finally, Jim knew that additional advertising was needed. The advertising had to be immediate and aggressive. Television and journal advertising had to be increased, and a good advertising company was needed. If these new changes were implemented now, there would be a good chance that Rentall would be able to maintain close to its 80 percent of the market. In order to confirm Jim's perceptions, the same marketing research firm was employed to analyze the effect of these changes, using the same sample of 1,000 customers.

The marketing research firm, Meyers Marketing Research, Inc., peformed a pilot test on the sample of 1,000 customers. The results of the analysis revealed that Rentall would only lose 100 of its original customers to Rentran and 20 to National if the new policies were implemented. In addition, Rentall would pick up customers from both Rentran and National. It was estimated that Rentall would now get nine customers from Rentran and 28 customers from National.

DISCUSSION QUESTIONS

1. What will the market shares be in one month?

2. What will the market shares be in three months?

3. If market conditions remain the same, what market share would Rentall have in the long run?

Rosewood Canning Company

26

Rosewood Canning Company, located in Tifton, Georgia, specializes in canning candied yams grown in the southeastern region of the country. The firm's headquarters, sales offices, and warehouses are open the entire year; the canning plant, however, is typically open from March 15 through October 15 each year, the season for harvesting and canning sweet potatoes. The actual harvest season is shorter than this seven-month period, but the potatoes are stored and refrigerated until the canning plant can process the accumulated inventory. At the end of each season, the canning equipment is cleaned, repaired, and "moth-balled" until the next season.

Farm cooperatives and brokers deliver the sweet potatoes to the plant in trucks; at the plant they are unloaded by conveyor and washed (water-sprayed) prior to storage in refrigeration units. Before the potatoes enter the cooking units, they are submerged in a strong alkaline bath which dissolves the peelings. Thereafter, the peeled potatoes are neutralized with a mild acid solution and washed thoroughly with water. They are then conveyed to the cooking units.

By Professors Jerry Kinard and Joe Iverstine, Southeastern Louisiana State University. Used by permission.

THE ORDERING PROBLEM

A major problem confronting Rosewood is the ordering of 50 percent caustic soda used in the peeling operation. The purchasing agent has historically struggled with the decision regarding the order quantity and the method of shipment of the caustic soda. He knows that caustic soda can be delivered by ten-ton tank trucks or 50-ton railroad tank cars. In the past, he has ordered seven tank trucks at the beginning of the season and one each day thereafter. (Each Friday, three truckloads of caustic soda are ordered for use during the weekend.) Approximately 380 tons of the solution are used each month; therefore, an extra tank truck is required every fourth day. The purchasing agent maintains a regular surveillance of inventory levels and has established a policy whereby the level should not drop below 20 tons.

Jim Stafford, a young assistant purchasing agent, was employed following the 1979 season. During his orientation program, he questioned why so many trucks were needed to deliver caustic soda. Specifically, he asked if bulk rail shipments would be more economical. The purchasing agent replied, "It is too much trouble fooling with the railroad." He advised his assistant, however, that he would welcome any suggestions Stafford might wish to make.

From an analysis of the canning operation and past practices, Stafford developed the following data: Monthly consumption of caustic soda was verified to be approximately 380 tons; clerical costs and laboratory analyses for each truck shipment totaled approximately $10; cost per ton for the caustic soda was $100; and inventory carrying cost was estimated to be one per cent of cost—primarily because of the use of steam to keep the product from freezing in storage.

After reviewing the unloading operations, Stafford noted that the average unloading rate was approximately five tons per hour. He also estimated the standard deviation to be 1.5 tons

Table 1.

Less Than (Tons/Hour)	Probability
2.0	.02
3.5	.16
5.0	.50
6.5	.84
8.0	.98

per hour. (See Table 1 for a schedule of unloading rates and probabilities.) Stafford concluded that the unloading rate could not be improved without extensive capital modifications.

If Rosewood Canning Company switched to 50-ton tank cars, the local railroad switch engine would spot the cars at the plant's unloading dock. A car puller would then be used to sequentially tow the cars in place for unloading. Rosewood Canning had 48 hours of free time to unload the spotted cars for release back to the railroad. A $50 per-car per-day demurrage penalty would be assessed on any car retained after the free time (48 hours) had expired. (The full penalty would be paid for any time over the free time. For example, a $50 penalty would be assessed if a car were held for 49 hours; another $50 would be levied if this car were held an additional 24 hours.) In addition, the railroad switch engine would only bring in loaded cars and remove empty cars once per day. A $250 fee was charged for additional switching.

These demurrage penalties and switching charges constituted the "trouble" alluded to by the purchasing agent. Stafford was not certain that his boss's decision to use trucks was wise, however. Unloading labor was the same for both truck and rail shipments. The latest price quotations for the 50 percent caustic soda indicated a $10/ton savings of rail shipments over shipments by tank trucks.

DISCUSSION QUESTIONS

1. What method of delivery would you choose?

2. How much caustic soda would you order each time?

Rosewood Canning Company

Ruth Jones's Heart By-Pass Operation

27

Ruth Jones, a robust 50-year-old insurance adjuster living in the northern suburbs of Chicago, has been diagnosed by a University of Illinois cardiologist as having a defective heart valve. Although otherwise healthy, Jones's heart problem could prove fatal if left untreated.

Firm research data are not yet available to predict the likelihood of survival for a woman of Mrs. Jones's age and condition without surgery. Based on his own experience and recent medical journal articles, the cardiologist tells her that if she selects to avoid surgical treatment of the valve problem, chances of survival would be approximately as follows: only a 50-percent chance of living one year, a 20-percent chance of surviving for two years, a 20-percent rate for five years, and a 10-percent chance of living to age 58. He places her probability of survival beyond age 58 without a heart by-pass to be extremely low.

The by-pass operation, however, is a serious surgical procedure, with five percent of the patients not living through the operation or succumbing in recovery. Furthermore, the first year after surgery is critical, with a nearly 45-percent

By Professor Barry Render, University of New Orleans.

mortality rate during that period. If Mrs. Jones were to survive beyond the first year, her chances of living five years would be approximately 20 percent. The survival rates for ten, 15, 20, 25 years, respectively, are as follows: 13 percent, eight percent, five percent, and four percent.

DISCUSSION QUESTIONS

1. Do you think Mrs. Jones should select the by-pass operation?
2. What other factors might be considered?

Seaburg Construction Company

28

Seaburg Construction Company, formed in 1950 by James Seaburg, was initially engaged in residential construction in Mobile, Alabama. Later, Mr. Seaburg's business was expanded to include the construction of office buildings and apartment complexes. In 1965, an industrial division was added to take advantage of the industrial expansion in the Gulf coast region.

Seaburg's industrial division performs both new plant construction and contract maintenance for existing plants. High quality work and strict adherence to deadlines have made Seaburg a favorite among the companies that have expanded their industrial capacity in the region. Moreover, Seaburg maintains good relationships with the local trade unions. He still carries a union card as a carpenter even though he has not worked at the trade for the past 20 years. As a result, Seaburg's jobs are rarely interrupted because of labor disputes.

Because of this positive image, several firms retain the Seaburg Construction Company to perform contract maintenance on the facilities that it built. Also, this reputation has enhanced the company's ability to capture contract maintenance for plants that were constructed by other firms. Seaburg's construction superinten-

By Professors Jerry Kinard and Joe Iverstine, Southeastern Louisiana State University. Used by permission.

dents work closely with the production managers of those plants that have signed maintenance contracts with Seaburg. Even though most contracts are cost-plus, Seaburg enjoys saving money for his client companies. In fact, he has instituted work sampling to ensure that his maintenance crews are productive. In particular, he takes pride in the work of his operations research staff. In this part of his company, Seaburg has adopted operations research techniques used by the Allied Forces in World War II. (The British Admirality used operations research teams to increase the size of convoys. Larger convoys reduced the vulnerability to German submarine attack.) While Seaburg's knowledge of operations research techniques was not acquired through formal training, he has been successful in acquiring, through individual effort, considerable expertise in the use of PERT/COST and other basic tools. Consequently, he now relies heavily on those techniques which he understands and which have application in the con-

struction industry. Seaburg particularly likes having his operations research staff reduce the complexity of a large scale maintenance turnaround. Through the use of network models, planning and control of turnaround activities are effected. Seaburg's superintendents are sensitive to the lost production incurred by their clients during these turnaround periods. They know that restoration of production is especially important for a "sold-out" plant.

THE TURNAROUND PROBLEM

In the spring of 1980, one of Seaburg's clients, a chlorine complex in nearby McIntosh, Alabama, was operating at 100 percent of capacity—"sold-out." A maintenance turnaround was scheduled, however, to perform major repairs to the facility. Turnaround activities, expected times for their completion, and sequencing constraints were as shown in the table below.

Job Initial	Job	t_e (hours)	Sequencing Constraint
alpha	Project start	0	—
A	Shut down plant and secure for maintenance	8	alpha
B	Shut down caustic evaporation plant and secure for maintenance	16	alpha
C	Remove existing chlorine compressor and install new unit	72	A
D	Clean chlorine coolers	16	A
E	Clean and repack acid towers	24	A
F	Retube liquefiers	36	A
G	Change ruptured discs and relief valves	10	A
H	Change leakage control valves	16	A
I	Clean salt saturation	24	B
J	Replace entrainment separators	24	B
K	Change control valves	16	B
L	Change impellers on circulating pumps	8	B
M	Dry and leak test chlorine equipment	24	C,D,E,F,G,H
N	Change heat exchanger on the first-effect evaporator	48	B,C
O	Leak test and start caustic evaporation plant	8	I,J,K,L,N
P	Start up chlorine plant	8	M,O
omega	Project end	0	P

Seaburg Construction Company

It should be noted from the above sequencing constraints that Job C (removal of the existing chlorine compressor and installation of a new unit) constrained Job N (changing the heat exchanger on the first-effect evaporator) because a large crane was needed for both jobs. Plans called for the crane to perform the compressor job (C) before moving to the heat exchanger job (N). Seaburg's staff advised the production manager that a second crane could be rented so that both jobs could be performed simultaneously. The rental of the crane would cost a base fee of $10,000, plus $8,000 per day. Contribution to profit and overhead from the production complex was estimated at $40,000 per day. Seaburg's superintendents and the production manager of the complex pondered their alternatives.

DISCUSSION QUESTIONS

1. Should the second crane be rented?

2. Is there any slack in the project?

St. Pierre Salt Company

29

St. Pierre Salt Company, located in Brusly, Louisiana, was formed in 1950 by Julian St. Pierre. The St. Pierre family owned 2,000 acres of land over huge salt deposits in West Baton Rouge Parish (County) which served as a source of salt, a vital raw material for the massive petrochemical industry located along the Mississippi River from Baton Rouge to New Orleans. Since the company was first formed, petrochemical firms have repeatedly attempted to purchase large tracts of land from the St. Pierre family. At the insistence of Julian St. Pierre, however, the family has steadfastly refused to liquidate its extensive property holdings.

Julian St. Pierre, a World War II veteran, attended a prominent southern university on the G.I. Bill and majored in geology. In addition, he worked for a major oil company for two years. His primary interest, however, was the huge salt dome formations under his family's land. Government geologists predicted that the salt deposits were virtually inexhaustible. In 1948, St. Pierre secured a bank loan to build two brine wells. (Brine wells are used to dissolve the salt in the dome by pumping and circulating water through the dome.) After the walls were drilled, a local chemical plant signed a contract with St.

By Professors Jerry Kinard and Joe Iverstine, Southeastern Louisiana State University. Used by permission.

Pierre to purchase brine from his field. The chemical firm secured a right-of-way and laid a pipeline from St. Pierre's wells, under the Mississippi River, to its complex located east of the river.

As St. Pierre received revenue from the chemical firm that purchased brine, he expanded his capacity to five wells. (Two additional water wells were required to service the five brine wells.) As the petrochemical complex expanded in the greater Baton Rouge area, the chemical firm that owned the pipeline began selling brine to other users in the area. Soon, all five wells were operating at capacity. Thereafter, St. Pierre drilled five additional brine wells and three supporting water wells, thereby doubling his capacity. Demand later stabilized at a level that could be satisfied from the brine of eight wells; consequently, two of St. Pierre's wells are kept in "reserve."

SALT EVAPORATION

In 1977, St. Pierre was contacted by an east coast chlorine producer who was attempting to secure purified (free of heavy metals) salt and have it shipped by rail to its three plants located in West Virginia, South Carolina, and Georgia, respectively. The chlorine producer had historically purchased his salt from the Bahamas; however, a 20-year contract with the Bahamian supplier was to expire in 1981. Early negotiations convinced the chlorine producer to find another source of salt.

To provide the salt, St. Pierre would have to install a purification plant, including salt evaporators, centrifuges, dryers, and a loading facility. The firm already had on its property a rail spur that previously serviced an abandoned sugar mill. After an extensive review of the project's economics, St. Pierre decided to proceed with the purification plant. In August, 1980, he signed a contract to supply purified salt to the chlorine producer, beginning February 1, 1982.

A key decision confronting St. Pierre and the engineering consulting firm he employed to design and construct the facility was the selection of centrifuges, which separate recrystallized salt from the brine solution. The separated salt is then fed to the salt dryers for the removal of residual moisture. Two major firms supplied such centrifuges suitable for salt service—AKZ, a German firm, and Century-Morris (CM), a U.S. corporation.

AKZ centrifuges are used widely in Europe and are considered the most reliable in the industry. These centrifuges had a stream factor of 96 percent.[1] However, in the event of a breakdown, the German firm cannot supply technical service or replacement parts immediately. Officials of AKZ projected that there was only a 20-percent probability that their centrifuges could be restored to service within 48 hours following a breakdown. Because parts had to be flown from Germany, immediate return to service for the centrifuges was unlikely. Moreover, AKZ had not established a U.S. distributorship or service center. Its organizational philosophy was based on centralization in order to control quality. Hence, its major service centers were located in Ludwigshafen, West Germany.

The CM centrifuges are used by most U.S. firms for salt separation. Corporate headquarters are located in Houston, Texas, and a service center is located in New Orleans, Louisiana. The CM centrifuge is not as reliable as the AKZ model; it can demonstrate only a 90-percent stream factor. The close proximity of the New Orleans' service center, however, supports a projected 85-percent probability of return to service within 48 hours after a breakdown.

Forty-eight hours was selected as the critical time by St. Pierre's engineers because of the in-process inventory normally maintained. This inventory permits the centrifuges to be down for

---

1. Stream factor is the percentage of time that a given piece of equipment is operable.

48 hours without curtailment of operations. A production curtailment would result in lost revenue for St. Pierre because his plant was "sold-out."

St. Pierre and his consulting engineers visited plants using both the AKZ and CM centrifuges. Installation and operating costs for both machines were estimated to be equal. Both have the same rated capacity of 30 tons/hr. St. Pierre had a gut feeling to select the AKZ because it "looked better." However, he knew his decision had to be made on a more rational basis.

DISCUSSION QUESTION

Which centrifuge would you select? Why?

Shale Oil Company

30

The Shale Oil Company contains several operating units that comprise its Aston, Ohio, manufacturing complex. These units process the crude oil that is pumped through and transform it into a multitude of hydrocarbon products. The units run 24 hours a day, seven days a week, and must be shut down for maintenance on a predetermined schedule. One such unit is Distillation Unit No. 5, or DU5. Studies have shown that DU5 can operate only 3½ years without major equipment breakdowns and excessive loss of efficiency. Therefore, DU5 is shut down every 3½ years for cleaning, inspection, and repairs.

DU5 is the only distillation unit for crude oil in the Aston complex, and its shut down severely affects all other operating units. Some of the production can be compensated by Shale refineries in other locations, but the rest must be processed before the shutdown and stored. Without proper planning, a nationwide shortage of Shale gasoline could occur. The timing of DU5's shutdown is critical, and the length of time the unit is down must be kept to a minimum to limit production loss. Shale uses PERT as a planning and controlling tool to minimize shutdown time.

By Professor Barry Render, University of New Orleans.

Table 1. *Preventive Maintenance of DU5*

	Activities	Time Estimates (in days)		
		Optimistic	Most Likely	Pessimistic
1–2	Circulate wash water throughout unit	1	2	2.5
2–3	Install blinds	1.5	2	2.5
3–4	Open and clean vessels and columns	2	3	4
3–5	Open and clean heat exchangers, remove tube bundles	1	2	3
3–6	Open and clean furnaces	1	2	4
3–7	Open and clean mechanical equipment	2	2.5	3
3–8	Inspect instrumentation	2	4	5
4–9	Inspect vessels and columns	1	2	3
5–10	Inspect heat exchanger shells	1	1.5	2
5–11	Inspect tube bundles	1	1.5	2
6–12	Inspect furnaces	2	2.5	3
6–17	Retube furnaces	15	20	30
7–13	Inspect mechanical equipment	1	1.5	2
7–18	Install new pump mechanical seals	3	5	8
8–19	Repair instrumentation	3	8	15
9–14	Repair vessels and columns	14	21	28
10–16	Repair heat exchanger shells	1	5	10
11–15	Repair tube bundles, retube	2	5	10
12–17	Repair furnaces	5	10	20
13–18	Repair mechanical equipment	10	15	25
14–20	Test and close vessels and columns	4	5	8
15–16	Install tube bundles into heat exchanger shells	1	2	3
16–20	Test and close heat exchangers	1	2	2.5
17–20	Test and close furnaces	1	2	3
18–20	Test and close mechanical equipment	1	2	3
19–20	Test instrumentation	2	4	6
20–21	Pull blinds	1.5	2	2.5
21–22	Purge all equipment with steam	1	3	5
22–23	Start up unit	3	5	10

The first phase of a shutdown is to open and clean the equipment. Inspectors can then enter the unit and examine the damage. Once damages are determined, the needed repairs can be carried out. Repair times can vary considerably depending on what damage the inspection reveals. Based on previous inspection records, some repair work is known ahead of time. Thorough cleaning of the equipment is also necessary to improve the unit's operating efficiency. Table 1 lists the many maintenance activities and their estimated complexion and their times.

DISCUSSION QUESTIONS

1. Determine the expected shutdown time and the probability the shutdown can be completed one week earlier.
2. What are the probabilities that Shale finishes the maintenance project one day, two days, three days, four days, five days, or six days, earlier?
3. Shale Oil is considering increasing the budget to shorten the shutdown. How do you suggest the company proceed?

Shale Oil Company

Sherman Motor Company

31

The Sherman Motor Company manufactured two specialized models of trucks in a single plant. Manufacturing operations were grouped into four departments: metal stamping; engine assembly; model 101 assembly; and model 102 assembly. Monthly production capacity in each department was limited as follows, assuming that each department devoted full time to the model in question:

	Monthly capacity	
Department	*Model 101*	*Model 102*
Metal stamping	2,500	3,500
Engine assembly	3,333	1,667
Model 101 assembly	2,250	—
Model 102 assembly	—	1,500

That is, the capacity of the metal stamping department was sufficient to produce stampings for either 2,500 model 101 trucks or 3,500 model 102 trucks per month if it devoted full time to either model. It could also produce stampings for both models, with a corresponding reduction in the potential output of each. Since each model 102 truck required five sevenths as much of the capacity of the department as one model 101 truck, for every seven model 102 trucks produced it would be necessary to subtract five from the capacity remaining for model 101. If, for example, 1,400 model 102 trucks were produced, there would be sufficient stamping capacity available for 2,500 − (5/7) (1,400) = 1,500 model 101 trucks. Thus, the capacity restrictions in the four departments could be represented by the straight lines shown in Exhibit 1. Any production combination within

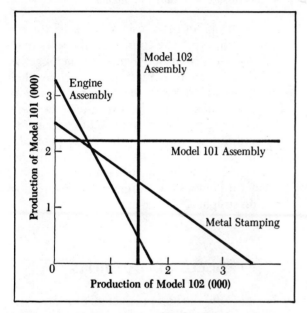

Exhibit 1. *Diagram Showing Production Possibilities*

the area bounded by the heavy portion of the lines was feasible from a capacity standpoint.

The prices to dealers of the two models, FOB the Sherman plant, were $2,100 for model 101 and $2,000 for model 102. Sherman followed the price leadership on one of the larger manufacturers in the industry.

As a result of a seller's market in 1953, Sherman was able to sell as many trucks as it could produce. The production schedules it had followed during the first six months of the year resulted in a monthly output of 333 model 101 trucks and 1,500 model 102 trucks. At this level of production, both the model 102 assembly and the engine assembly departments were operating at capacity, but the metal stamping department was operating at only 56.2 percent of capacity and the model 101 assembly department was at only 14.8 percent. Standard costs at this level of production are given in Exhibit 2, and further details on overhead costs are given in Exhibit 3.

At a monthly planning session of the company's executives in July 1953, dissatisfaction was expressed with the company's profit performance as reported in the six-month income statement just prepared (see Exhibit 4). The sales manager pointed out that it was impossible to sell the model 101 truck to yield a profit and suggested that it be dropped from the line in order to improve overall profitability.

Exhibit 2. *Standard Costs of Two Truck Models*

		Model 101		Model 102
Direct materials		$1,200		$1,000
Direct labor				
Metal stamping	$ 40		$ 30	
Engine assembly	60		120	
Final assembly	100	200	75	225
Overhead*				
Metal stamping	$216		$169	
Engine assembly	130		251	
Final assembly	445	791	175	595
Total		$2,191		$1,820

*See Exhibit 3.

Exhibit 3. *Overhead Budget for 1953*

Department	Total overhead per month*	Fixed overhead per month†	Variable overhead/unit Model 101	Variable overhead/unit Model 102
Metal stamping	$ 325,000	$135,000	$120	$100
Engine assembly	420,000	85,000	105	200
Model 101 assembly	148,000	90,000	175	—
Model 102 assembly	262,000	75,000	—	125
	$1,155,000	$385,000	$400	$425

*Based on planned 1953 production rate of 333 model 101 trucks and 1,500 model 102 trucks per month.
†Fixed overhead was distributed to models in proportion to degree of capacity utilization.

The controller objected to this suggestion. "The real trouble, Dick, is that we are trying to absorb the entire fixed overhead of the model 101 assembly department with only a small number of units production. Actually these units are making a contribution to overhead, even though it's not adequate to cover fixed costs, and we'd be worse off without them. In fact, it seems to me quite possible that we'd be better off by *increasing* production of model 101 trucks, cutting back if necessary on model 102 production."

The production manager pointed out that there was another way in which ouput of model 101 trucks could be stepped up, which would not require a cutback in model 102 production. This would be through purchase of engines from an outside supplier, thus relieving the present capacity problem in the engine assembly department. If this course of action were followed, Sherman would probably furnish the necessary materials but would reimburse the supplier for labor and overhead.

Exhibit 4. *Income Statement for Six Months Ending June 30, 1953 (Thousands of Dollars)*

Net sales	$21,950
Cost of goods sold	20,683
Gross Margin	$ 1,267
Selling, administrative, and general expense	1,051
Net income before taxes	$ 216
Taxes on income	115
Net income after taxes	$ 101

Sherman Motor Company

At this point the president entered the discussion. He asked the controller, the sales manager, and the production manager to get together to consider the two questions raised by their comments and to report their recommendations to him the next day. The two questions were: (1) Assuming no change in present capacity and demand, what would be the most profitable product mix? (2) What was the maximum labor and overhead charge that Sherman could afford to pay for engines if it purchased them from an outside supplier?

DISCUSSION QUESTIONS

1. **a.** Find the best product mix for Sherman Motors first when the capacities are those of the case and then with the engine capacity raised to 3,334 units of 101 engines. What is a unit of engine assembly capacity worth?*

   b. The second unit of capacity added is worth the same as the first. Verify that if the capacity were increased to 4,333 the increased contribution is 1,000 times that in part **a.**

---

*Discussion questions 1, 3, and 4 are used by permission of the author, Professor James S. Reece, University of Michigan. Distributed by the Intercollegiate Case Clearing House, Soldiers Field, Boston, Mass. 02163. All rights reserved to the contributors.

c. How many units of 101 engine capacity can be added before there is a change in the value of an extra unit?

2. Sherman Motors is considering introducing a new economy truck, to be called Model 103. The total metal stamping capacity would be sufficient for 3,000 Model 103s per month, while the total engine assembly shop would be enough for 2,500 Model 103s. The 103s could be assembled in the 101 assembly department; each 103 would require only half as much time as a 101. Each Model 103 truck would give a contribution of $225.

   a. Formulate the production decision with the three trucks as a linear programming problem and then verify that no Model 103s should be produced.

   b. How much would it cost in terms of contribution if, for some other reasons, management insisted that at least one Model 103 be made?

c. How high would the contribution on each 103 have to be before it became attractive to produce the new model?

3. The engine assembly line can be put on overtime. Suppose that efficiencies do not change and that 2,000 units of 101 overtime capacity are available. If direct labor costs increase by 50 percent on overtime and if the fixed overhead on the line on overtime is $40,000, the variable overhead remaining the same, would it pay to go on overtime?

4. The marketing manager, in arguing that maximizing short-run contribution was not necessarily to the long-run good of the company, wanted to produce as many Model 101s as possible. It was agreed to maximize the contribution for the month as long as the number 101s produced was at least four times the number of 102s. What is the resulting product mix?

State University Motor Pool

32

In his 1975 report to the Board of Regents, State University President Theodore Rawlings summed up the past year and offered a gloomy forecast for the future: "To cope with the invidious forces of inflation and recession, SU has taken strong measures of retrenchment. The continuing economic doldrums are affecting everyone and everything and higher education must bear its share of adversity. The institution has had to cut back on many types of expenditures to cover increases in vital services such as energy costs. Future austerity plans will include paring administrative and operating costs in an attempt to further 'tighten the belt.' "

In March, 1976, Dr. Harrison Ely, Vice-President for Business and Finance, expressed his concern about the cost effectiveness of SU's Division of Transportation Services during a conversation with some College of Business faculty. Dr. Ely felt that the motor pool was not operating efficiently, although he indicated that the basis for this belief was primarily intuition, not specifically supported by any "hard" evi-

This case was prepared by Dr. William W. Williams of Louisiana State University as a basis for class discussion rather than to illustrate either effective or ineffective handling of an administrative situation. Presented as a Case Workshop and distributed by the Intercollegiate Case Clearing House, Soldiers Field, Boston, Mass. 02163. All rights reserved to the contributor. Printed in U.S.A.

dence. He was of the opinion that in light of the University's continuing budgetary squeeze an analysis of the motor pool's operation might provide significant avenues for cost savings.

BACKGROUND

State University is one of the largest land-grant institutions for higher education in the United States. Founded in 1798, it became the official state university in the late 1800's. Since that time SU has matured into a full-fledged "multiversity" consisting of over 25 different colleges and schools dispersed geographically across the state at five primary campuses. Of over 50,000 total enrollments, nearly 30,000 students are in residence at the University Park campus. University Park is also the location of the system-wide coordination, integration, and administration office.

Under SU's dual-pyramid type of organization structure, each campus remains largely autonomous, administered by a chancellor and staff. The entire state-wide system is headed by a president, and the various administrative, research, and ancillary functions are the immediate responsibility of system vice-presidents (see Exhibit 1).

Among other responsibilities, a major task of the Vice-President for Business and Finance is the supervision of system-level transportation services. Despite the fact that some campuses had opted to subsume the transportation function under the domain of the campus chancellor, the University Park motor pool continued to remain accountable to the system vice-president. Reporting directly to Dr. Ely was Mr. Robinette, Director of Transportation Services.

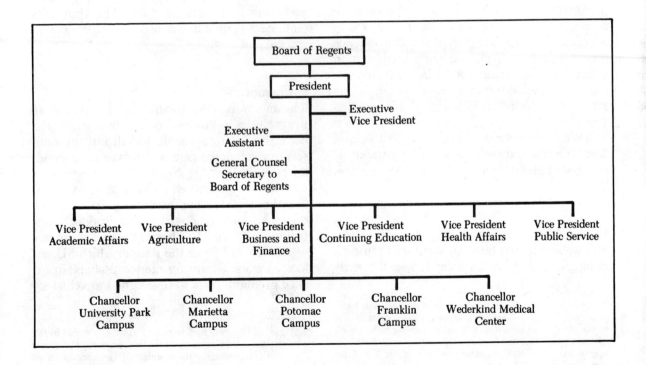

Exhibit 1. *State University System Organization*

UNIVERSITY PARK MOTOR POOL OPERATIONS

The University Park motor pool is by far the largest of all SU's transportation services.[1] Nearly 900 vehicles of various types are owned and maintained by the motor pool. The majority of these vehicles are permanently or semi-permanently assigned to specific activities: safety and security; maintenance; utilities; and administration. However, a large number of vehicles are maintained on a demand basis to facilitate institutional-related travel by faculty, staff, and students. As of fiscal 1975 the dispatch fleet consisted of 145 vehicles. Typically requests are made to the dispatch office which determines vehicle availability and assigns cars to fill the requests.

University policy encourages the use of these vehicles for official travel, but does allow employees some discretion. Employees using personal vehicles for their own convenience are reimbursed operating costs only. If travel is in a personal vehicle for University convenience (i.e., a dispatch vehicle was not available upon request) reimbursement must be on a full cost basis (i.e., including some depreciation). Currently, these respective costs are $.10 and $.15 per mile.[2]

When an individual utilizes a pool vehicle for University travel, his/her department is charged. The rate structure is shown in Exhibit 2.

Vehicle Purchasing Procedures

Mr. Robinette had been Director of Transportation Services since its inception in the early 1950s. During this era the motor pool remained relatively small. Throughout the 1960s, however, as the University experienced a sharp increase in enrollments, requests for dispatch vehicles accelerated rapidly. During this period a large number of vehicles were added to the fleet to keep pace with demand (see Exhibit 3 for the trend in fleet mileage growth). Although no formal methods were utilized to determine how many vehicles to acquire, over the years relatively few requests were ever unsatisfied. In fiscal 1975 only 11 requests were denied due to vehicle unavailability.

In general, orders for new vehicles are placed during the fall with the automobiles arriving in March and April. At this time, vehicles ready for retirement are disposed of via sealed-bid auctions. It has been motor pool practice to keep vehicles three years. In 1974–1975 the average price paid for a new vehicle was estimated to be approximately $3,700 with a salvage value averaging approximately $700. The University employed straight line depreciation for accounting purposes.

Operations

The motor pool maintained and repaired all fleet vehicles in-house. A complete machine and body shop were available for all but the most severe accident damage as well as routine service operations. Variable costs of operating a fleet vehicle were distributed on a per mile basis; during the most recent accounting period, operations costs (e.g., fuel, lubrication, tires, maintenance, etc.) had been allocated at the rate of $.048/mile.[3] Since the state in which SU was located is a self-insuring agency, no fixed insurance premium costs were assigned to vehicles.

---

1. Marietta and Potomac operated their motor pools independently of the System. Franklin's motor pool fleet was negligible due to its status as a commuter/evening school. Although the Medical Center operated a small fleet, the operation of the fleet was the responsibility of the Vice-President for Health Affairs.

2. These rates were also effective during fiscal 1975.

---

3. Although this rate had remained relatively stable in the past, there was some uncertainty as to the future. The motor pool had been reducing the number of large sedans in an attempt to increase fuel efficiency. This effort had, to some extent, been offset by increasing fuel costs.

Exhibit 2. *Rate Structure for Motor Pool Fleet, Fiscal 1975*

| | Rate | | |
	Per Mile	Per Day*	Number in Fleet
Compacts	$.10	$ 8.00	42
Sedans	$.12	$ 9.00	60
Station Wagons	$.14	$10.00	11
Club Wagons			
8 person	$.15	$11.00	
12 person	$.17	$12.00	32
14 person	$.19	$14.00	

*Daily rentals are charged at the daily rate or the mileage rate, whichever is higher.

Transportation Services overhead costs assigned to motor pool operations were not considered relevant. It was felt that since the dispatch fleet comprised about only 20 percent of Transportation Services' resource base, no significant alterations in burden would result from alterations in the size of the fleet or changes in purchasing policies.

PRELIMINARY INVESTIGATION

After discussions with Dr. Ely, Mr. Robinette and their respective staffs, two management professors and a small group of students began to plan how best to analyze the operations of the dispatch fleet. It was decided that the primary thrust of the initial investigation should focus on

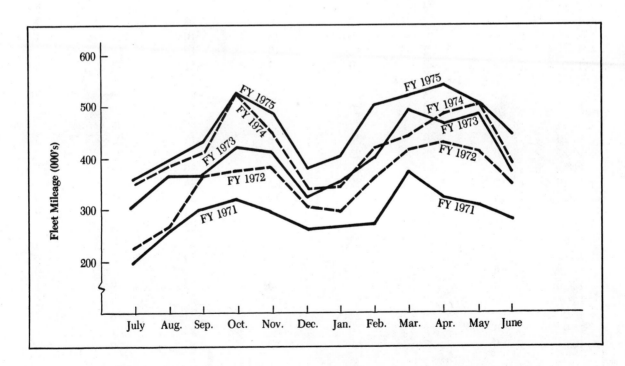

Exhibit 3. *Total Fleet Mileage by Month, Fiscal 1975 (Permanently Assigned and Dispatch Vehicles)*

State University Motor Pool

the collection and organization of raw data obtained from Transportation Services documents.

All information concerning a vehicle rental is recorded on a transfer voucher: expected and actual departure, expected and actual return, destination, purpose of trip, department to be charged, and mileage driven. The initial step of the data aggregation process involved a determination of the number of vehicles requested by day of week. Exhibit 4 shows the results from this compilation. After cursory review of these data, the consulting team agreed that the demand rate for vehicles might be closely associated with the University calendar (Exhibit 5).

The next stage of the investigation centered on ascertaining how long vehicles were kept out on rentals. A problem arose, however, in that dispatches occurred continuously during the course of a day and conceivably there could be an infinite number of different trip durations

Exhibit 4. *Number of Vehicles Demanded by Day of Week, Fiscal 1975*

Week of	Sunday	Monday	Tuesday	Wednesday	Thursday	Friday	Saturday
6/30	0	34	8	11	0*	5	0
7/7	1	21	20	18	8	16	0
7/14	0	13	10	15	9	21	2
7/21	0	27	16	25	11	17	1
7/28	0	14	11	14	26	16	8
8/4	0	25	22	18	10	17	4
8/11	0	11	12	21	13	14	3
8/18	0	29	15	22	15	6	5
8/25	0	23	12	20	13	13	2
9/1	3	0*	20	17	16	14	1
9/8	0	12	18	19	18	16	1
9/15	1	25	9	23	21	13	1
9/22	1	15	14	9	18	19	2
9/29	3	23	36	29	22	26	2
10/6	0	30	30	18	18	19	2
10/13	0	24	27	23	32	23	5
10/20	0	40	30	28	14	23	5
10/27	0	26	25	26	30	22	3
11/3	0	30	35	27	30	25	6
11/10	2	37	22	20	25	18	4
11/17	0	25	26	19	25	35	6
11/24	0	18	13	9	0*	3*	0
12/1	0	22	30	18	25	14	6
12/8	0	27	27	39	15	15	3
12/15	0	23	8	12	10	3	0
12/22	0	0*	0*	0*	1*	1*	0
12/29	0	5	3	0*	12	8	1
1/5	0	34	16	25	25	14	2
1/12	1	26	27	31	31	18	7
1/19	0	38	26	21	23	31	10
1/26	0	37	23	26	37	30	3

(Continued)

Exhibit 4. *(Continued)*

Week of	Sunday	Monday	Tuesday	Wednesday	Thursday	Friday	Saturday
2/2	1	23	30	33	25	33	3
2/9	0	38	32	30	23	34	4
2/16	1	26	31	27	29	26	6
2/23	0	33	22	28	26	30	12
3/2	2	29	32	27	22	26	6
3/9	1	20	27	31	20	22	4
3/15	0	27	20	30	24	15	5
3/23	1	20	14	13	13	1	0
3/30	1	29	21	32	29	27	4
4/6	1	38	24	25	31	28	5
4/13	1	32	20	34	38	17	1
4/20	1	19	23	28	35	23	6
4/27	3	26	32	32	37	18	6
5/4	0	42	37	32	32	18	6
5/11	0	38	36	37	44	30	3
5/18	0	22	39	41	30	12	9
5/25	0	25	30	28	29	22	5
6/1	13	34	23	16	19	33	0
6/8	1	20	18	18	12	13	0
6/15	1	31	11	23	17	19	1
6/22	1	22	17	9	17	19	4

*Denotes University Holiday.

Exhibit 5. *State University Academic Calendar*

Summer Quarter 1974
    6/14—Classes begin
    8/21—Classes end
    8/23—Commencement

Fall Quarter 1974
    9/26 —Classes begin
    12/10—Classes end
    12/13—Commencement

Winter Quarter 1975
    1/8 —Classes begin
    3/18—Classes end
    3/21—Commencement

Spring Quarter 1975
    4/2 —Classes begin
    6/5 —Classes end
    6/10—Commencement

(Exhibit 6). In an attempt to simplify the collection process, it was decided that if a vehicle was requested for departure after 4 PM, the day of dispatch would not count in the calculation of trip duration time. However, a request for departure prior to 4 PM would be the equivalent of "reserving" a vehicle for an entire day and would count toward the service time calculations.[4] Consistent with the above decision, trip

4. The rationale behind this decision may best be explained via a typical example. In many instances vehicles were checked out for brief overnight trips, departing in late afternoon and returning the next day in mid-morning. If this were to be counted as two (2) days, it would understate the actual number of requests that could be served by a vehicle. What actually happens is that upon return, the vehicle is serviced and made ready for a subsequent dispatch the same day. Basically, this is the manner in which motor pool dispatchers planned (i.e., for the above situation, the vehicle was not reserved for two days, but just for one). Although the 4 PM "cutoff" was an arbitrary choice of the consultants, it does make trip duration times conservative and admits a margin for error in following analysis.

State University Motor Pool

Exhibit 6. *Random Sample of Departures and Returns for Selected Time Intervals*

Time	Number of Departures	Number of Returns
before 8 AM	13	21
8 to 9 AM	35	27
9 to 10 AM	21	33
10 to 11 AM	28	23
11 to 12 PM	10	9
12 to 1 PM	17	20
1 to 2 PM	17	5
2 to 3 PM	10	9
3 to 4 PM	21	11
4 to 5 PM	63	11
after 5 PM	2	70

durations were recorded for each month and are presented in Exhibit 7.

The final phase of the data collection process concentrated on the assessment of fleet generated mileage. For each month, total mileage accumulated for trips of a specific duration were tallied. This sum was then divided by the total number of trips of that duration (Exhibit 7) to arrive at the average trip distance. The results of these computations are shown in Exhibit 8.

At this juncture the consulting team met once again to consider the direction their analysis should take.

Exhibit 7. *Absolute Frequencies of Trip Length by Month, Fiscal 1975*

Trip Duration (days)	July	August	September	October	November	December
1	101	120	87	175	123	53
2	66	81	94	172	138	87
3	44	52	49	86	84	39
4	35	27	33	52	40	38
5	27	27	24	48	32	22
6	18	13	12	24	22	11
7	9	13	8	8	7	4
8	10	10	7	6	9	4
9	1	2	1	1	8	7
10	3	3	3	5	2	7
11–12	5	5	7	7	4	12
13–14	5	4	5	1	2	5
15–16	0	2	7	1	2	4
17–20	3	4	6	3	3	3
21–25	1	5	1	1	0	3
26–30	0	7	2	10	7	4
31–40	16	17	2	5	6	3
41–60	2	1	1	4	3	2
61–120	2	0	1	1	0	0

(Continued)

State University Motor Pool

Exhibit 7. (*Continued*)

Trip Duration (days)	January	February	March	April	May	June
1	124	181	113	167	167	105
2	208	188	144	176	249	92
3	79	61	66	64	99	41
4	65	77	38	60	68	43
5	38	31	31	54	47	37
6	20	24	16	34	25	12
7	11	8	17	14	13	13
8	7	5	9	5	11	11
9	2	6	4	1	1	8
10	3	1	5	10	3	4
11–12	7	4	10	5	7	12
13–14	4	1	8	3	2	6
15–16	0	1	5	1	1	4
17–20	1	2	4	2	0	5
21–25	1	0	3	9	2	4
26–30	7	3	3	7	2	9
31–40	4	0	8	10	3	3
41–60	1	0	0	3	1	0
61–120	0	1	0	0	0	9

Exhibit 8. *Average Mileage Accumulated for Various Trip Durations*

Trip Duration (days)	July	August	September	October	November	December
1	139	133	166	125	112	150
2	216	248	243	279	240	220
3	359	401	344	398	414	351
4	445	421	413	463	506	393
5	402	553	502	586	442	552
6	499	681	1050	898	760	630
7	851	834	604	779	1507	596
8	463	849	857	473	1000	919
9	856	2180	1234	4369	1055	840
10	659	1493	1399	1321	2107	834
11–12	1256	921	803	1240	1225	611
13–14	1217	1496	453	94	938	560
15–16	—	1782	768	508	315	804
17–20	1202	1928	1201	307	739	1140
21–25	1866	2279	2496	1019	—	2043
26–30	3549	1308	856	890	1348	1388
31–40	1940	1713	1833	947	1324	854
41–60	1903	2390	742	1184	2234	330
61–120	11,804	—	3085	3529	—	—

(*Continued*)

State University Motor Pool

Exhibit 8. (*Continued*)

Trip Duration (days)	January	February	March	April	May	June
1	75	121	137	136	85	170
2	202	220	243	260	202	213
3	322	381	389	394	296	344
4	439	515	468	518	385	473
5	525	572	623	645	563	561
6	744	516	720	646	560	793
7	1069	767	830	688	764	889
8	977	854	917	1325	842	696
9	1143	945	909	2540	1147	688
10	934	1160	717	1175	356	1060
11–12	607	313	930	1030	788	1168
13–14	1275	1437	1230	787	1631	792
15–16	—	993	2045	1332	1228	763
17–20	1011	1282	463	883	—	1384
21–25	611	—	982	1094	594	2113
26–30	1075	928	1945	1306	1690	1060
31–40	1323	—	923	1328	563	618
41–60	4225	—	—	161	10,964	—
61–120	—	6914	—	937	—	3752

DISCUSSION QUESTION

Explain the procedure you think the team should follow and describe the steps that will be involved.

Touro Infirmary

33

Touro Infirmary is a medium-sized teaching hospital located in New Orleans. The department of dietetics must meet the varying needs for the feeding of patients, staff, and visitors of the facility. The nutritional requirements of the patients are diverse, necessitating a complex menu structure. Diet options include sodium-restricted, bland, calorie-restricted, and numerous other regimes.

The bed capacity for the institution is 500, indicating a maximum of approximately 1,500 meals daily. Since Touro has a large number of Jewish patients, a unique demand is the frequent serving of kosher food. Kosher food must be prepared and served in accordance with strict religious rules. For example, the food must be blessed by a rabbi and prepared with equipment that is used exclusively for kosher products. Additionally, there are restrictions placed upon the food combinations that can be offered in a kosher meal and certain types of meats and fishes may not be served.

Approximately 1,825 kosher meals are served to Touro patients over a one-year period. Because the hospital cannot prepare these meals in its kitchens, all kosher meals are ordered from Schreiber Foods in New York, and are shipped by air mail. The cost per dinner is $3.50. If more

By John J. Fedorko. Used by permission.

than 150 dinners are ordered at once, the price is reduced to $3.25 per dinner. The order is placed by telephone and shipment can be expected to be received in three working days. The cost of placing an order is $10. It is estimated that carrying costs are 25 percent of the meal cost; the many additional requirements of religious laws, including special silverware, are part of the reason for this high cost.

A problem arises when a patient orders a kosher meal and the hospital has run out of stock. An alternative source is available in New Orleans but at a premium of $10. Another unusual problem is storage. A separate freezer must be used to store the kosher food. The present freezer has a capacity of 75 dinners. Patton Industries offers a commercial freezer that has a capacity of 225 dinners. The cost of the freezer is $1,800 and it has a useful life of ten years.

The head of the dietary department, Mrs. Kathy Fedorko, has requested an inventory analysis to determine a method for inventory control that will minimize costs.

DISCUSSION QUESTIONS

1. What is the optimal amount to be ordered and how often? At what point should the hospital reorder?

2. Besides quantitative methods to determine proper inventory control, what other considerations should be taken into account? Is there an alternative method that will minimize costs?

Touro Infirmary

Trading in Northern Steel Stock

34

Gordon Maussy, Sr., is chief economist for the Federal Reserve Bank of Delaware. With a Ph.D. from Yale University and four master's degrees from various universities, he has diverse research interests that extend to econometric studies of the New York Stock Exchange. Maussy's 17-year-old son, Gordon, Jr., has been a curious onlooker to his father's obsession with numbers ever since he completed a college algebra course at Delaware Township High School.

One day, Gordon, Sr., returned home from the office early to find his son sifting through stacks of papers in the study. "What are you doing with my files?" asked Gordon, Sr. "Dad, I was just looking at the figures you have on the Northern Steel Company stock. I've been watching the closing price per share for the past eight months now. I kind of like this stock," replied the son. "And just what did you observe?" asked Gordon, Sr., suddenly becoming both interested and amused at his son's hitherto secret hobby.

Going to his bedroom to retrieve a table he had prepared, Gordon, Jr., returned and handed his father the paper shown in Exhibit 1. "This is my analysis of the chance Northern stock will go up or down. A lot depends on what happened the day before," said Gordon, Jr.

By Professor Barry Render, University of New Orleans.

Exhibit 1.

Price Change in Northern Stock on Any Given Day (to the nearest $)	Price Change in Northern Stock the following Day				
	Down $2	Down $1	Unchanged	Up $1	Up $2
Down $2	0.10	0.25	0.25	0.30	0.10
Down $1	0.05	0.15	0.30	0.35	0.15
Unchanged	0.05	0.20	0.40	0.25	0.10
Up $1	0.15	0.35	0.25	0.20	0.05
Up $2	0.15	0.30	0.35	0.10	0.10

Impressed by his son's quantitative approach to tracking the stock, three days later Gordon, Sr., presented the young man with 100 shares of Northern Steel. The stock had just closed up $1 to $20 per share. This gift, however, was not without a specific condition. At the end of 30 trading days, Gordon, Jr., must cash in his shares. The value of the stock at that time would become his expense money in the freshman year of college.

Concerned with having plenty of money for extracurricular activities while away at school, Gordon, Jr., quickly devised an investment strategy that "can't lose." He decided to do the following:

1. Sell all shares owned at the end of a trading day whenever the price of the stock increases two days in a row.
2. Buy as many shares as cash allows whenever the price of the stock has declined at the end of a trading day.

3. Do nothing if the price remained the same.

Gordon, Sr., has agreed to pay all brokerage commission fees incurred in order to stimulate his son's speculative interests. Gordon, Jr., asks if there is any way to "experiment" with the proposed strategy on paper before he begins his real trading the next day with $2,000 worth of stock on the line. His father replies with one word, "simulation."

DISCUSSION QUESTIONS

1. What will Gordon, Jr.'s financial picture look like at the end of 30 days?

2. Can you develop an alternative strategy that yields a better financial picture?

Western Ranchman Outfitters

35

Western Ranchman Outfitters (WRO) is a family-owned and -operated mail order and retail store business in Cheyenne, Wyoming. It bills itself as "The Nation's Finest Western Store" and carries high quality western apparel and riding supplies. Its catalog is mailed all over the world; the store and its president, John Veta, have appeared in a short article in *Fortune* magazine; and clothes from WRO were featured in the August 1980 *Mademoiselle*.

One of WRO's most staple items is the button front, shrink-to-fit blue jean made by Levi Strauss (model no. 501). This is the original riveted denim pant that cowboys shrunk by sitting in a tub of hot water. It is the epitome of durability and fit and is still a popular jean. When Mr. Veta was asked his stockout philosophy for this item, he answered, "Would you expect a drugstore to have aspirin?" Further, Mr. Veta has had a pleasant relationship with Levi Strauss for all the years of his business career.

Don Randell, director of merchandising, takes a physical inventory of this item once a month. His records show annual usage, amount on hand, quantity ordered, and quantity received (which has been averaging 185 pairs per month, except in January–March when it aver-

By Sharon Veta Snyder. Used by permission.

ages 150 pairs per month), all dated by the month. The store attempts to keep a safety stock adequate for 60 days for two reasons: production problems of the supplier and a hedge against unusually large orders.

Mr. Randell described the problems of ordering. "The rag business," as it is known, "is made up of the most disorganized group of people I've ever had the opportunity to be associated with," according to Randell. The problems he cited include not specifying a delivery date, unexplained late deliveries, a general lack of productivity, and lead times of up to six months.

Randell contrasted this situation with his experience in the flexible packaging industry, where reliability was a hallmark, and a delay of a single day warranted notification to the customer.

The most recent eight-month period is used to illustrate WRO's ordering difficulties. While the sample figures in Exhibit 1 may seem peculiar, they reflect WRO's philosophy of offering a full range of sizes and Mr. Randell's attempts to predict Levi Strauss' delivery pattern so that the store is close to obtaining the stock it needs. For example, in the last eight months, no one bought a pair sized 27 × 36. Nevertheless six were ordered and received so that should such a customer appear, he would be able to satisfy his needs. For size 27 × 34, 33 were ordered, but only 21 were received, which is very close to the 18 sold in the eight months of the previous year. The 27-inch and 28-inch waist sizes shown in the exhibit are but two of the many available waist sizes, of course—waist sizes up to 60 inches are produced and sold.

Randell places an order for Levi blue jeans every month, doing his best to ensure an adequate supply for the business. Normally, WRO customers are not disappointed when requesting the Levi 501. However, in the past two months, the Wyoming Game and Fish Department has been requiring extra pairs of this jean, and WRO has not always had this exact jean in stock. Since

Exhibit 1. *Usage and Ordering of the Levi "501" for Selected Sizes*

Size (in inches) Waist × Length	Usage	Number Ordered	Number Received
27 × 28	11	—	—
27 × 29	1	—	—
27 × 30	6	—	—
27 × 31	0	—	—
27 × 32	4	—	—
27 × 33	—	—	—
27 × 34	18	33	21
27 × 36	—	6	6
28 × 28	—	—	—
28 × 29	—	—	—
28 × 30	—	—	—
28 × 31	—	3	3
28 × 32	4	—	—
28 × 33	7	—	—
28 × 34	8	21	12
28 × 36	27	30	18
	86	93	50*

*Approximately 54 percent of the number ordered were received.

Western Ranchman Outfitters

there are at least four styles that satisfy the state requirements, the problem is usually overcome with other styles or brands.

Annual demand at WRO for the Levi 501 is 2,000 pair. The cost of placing an order is about $10, the carrying cost is 12 percent, and the cost of the Levi to WRO is $10.05 per pair.

DISCUSSION QUESTION

Evaluate Randell's ordering policy. How does it compare with formal mathematical approaches?

Western Ranchman Outfitters

WTVX

36

WTVX, Channel 6, is located in Eugene, Oregon, home of the University of Oregon's football team. The station is owned and operated by George Wilcox, a former Duck (University of Oregon Football player). Although there were other television stations in Eugene, WTVX was the only station that had a weatherman who was a member of the American Meteorological Society (AMS). Every night, Joe Hummel would be introduced as the only weatherman in Eugene that was a member of the AMS. This was George's idea, and he believed that this gave his station the mark of quality and helped with market share.

In addition to being a member of AMS, Joe was also the most popular person on any of the local news programs. Joe was always trying to find innovative ways to make the weather interesting, and this was especially difficult during the winter months when the weather seemed to remain the same over long periods of time. Joe's forecast for next month, for example, was that there would be a 70-percent chance of rain *every* day, and that what happens on one day (rain or shine) was not in any way dependent on what happened the day before.

One of Joe's most popular features of the weather report was to invite questions during

By Professor Ralph M. Stair, Florida State University.

the actual broadcast. These questions would be phoned in, and they were answered on the spot by Joe. Last week, a ten-year-old boy asked what caused fog, and Joe did an excellent job of describing some of the various causes.

Occasionally, Joe would make a mistake and this was the case during a recent weather broadcast. A high school senior asked Joe what the chances were of getting 15 days of rain in the next month (30 days). Joe made a quick calculation: 70 percent (15 days/30 days) = 70 percent (½) = 35 percent. Joe quickly found out what it is like being wrong in a university town. He had over 50 phone calls from scientists, mathematicians, and other university professors, telling him that he had made a big mistake

in computing the chances of getting 15 days of rain during the next 30 days. Although Joe didn't understand all of the formulas the professors mentioned, he was determined to find the correct answer and make a correction during a future broadcast.

DISCUSSION QUESTIONS

1. What are the chances of getting 15 days of rain during the next 30 days?

2. What do you think about Joe's assumptions concerning the weather for the next 30 days?

PART TWO

Readings

Forecasting

Every day, managers are forced to make decisions involving thousands, and even millions, of dollars without knowing what will happen in the future. New equipment is acquired without knowing the demand for products, inventory is ordered without knowing what sales will be, and investments are made without knowing what the future revenues will be. Managers and decision makers, in making decisions whose outcome is a function of the future, are always trying to reduce uncertainty and to make better estimates of what will happen in the future. Reducing this uncertainty and making estimates or predictions about the future is the main emphasis of forecasting.

There are literally thousands of quantitative forecasting techniques, and numerous forecasting techniques use subjectivity and intuition. Some of the more typically used quantitative forecasting techniques include moving average, exponential smoothing, trend projection, simple regression, and multiple regression. An example of a popular subjective forecasting technique is the Delphi Method.

Irrespective of the forecasting technique chosen, there exists an overall framework that is used to make forecasts of future events. The first step is to determine the use and objectives of the forecast. Next, the items or quantities to be forecasted are determined. Once this is done, the time horizon of the forecast is established and a particular forecasting method or model is selected. Then data can be gathered, the forecasting model can be validated, the actual forecast can be made, and the results can be implemented into the decision-making process.

In monitoring a forecasting technique, a number of approaches can be used to ascertain the accuracy of the forecasting methodology. One of the popular techniques for measuring forecast accuracy is mean absolute deviations. With this approach, the absolute differences between the forecast and the actual demand figures are totaled and then averaged. This average is the mean absolute deviation.

Forecasting Nursing Staffing Requirements by Intensity-of-Care Level

Determining personnel requirements in a hospital environment is perhaps one of the most difficult activities facing the hospital administrator. This is especially true in determining the needed level of nurse staffing requirements. Furthermore, the further in advance that the nursing staff requirements can be forecasted, the easier it is to develop plans and schedules for staffing, training programs, and vacation time. In some cases, nursing salary costs can represent as much as 50 percent of the operating cost of a short-term, acute-care hospital. For these types of health care delivery systems, forecasting nursing staff requirements is essential.

In this article, Helmer and Suver describe how they employed various forecasting approaches in estimating nursing staff requirements. In developing their model, such factors as intensity-of-care levels, total census, and type of ward were included in the analysis. The health care delivery system discussed in the article is a 200-bed hospital.

In order to develop forecasts for nursing staff requirements, a number of regression models were developed. These models utilized input data from daily reports by shift, ward, and intensity-of-care levels. The number of patients in each level of care was forecasted using ward, month, day, shift, and time variables as the major independent variables. Then, the number of patients as a function of these levels was used to predict nursing workhour requirements. Furthermore, using only time, beds, ward, and month as independent variables, the model was also able to predict total hospital census for a specific month and a particular ward. Then, using this forecasted census, levels of care for these wards for various months can be predicted.

As a result of using regression analysis to forecast nursing staff requirements, there was a reduction of approximately three full-time equivalent nurses with a potential annual dollar savings of nearly $50,000. This cost savings averaged out to be approximately one dollar per patient per day. The hospital administrator felt that these savings were achievable without any reduction in the quality or level of health care.

Incorporating Judgments in Sales Forecasts: Application of the Delphi Method at American Hoist & Derrick

This article by Basu and Schroeder demonstrates the successful use of a judgmental forecasting technique. In the past, subjective forecasts were made that relied primarily on subjective judgments of a few top-level managers. These forecasts, unfortunately, were subject to a significant amount of error. As a result, a Delphi approach was implemented. This approach used a panel of experts, a series of three rounds, and a questionnaire for each round. A total of 23 key individuals who were considered knowledgeable personnel from different functional areas were chosen to participate in the Delphi forecasting technique.

The results of the Delphi approach were greater sales accuracy and more convergence of some of the forecasting estimates. In 1975, the Delphi sales forecast had an error of less than one-third of one percent. This represented a significant increase in forecast accuracy over the previous methods, which had errors of plus or minus 20 percent in some cases. Furthermore, the Delphi approach produced reasonably uniform estimates of sales among different managers. This congruence in outlook on business conditions and corporate sales was considered valuable by the managers of American Hoist & Derrick.

Forecasting Nursing Staffing Requirements by Intensity-of-Care Level

F. Theodore Helmer
Edward B. Oppermann
James D. Suver

1

The continuing escalation of health care costs has become a matter of considerable national concern. Research is being conducted throughout the nation on cost containment, and much of this effort has recently been devoted to the macroquestions on regulation of health care costs. The purpose of this research is to develop a micro approach into nursing cost containment from the viewpoint of the hospital administrator at a 220-bed, nonprofit community hospital in an urban setting. When cost containment is approached from this perspective, we have found that nursing requirements can be influenced by proper planning, and it is in this area where the greatest control over costs can be exerted. Considerable savings can result from reduction, or more efficient utilization, of nursing man-hours. Since payroll expenditures typically account for over 50% of the operating budget of most hospitals, this area would seem to provide the greatest potential for savings.

In [a] recent study, [the] relationship between nursing salary expenses and workloads was determined, and models were developed to

Reprinted by permission of F. Theodore Helmer, Edward B. Oppermann, and James D. Suver, "Forecasting Nursing Staffing Requirements by Intensity–of–Care Level," *Interfaces*, Vol. 10, No. 3, June, 1980, Copyright 1980 The Institute of Management Sciences.

forecast nursing salary expenses from independent workload input variables [Helmer, Levy, and Suver, 1978]. This study reinforced the need for more efficient nursing man-hour budgets, workload forecasts, and control procedures.

RESEARCH OBJECTIVES

The overall goal of the research was to enable hospital management to predict nursing man-hour requirements by ward, shift, day of the week, and month of the year. Since the nursing man-hours required by ward and by shift for any given day are a function of both the number of patients by care level and the standard hours (for that level of care), the research has focused first on the demand, or patient forecast. Future efforts will continue into the evaluation of the standards for control purposes. The first models will be expected to predict required nursing hours by ward and shift with greater accuracy and less effort than is currently being accomplished manually. It is important to note that approximately 50% of the nursing hours in the hospital were "variable" costs and could be varied with patient requirements. Other hospitals may not have this degree of freedom, but it is desirable to develop, if possible, for management flexibility.

METHODOLOGY

In order to obtain estimates of the required nursing man-hours, statistical model[s] were developed to predict the number of patients by six intensity-of-care levels for each hospital ward by month, day, and shift. The magnitude of the distribution of care levels is shown in Table 1. With the support of a nonprofit 220-bed short-term acute-care hospital, intensity-of-care census data for each shift for the year 1978 were gathered. This information was collected on the Nursing Staffing Report, and each of the 9687 observations was keypunched, verified, and used

as input to the Statistical Package for Social Sciences multiple regression routine. Numerous regression runs were made with the following as independent indicator variables:

WARDS:	ICC/CCU	Intensive Care, Coronary Care
	2N	Psychiatric Cases
	3N	Medical Cases + Surgical and Orthopedic Overflow
	3T	Medical Cases
	4T	Surgical Cases
	5T	Orthopedic Cases
	PEDS	Pediatrics
	OB	Obstetrics— Maternity and Gynecology Cases
	NSY	Nursery
MONTH:	January through December	
DAY:	Sunday through Saturday	
SHIFT:	Day, Evening, Night	
TIME:	Day of the year, numbered 1 through 365	

The Ward 2N, the month of May, the day of Wednesday, and the day shift were selected as the reference point and set equal to zero (this is reflected in the constant term). The resulting models predict the number of patients by care level, shift, ward, month, and day of the week. The impact of the shift, day of the week, and other independent variables on the workloads can be easily determined from the model coefficients.

RESULTS

The results of the numerous regression runs are summarized in Table 2, which is based on the 9,687 observations made in 1978. For example,

Table 1. *Totals by Level of Care*

	Total Census in 1978	Average Patients per Day (3 Shifts)	Average Patients per Shift
CL1	15,226	41.72	13.91
CL2	94,234	258.18	86.06
CL3	41,115	112.64	37.55
CL4	8,131	22.28	7.43
CL5	1,720	4.71	1.57
CL6	385	1.05	.35

the model for care level #1 contains only significant coefficients (at the .05 level) and is:

No. of Patients

$$= 1.03 + .49(3N) + .67(3T) + 1.75(4T)$$
$$+ .84(5T) + .27(PEDS) + 5.12(OB)$$
$$+ 5.72(NSY) - .45(APRIL) - .30(JUNE)$$
$$- .35(AUGUST) - .36(SUNDAY)$$
$$- .33(MONDAY) - .31(TUESDAY)$$
$$- .18(FRIDAY) - .34(SATURDAY)$$
$$- 1.31(NIGHT SHIFT)$$
$$- .00097 (TIME).$$

Statistics on Model:
$R^2 = .61$, and Standard Error of Estimate is 1.8.

For example, if this model were to be used to predict the number of patients requiring level #1 of care in Ward 4T (Surgical Cases) on Monday, July 17, 1978, during the day shift, we would have 4T = 1, Monday = 1, Time = 195, and the following equation:

Estimated No. of CL1 Patients

$$= 1.03 + 1.75(1) - .33(1) - .00097(195)$$
$$= 2.26 \text{ patients.}$$

(Actual number of patients was 2.)

The results of the seven models developed are particularly helpful when compared in the format of Table 2. A review of this table by ward clearly shows the distribution of care levels by ward and can be extremely valuable in the dis-tribution of the nursing skill mix (RN's, LPN's, and other) by ward. For example, the care level mix for the Surgical Ward (4T) reflects the fact that most of the patients require care specified by care level #2 with the following distribution for July 15, 1978, during the day shift:

Care Level	Estimated No. of Patients
CL1	2.26
CL2	24.84
CL3	5.70
CL4	.05
CL5,6**	.00

An evaluation of the time constant shows that there is relatively little change over time in the number of patients in any care level. However, a review of the monthly data suggests an increase in care level during the later months of the year. The second year (1979) of data which has now been collected will be used to clarify these points. Obviously, such information is crucial to the hospital administrator in planning nursing work loads. For weekly scheduling, an evaluation of the daily data is helpful to the administrator. The data clearly show a decreased demand for nursing staffing on Fridays, Saturdays, Sundays, and Mondays, which is not un-

---

**These patients are not normally admitted to this ward.

Table 2. *Regression Models by Care Levels (1978 Data, **n** = 9,687)*

	CL1	CL2	CL3	CL4	CL4,5	CL5,6	CL4,5,6
CONSTANT	1.03	4.99	1.22	.98	1.07	.42	1.50
TIME	-.00097	.00040	.00209	-.00250	-.00279	-.00283	-.00601
(SHIFTS)							
DAY[a]							
EVE		-1.45	.66		.06		
NITE	-1.31	-.24	.65				
(WARDS)							
ICU/CCU			-2.03	3.19	4.44	1.64	4.84
2N[a]							
3N	.49	2.03	1.38	-.66	-.70	-.06	-.72
3T	.67	18.90	5.89	-.68	-.71	-.06	-.73
4T	1.75	21.75	3.82	-.44	-.46		-.45
5T	.84	22.49	4.93	-.53	-.57	-.06	-.59
PEDS	.27	-.136	1.40		-.42		-.39
OB	5.12	2.06	-.31		-.13	-.06	-.15
NSY	5.72	.64	-1.56	-.59	-.62	-.06	-.64
(MONTHS)							
JAN				-.23	-.30	-.36	-.67
FEB						-.22	-.30
MAR			.21		-.19	-.21	-.36
APR	-.45	.88					
MAY[a]							
JUN	-.30				.25	.12	.38
JUL		-.45			.27	.15	.54
AUG	-.35	-1.42	.38	.35	.33	.26	.67
SEP		.21	.54	.32	.31	.40	.80
OCT			.38	.23	.29	.48	.81
NOV				.43	.50	.62	1.17
DEC				.58	.67	.69	1.43
(DAYS)							
SUN	-.36	-1.79	-.55				
MON	-.33	-1.98	.25				
TUE	-.31	-.98	.30				
WED[a]							
THR					.07		.07
FRI	-.18	-.77	.16	.07	.01		.08
SAT	-.34	-1.89	-.17				
R^2	.61	.89	.61	.64	.74	.56	.77
STD ERROR	1.80	3.51	2.21	.87	.93	.47	.93

[a] These variables included in constant term.

Forecasting Nursing Staffing Requirements by Intensity-of-Care Level

usual. However, the model supports intuition with more precise information. Obviously, with the availability of numerous part-time nurses whose schedules can be a management "variable," management has the ability to bring in this resource as the forecast and actual demand indicates. Predictably, the more acutely ill patients, while showing a seasonal pattern, do not demonstrate any significant daily or by-shift variation.

In a further attempt to make these results meaningful, six years of monthly data on total patient-days were collected. These data were regressed with time, ward, and month as the independent variables to predict total hospital patient-days for a specific month and by ward. The resulting model is:

Total census for any ward and month is found from the equation

$$177.30 + .46813 \text{ (time in months} \\ \text{where } t = 1 \text{ for July, 1972)}$$

plus indicator variable coefficient values (significant at the .05 level):

$$(R^2 = .96 \text{ and STD ERROR} = 68.9)$$

− 40.52 for February	+ 141.95 for 3N
+ 22.58 for March	+ 730.17 for 3T
− 37.13 for June	+ 818.49 for 4T
− 23.43 for July	+ 769.27 for 5T
− 26.05 for August	+ 20.51 for PEDS
− 24.44 for November	+ 145.89 for OB
− 48.54 for December	+ 117.76 for NSY

An example of the application of this model is as follows:

Census for Ward 4T for July 1978:

Census = constant + .46813(months since t = 0) − 23.43(July) + 818.49(4T)
Census = 177.30 + 34.17 − 23.43 + 818.49

Census = 1,006.53 or 1,007 patient-days for Ward 4T for July, 1978.

The care level mix for Ward 4T for the day shift for July, 1978 as previously estimated from the models in Table 2 is:

Care Level	Number of Patients	% of Patients
CL1	2.26	6.88
CL2	24.84	75.62
CL3	5.70	17.35
CL4	.05	.15
CL5,6	.00	.00
Total	32.85	100.00

The July, 1978 estimate of number of patients by level of care for the day shift for Ward 4T becomes:

Care Level	Number of Patients
CL1	69.3
CL2	761.5
CL3	174.7
CL4	1.5
CL5,6	0.0
Total	1,007.0

Applying standard nursing hours by intensity of care would estimate the following day shift staffing necessary in Ward 4T during July, 1978:

Care Level		Hours of Care per Patient	Standard Hours for Month
CL1	69.3	1.5	104.00
CL2	761.5	2.1	1,599.2
CL3	174.7	3.5	611.4
CL4	1.5	4.7	7.0
CL5	0.0	6.5	0.0
CL6	0.0	8.0	0.0
Total			2,321.6 hours or 290.2 nurse-days

Our results to date have been extremely useful to the hospital administrator. The output of the models has been compared with the standard hours of nursing care estimated by the nursing staff. The insight on the distribution of these requirements by shift, day of the week, and month of the year has pointed out several areas for more detailed analysis by the nursing staff.

CONTINUING RESEARCH

The models developed are now being expanded by the inclusion of the 1979 data. The early indicators reaffirm the validity of the existing models, and we are encouraged by this reinforcement. The next critical area of investigation is in the area of the standard hours specified and the nursing skill mix. The data include both the actual hours experienced and the standard hours for every shift by ward, day, and month for 24 months of data. It is anticipated that this research will continue to provide the administrator with an effective and logical framework for decision making on nursing staffing.

ENDNOTE

Helmer, F. Theodore, Levy, Paul D., and Suver, James D., 1978, *A Methodology for Nursing Salary Forecasting*, USAF Academy Technical Report No. 78–10, February.

DISCUSSION QUESTIONS

1. What forecasting techniques were used in this study, and what assumptions had to be made in using this particular technique?

2. Would another forecasting technique, such as exponential smoothing or moving average, be more appropriate for forecasting nursing staffing requirements for this particular situation?

3. Briefly describe some of the results that were obtained from this particular study.

4. What types of savings were obtained or made possible using this particular approach?

5. Would this type of forecasting technique be appropriate for staffing requirements in the private sector?

Incorporating Judgments in Sales Forecasts: Application of the Delphi Method at American Hoist & Derrick

Shankar Basu
Roger G. Schroeder

2

INTRODUCTION

American Hoist & Derrick is a well-known manufacturer of construction equipment, with annual sales of several hundred million dollars. Their sales forecast is an actual planning figure—not merely a goal—since it is used to develop the master production schedule, cash flow projections, and work force plans. Consequently, the top management personnel at American Hoist & Derrick are extremely concerned with predicting sales as accurately as possible. Due to this concern, management is reluctant to rely upon any single forecasting method. Thus, while the Delphi method of sales forecasting is emphasized in this paper, the 1975 sales forecast was developed using a number of methods.[1]

In the past, American Hoist & Derrick sold everything they could make. Sales forecasts were derived by a few key individuals, who utilized various methods to analyze the data from plant managers and sales personnel, but relied principally upon subjective judgment. Over the past ten years, these subjective forecasts have been

Reprinted by permission of Shankar Basu and Roger G. Schroeder, "Incorporating Judgements in Sales Forecasts: Application of the Delphi Mehod at American Hoist & Derrick," *Interfaces*, Vol. 7, No. 3, May, 1977, Copyright 1977 The Institute of Management Sciences.

in significant error and this has caused a great deal of concern in top management.

Beginning with the 1975 sales forecast, top management wanted to assess the sales potential accurately, in order to determine just how fast the production capacity should be expanded. Such an estimate could not be based solely upon historical sales, since these only reflected previous production constraints. Additionally, rapidly changing economic conditions made the past a relatively poor predictor of the future—for production costs as well as expected sales. Consequently, the managers decided to temper historical data with informed judgment by utilizing the Delphi method to develop a five-year sales forecast. However, alternate forecasts were also prepared, using regression analysis and exponential smoothing, in order to avoid undue reliance on any single method and to provide a bench mark with which the other results could be compared.

Due to space limitations, only the Delphi method is discussed in this paper. The next section describes the actual use of the Delphi method at American Hoist & Derrick; the following section summarizes the results and conclusions of its use. The last section, an Appendix, details the general Delphi technique with particular emphasis on developing sales forecasts, for those unfamiliar with the basic method.

DELPHI METHOD USE AT AMERICAN HOIST & DERRICK

Formulating the Delphi study

The well-known Delphi method consists of: (1) a panel of experts, (2) a series of rounds, and (3) a questionnaire for each round. Each member of the panel responds anonymously to the questionnaire on each round and the summarized responses of the panel are fed into the next round. At AH&D it was decided to use three rounds for the Delphi study, based on the rationale described in the Appendix.

In constructing the panel a total of 23 key individuals were selected. The panel selection was based on the following criteria:

- personnel who had been doing these forecasts intuitively,
- personnel who were responsible for using these sales forecasts,
- personnel whose activities were affected by these forecasts,
- personnel who had a strong knowledge of market place and corporate sales.

Care was taken to include knowledgeable personnel from different functional areas of the corporation.

In the case of sales forecasting the Delphi questionnaire should request not only sales estimates of interest, but also such information as an industry projection and a business indicator. This additional information will provide a check against the sales figure through correlation and it also helps the respondents develop their process of estimation. A close look at the corporate revenue for American Hoist & Derrick over the last five years revealed that the construction equipment group generated approximately 60 percent of the total revenue. The most logical industry that total company sales would correlate with is, therefore, the construction equipment industry. A graphical and analytical check demonstrated that these two time series were indeed correlated. Next, leading, roughly coincident, and lagging indicators were tried for best fit with the construction equipment industry. The closest fit was obtained with GNP in current dollar series and GNP was therefore determined to be the business indicator of interest.

The questionnaire then requested the following four estimates on each of the three rounds:

- Gross National Product, current dollars;
- Construction equipment industry shipments, current dollars;

- American Hoist & Derrick construction equipment group shipments, current dollars;
- American Hoist & Derrick, corporate value of shipments, current dollars.

The first round
To help obtain a realistic median on the first round, all four estimates which were being requested had data input. The data input were actual figures for the past five to seven years. Compound growth rate and graphical representation of each series were included. Opinion on percent increase expected for the next five years was requested. Exhibit 1 is a part of the first round questionnaire for the construction industry estimate. A similar page was included for each of the other three estimates requested.

Construction Industry Estimate
The following figures and graph show historical sales figures for power cranes, shovels, walking draglines and walking cranes for the last seven years. Please indicate your estimate for each of the next six years. (% increase expected and graphically).

Year	% Increase	Industry Sales Mil $	Calendar Year	% Increased Expected
1967		511	1974	———
1968	2.5	524	1975	———
1969	9.7	575	1976	———
1970	.4	598	1977	———
1971	6.5	637	1978	———
1972	12.8	719	1979	———
1973	35.4	974		

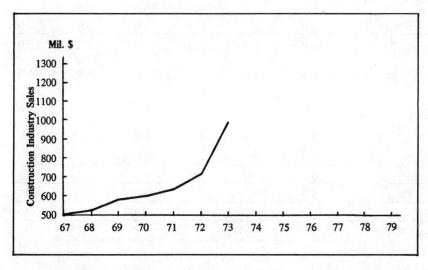

Exhibit 1. *Sample: Partial First Round Request for Information*

Incorporating Judgments in Sales Forecasts

132

The responses on the first round were collected and summarized. A standard statistical analysis of the responses was conducted which generated for each of the four series—number of observations, largest observation, smallest observation, range of observations, mean, confidence limits, standard deviation and median.

The second round

The second round questionnaire included feedback on actual responses together with the above standard statistical analysis. Each panel member's response was indicated and his revised estimate was requested in the second round. (See Exhibit 2 for a sample of the data feedback for

Exhibit 2. *Sample: Partial Second Round Feedback of Estimates*

You Are	1974	1975	1976	1977	1978	1979
1	5.0	7.0	7.0	6.0	6.0	6.0
2	25.0	20.0	15.0	20.0	20.0	15.0
3	6.5	5.4	7.6	8.2	10.0	10.0
4	15.0	10.0	8.0	0.0	2.0	5.0
5	20.0	20.0	8.0	8.0	6.0	7.0
6						
7						
8	15.0	3.0	7.0	6.0	6.5	4.0
9						
10	20.0	10.0	5.0	10.0	10.0	10.0
11	7.0	8.0	5.0	5.0	6.0	
12	20.0	4.0	5.0	16.0	2.2	4.0
13	13.0	5.0	4.5	8.5	8.8	10.2
14	25.0	2.0	3.0	6.0	7.0	8.0
15	20.0	10.0	5.0	5.0	5.0	7.0
16	35.0	0.0	7.0	9.0	0.0	(10.0)
17						
18	30.0	5.0	6.0	6.0	6.0	6.0
19	(20.0)	5.0	9.0	3.0	3.0	3.0
20	10.0	5.0	7.0	10.0	8.0	10.0
21						
22	20.0	10.0	20.0	35.0	25.0	15.0
23						
High	35.0	20.0	20.0	35.0	25.0	15.0
Low	(20.0)	0.0	3.0	0.0	0.0	(10.0)
Range	55.0	20.0	17.0	35.0	25.0	25.0
Mean	15.7	7.6	7.6	9.5	7.7	7.1
Std. Dev.	12.3	5.5	4.1	8.0	6.3	5.7
95% Confidence	9.3/22.0	4.7/10.4	5.4/9.7	5.4/13.6	4.5/10.0	4.0/10.2
Your Revised Estimate	——————			——————		——————
Explanation						

the construction industry estimate.) On the second round all members of the panel were asked for explanations of their responses, irrespective of whether their responses fell in the top, bottom or interquartile range. The logic behind including the entire population was that the explanations of any person might be important and meaningful for the total population.

The response to the second round was of a "brain storming" nature. There was an outpouring of explanations from the panel members. The individual reasons for estimates were collected, summarized and listed under separate headings of GNP, CE Industry, AH&D Construction Equipment group and AH&D total shipments. All these explanations were then categorized into positive and negative factors for each of the four estimates. Relevant published data and opinion of well-known economists were also collected and prepared for input into the third round.

The third round

The third and final round questionnaire was designed with extreme care. The format for this round was:

- restatement of the initial question,
- feedback of a respondent's first and second estimates,
- second round response, standard statistical analysis,
- factors that were considered important by the respondents in reaching their estimate in the second round,
- related facts, figures and views of external experts,
- a request for the respondent's revised estimate,
- a request for comments or opinions.

Exhibit 3 shows that portion of the third round questionnaire applicable to sales in the entire construction equipment industry; similar formats were used for Gross National Product

(GNP) sales in the AH&D construction equipment group, and total sales for American Hoist & Derrick.

Statistical analysis on the third round was considered as the final forecast by the panel. The standard deviation and 95 percent confidence band had narrowed sufficiently to consider this forecast a reasonable consensus of the panel.

RESULTS AND CONCLUSIONS

Sales forecast accuracy

The use of the Delphi method had a direct and definite impact on the American Hoist & Derrick sales projection. Top management was presented three forecasts: one developed using the Delphi method; another using regression analysis; and a third forecast developed using exponential smoothing. The Delphi forecast was considered most credible by top management because it incorporated the experienced judgment of 23 key corporate individuals. This confidence was subsequently justified, as indicated in Exhibit 4. The 1975 Delphi sales forecast was within $1.1 million of the actual 1975 sales, that is, *the sales forecast error was reduced to less than one-third of one percent.* Due to an extensive management reorganization and reassignment of key individuals in 1976, the Delphi method was not used to develop a new five-year sales forecast or update the previous one. In spite of this, the 1976 sales forecast—corresponding to the second year of the original five-year projection—was within $13 million of actual 1976 sales, resulting in a forecast error of less than four percent. *This was considerable improvement over the previous forecast errors of plus or minus 20 percent.* Additionally, the Delphi forecasts were more accurate than the forecasts developed using regression analysis of exponential smoothing. The forecasts developed using these latter techniques were incorrect by $30–50 million, indi-

Exhibit 3. Sample: Partial Third Round Input of Data and Request for Final Estimate Construction Equipment Industry

1) <u>Question Restated</u>: Estimate percent increase in CE industry shipments in current dollars for calendar years.

	1975	1976	1977	1978	1979
2) <u>Your 1st est.</u>:					
Your 2nd est.:					
3) 2nd Round Response:					
High	10.0	10.0	10.0	10.0	10.0
Low	4.0	5.0	6.0	5.0	6.0
Range	6.0	5.0	4.0	5.0	4.0
Mean	7.14	7.56	7.92	6.7	7.75
Std. Dev.	2.29	1.34	1.79	1.51	1.51
95% Conf.	5.5/8.8	6.6/8.5	6.6/9.2	5.6/7.8	6.6/8.8

4) Factors that were considered by the respondents:

Negative—Long delivery time
—Slow recovery in industry from recession
—Interest rate, financial control over expansion, repair and maintenance of current equipment
—Continued slowdown in housing
—Environmental factors causing project delays
—Drying up of federal funds
—Downtrend in backlogs
Positive—Price increases
—Accelerated export business, continued worldwide demand of machinery for energy related projects

5) Related figures for your consideration:

Source: F. W. Dodge
Construction contract awards in April and May were 32% above the depressed 1st quarter average. First quarter capital appropriation jumped 66% to 16.9 billion. This follows a 104% increase between the 3rd and 4th quarters of 1974.

6) Your revised estimate:

	1975	1976	1977	1978	1979
Percent increase expected:					

7) Comments, other facts and figures you would like to see or show:

cating a forecast error on the order of 10–15 percent.

One negative aspect of the study is the time period required to develop the forecast: approximately three months to complete all three rounds, evaluate the results, and produce a final consensus. However, the authors estimate that the next Delphi sales forecast, to be developed in late 1977, will be completed in only four to six weeks. This improved response time is expected to result from a Delphi education training program and the use of precoded input

Exhibit 4. Actual vs. Forecast Sales (American Hoist & Derrick)

	1975	1976
Actual Sales (millions)	$359.1	$410
Forecast Sales (millions) Using Delphi Method	$360.2	$397
Forecast error	+.3%	−3.3%

Incorporating Judgments in Sales Forecasts

forms in conjunction with a General Electric Statistical analysis system for data analysis.

Uniform sales estimates

Apart from the improvement in forecast accuracy, the next most beneficial aspect of the Delphi study was that it provided a reasonably uniform estimate of sales among different managers. The managers on the panel were presented with accurate past and present economic conditions and data on the business environment. Through successive rounds of Delphi, they developed a congruence in outlook on business conditions and corporate sales. Exhibit 5 indicates the median, standard deviation, and range of the responses for each of the three rounds for estimates of the GNP and total sales in the construction equipment industry. The tendency toward consensus is indicated by the reduction in range, standard deviation, and in the 95% confidence interval from one round to the next. All numerical estimates exhibited this type of reduction in variance.

This tendency toward congruence resulted in a relatively uniform base for future decision making among the participants in the study.

Managers reacted very favorably to involvement in the forecast, and exhibited interest by requesting the results of the study. Particular enthusiasm was shown in the second round, when each manager was asked for the reasons behind his/her forecasts. A great many corporations lack this uniformity of outlook, and often quite divergent assumptions are made about sales potential. Even if there is a published forecast for sales, it probably will not have been internalized by managers to the extent that occurs from participation in a Delphi study. At American Hoist & Derrick there was a very marked divergence in sales estimates among managers in the first round; this divergence was greatly reduced upon completion of the third round.

Conclusions

The following conclusions were arrived at by the authors in conducting the Delphi study for sales forecasting:

1. Delphi has definite utility as an analytical tool for predicting sales of a corporation. As the forecasts incorporate anticipation of the future by experienced and qualified

Exhibit 5. *Convergence of Some Estimates*
GNP Estimates 1978
% Growth

	High	Low	Range	Standard Deviation	Median
Round 1	12.0	0.0	12.0	2.9	6.5
2	10.0	0.0	10.0	2.6	6.0
3	8.5	5.0	3.5	1.5	5.9

Construction Equipment Industry Estimates 1978
% Growth

	High	Low	Range	Standard Deviation	Median
Round 1	25.0	0.0	25.0	6.3	5.9
2	15.0	0.0	15.0	3.9	6.0
3	13.0	5.0	8.0	2.4	6.3

individuals, the results seem to be meaningful and realistic. Though the results can be used singularly, it is suggested that they be used in conjunction with other quantitative approaches to sales forecasting.

2. Apart from its analytical value, a Delphi study has an inherent educational value. The corporate officers are presented with past and present economic conditions and status. As a result, there is the development of a congruence in outlook on business conditions and corporate sales volume. This provides for a more uniform singular base for decision making by the different managers involved in the study.

APPENDIX

The Delphi technique

The Delphi method, which can also be called "opinion methodology," is a relatively new technique. It has been used primarily for predicting technological innovations and business indices.[2,3,4] No reported uses of Delphi for sales forecasting have been found in the literature.

The Delphi technique is a method for obtaining a reliable consensus from a group of experts.[5] Structurally, it consists of (1) a questionnaire which is responded to anonymously; (2) a sequence of rounds which successively refine the forecast; and (3) controlled data input, including opinion feedback and statistical analysis. The sequence of steps that might be followed in utilizing Delphi for sales forecasting is shown in Figure 1.

In using the Delphi technique four factors should be considered: the panel of experts, the questionnaire, number of rounds, and controlled data input.

Panel of experts. There are three significant considerations in choosing a panel of experts.

First, the number of experts in the panel is important, since too low a number will have a high average group error while too high a number will constitute too great a physical workload. A suitable number in the panel is desired so that the results are reliable and reproducible. Dalkey indicates that 15 to 20 members seem to be a good panel size considering the tradeoff between workload and group error.[6]

The second consideration in selecting a panel is the expertise of each panel member. One should consider such factors as years of professional experience, educational background, access to information, and responsibility and authority. The main criterion for inclusion on the panel, however, should be a high degree of knowledgeability about the subject being considered.

Thirdly, the ideal panel environment is one where there is no direct confrontation, and the channel of communication is through data input and opinion feedback in successive rounds. Anonymous response is of prime importance to avoid bias, unwarranted pressure, and the "band wagon" effect so commonly observed in open group meetings.

The questionnaire. The Delphi method includes a questionnaire for each round that is completed by the panel members. In the case of sales forecasting, the questionnaire should request not only the sales estimates of interest, but additional information, such as a business indicator, and industry projections. This additional information should be used as a check against the sales figure through correlations and it helps the respondents develop their process of estimation. Since sales are generally influenced by the economy and the industry, additional estimates provide valuable data for correlation analysis. It is suggested that respondents be asked to estimate a business indicator first, then their industry sales, and finally their company's sales. This provides a logical flow of dependence in the estimating procedure.

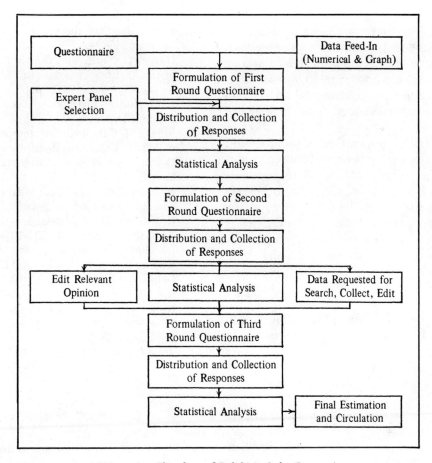

Figure 1. *Flowchart of Delphi in Sales Forecasting*

Number of rounds. The number of rounds is an important consideration because it affects the quality of the forecast as well as the effort expended. Dalkey has shown that the convergence of the forecast improves with each round, but reaches a saturation level in about three to five rounds.[7] Delphi studies almost always utilize three rounds to allow significant feedback and convergence. Sometimes a fourth or fifth round is added depending on the rate of actual convergence and the willingness of participants to continue.

Controlled data input. The quality of estimation depends to a great extent on the quality of data that is fed-in with the questionnaire. Three types of input should be an integral part of all Delphi studies—the statistical group response, relevant outside data input, and opinions of the panel members.

To help achieve consensus, the previous round estimates should be statistically analyzed and fed back to the panel members. The statistical analysis can be done either on the total population or on the interquartile population. The group response can be identified by the median, mean, or mode of the responses. Based on our limited experience, a good combination for sales forecasting appears to be statistical analysis on the total population with median as the response of the group.

Relevant data from outside the panel should be fed into the panel to provide a source of outside expertise. The opinions of respondents from the previous round should also be collected, summarized and edited for input into the next round of the Delphi study to allow panelists to study the reasons that other panelists give for their responses. Such data input usually facilitates convergence of the forecast through successive rounds of the Delphi.

Group discussion. The use of face-to-face group discussion was considered as an alternative to the Delphi method. Group discussion in sales forecasting has the following disadvantages or pitfalls which the Delphi technique avoids:

- inclination toward hasty formulation of pre-conceived notions;
- tendency to defend a stand once publicly taken;
- effect of persuasively stated opinion of others;
- effect of opinion of greatest supposed authority;
- effect of loudest, longest, or best formatted presentation;
- effect of redundant and irrelevant information;
- band wagon effect of majority opinion.

Because of these problems, the anonymity of the Delphi method was considered superior for sales forecasting.

ENDNOTES

1. J. C. Chambers, S. K. Mullich, and D. D. Smith, "How to Choose the Right Forecasting Technique," *Harvard Business Review,* July–August 1971, pp. 45–74.
2. Harper Q. North, and Donald L. Pyke, "Probes of the Technological Future," *Harvard Business Review,* May–June 1969, p. 68.
3. H. Q. North, "TRW Looks at the Future," TRW Systems, Inc., 1967.
4. Robert M. Campbell, "A Methodological Study of Expert Utilization in Business Forecasting," Doctoral dissertation, University of California, Los Angeles, 1966.
5. Norman Dalkey and Olaf Helmer, "An Experimental Application of the Delphi Method to the Use of Experts," *Management Science,* Vol. 9, April 1963, p. 458. Also, RM-727, the Rand Corporation, July 1962.
6. Bernice Brown, S. Cochran and N. Dalkey, "The Delphi Method II: Structure of Experiment," RM-5957-PR, the Rand Corporation, June 1969.
7. Norman Dalkey, Bernice Brown and S. Cochran, "The Delphi Method III: Use of Self Ratings to Improve Group Estimates," RM-611-PR, the Rand Corporation, November 1969.

DISCUSSION QUESTIONS

1. Why was it so important to develop a more accurate forecasting method for American Hoist & Derrick?

2. What types of forecasting techniques were used in the past and how accurate were they?

3. How would you compare the Delphi to other forecasting techniques, such as exponential smoothing and regression analysis?

4. What were some of the advantages of using the Delphi approach?

5. What are some of the negative aspects of using the Delphi technique versus other forecasting techniques?

Decision Theory

Decision theory is an analytic approach to making sound management decisions. It is especially useful when there are several decision alternatives and an uncertainty in future events. The technique has been successfully applied to such diverse problem as whether or not to expand a hospital, whether to conduct marketing research before developing a new product, selecting the best stock portfolio, and deciding which product among many to produce and how to produce it.

Whether the decision being made is to build a new factory or to just select a backyard lawnmower, the steps in making a good decision are basically the same. They are: (1) define the problem, (2) list the alternatives, (3) identify the possible outcomes, (4) list the payoff of each combination of alternatives and outcomes, (5) pick a decision theory model, and (6) apply the model to help make a decision.

There are several decision theory models to choose from—decision trees, decision tables, utility theory, and marginal analysis to the minimax, maximin, and maximax approaches. *Decision trees* are graphic representations that are particularly useful when sequential decisions must be made.

Communicating Model Based Information for Energy Debates

The reading in this section, "Communicating Model Based Information for Energy Debates," is written by Stephen Peck, a staff member of the Electric Power Research Institute in Palo Alto, California. His article discusses two examples of how decision theory was used to help provide unbiased information to managers in their debate to decide an energy policy. In the first example, a decision tree was employed to define a set of scenarios associated with a moratorium on the construction of new nuclear power facilities. In the second example, Peck describes an interactive computer program written to help a group think through the implications of alternative nuclear research and development strategies.

Communicating Model Based Information
for Energy Debates: Two Case Studies

Stephen C. Peck

3

The Electric Power Research Institute (EPRI) was founded in 1973. Its mission is to fund and manage a significant proportion of the research projects of the electric utilities industry. The research is mostly conducted by outside contractors and, in 1980, will amount to approximately $230 million. The money is provided by voluntary contributions from utilities, both private and public, which generate approximately 70% of the kilowatt hours sold in the U.S.

The Systems Program of EPRI's Energy Analysis and Environment Division is charged with integrating economic and environmental inputs to provide information and analysis to three client groups: R&D planners at EPRI, analysts and decision makers at electric utility companies, and those involved in the complex tasks of formulating and deciding on energy policy. In interacting with the latter group, we and our contractors have found that decision analysis is a very powerful tool.

A NUCLEAR MORATORIUM

Modeling is frequently used to advocate a particular policy position. This is unfortunate be-

Reprinted by permission of Stephen C. Peck, "Communicating Model Based Information for Energy Debates: Two Case Studies," *Interfaces,* Vol. 10, No. 5, October, 1980, Copyright 1980 The Institute of Management Sciences.

cause once the report summarizing the analysis and advocating a particular position is published, there is little in the analysis that can inform a debate on the issue. In this case the report is either neglected because it can only be used to advocate one position or the model must be used to make additional runs in an adversary proceeding called "counter-modeling" [Greenberger et al., 1976]. The additional runs can be made either by the modeler or by representatives of the opposing policy position who learn to use the model.

Model builders can provide information to model users about the implications of particular policies in combination with a number of important future uncertain events. In this way the modeler can provide information to both sides engaged in a policy debate. This is more likely to lead to the use of the analysis. A useful tool to structure model runs and provide input for such a debate is a "decision tree."

An example of the use of a decision tree is provided in an analysis [Dale W. Jorgenson Associates, 1979] which investigated the implications of a nuclear moratorium on the economy, the energy sector, and the electric utility industry. The Hudson-Jorgenson model of energy-economy interactions [Hudson and Jorgenson, 1974] was first linked to the REM, a regionalized representation of the US electric utility industry [Joskow and Baughman, 1976].

The Hudson-Jorgenson model was first developed in 1973. It is a relatively large model of the US economy focused on how developments in the energy sector will influence the process of economic growth. However, it does not include a detailed description of the electric utility industry. The REM does provide a detailed picture. It treats all electric utilities in a census region as a single company. It repeats this description for all nine census regions. Each "company" is represented by a demand module, a production-investment module, and a financial module.

By linking the Hudson-Jorgenson model and the REM, it is possible to investigate in some detail how quite specific developments in the electric utilities industry impact the national economy. The combined model system was exercised to investigate the implications of a nuclear moratorium for the electric utility industry and for the nation as a whole.

The tree shown in Figure 1 was used to structure the model runs. It was constructed from three sets of uncertainties; the first uncertainty was whether there would be a nuclear moratorium beginning in 1978 on the construction of all new nuclear plants; the second uncertainty was whether coal and oil prices would rise significantly from today's levels and whether the environmental costs associated with coal plants would be high or low; the third uncertainty was whether the growth rate of coal burning plants would be unrestricted or whether environmental pressures would significantly reduce their construction. Since it was assumed that each of the three uncertainties could take one of two values, there were eight possible scenarios: these are shown as nodes 1 through 8 in Figure 1.

The Hudson-Jorgenson/REM system could then be exercised to compute the implications associated with each branch of the tree. To show how the decision tree could be used to structure a debate, let us concentrate attention on the present value of real measured gross national product (GNP) between 1978 and 2000 denoted as $PV_i(GNP)$, where the subscript i identifies the ith branch of the tree.

A nuclear advocate might make one of the following two types of arguments. (a) Coal prices, oil prices, and environmentally related capital costs of coal plants are likely to rise in the near future due to union action (on coal), OPEC's behavior (on oil), and EPA decisions (on environmental costs); there are also likely to be restrictions on the allowed rate of increase in the number of coal plants. A nuclear moratorium would cause a movement to node 1, whereas no moratorium would mean that node 5 would be reached. The cost of a moratorium would then be $PV_5(GNP) - PV_1(GNP)$. (b) With no mora-

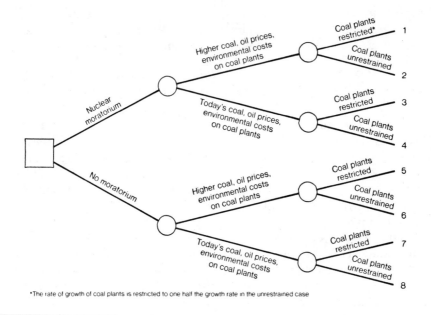

*The rate of growth of coal plants is restricted to one half the growth rate in the unrestrained case

Figure 1. *Scenario Design for Hudson-Jorgenson Study*

torium, it is unlikely that coal and oil prices and environmentally related capital costs of coal plants would rise much beyond current levels, and it is unlikely that there would be restrictions on the growth rate of coal plants; in this case node 8 would be reached. On the other hand, with a moratorium, US demand for imported oil would rise and consequently the world oil price; in addition, competition between coal and uranium would be lessened, thus causing coal prices to rise either by collusive behavior between coal companies, increased union pressure, or increased severance taxes; furthermore, because there would be fewer nuclear and more coal plants, the emissions from each coal plant would have to be controlled more stringently and the capital costs associated with environmental control on each coal plant would be increased. Even the increased emissions controls might not satisfy environmental intervenors concerned with the construction of coal plants in rural environments and the effects of strip mining; consequently, the rate of increase in the growth of coal plants might be restrained to reduce emissions. In this case, node 1 would be reached and the cost of a nuclear moratorium would be $PV_8(GNP) - PV_1(GNP)$.

A nuclear opponent could use the scenarios investigated by the use of the Hudson-Jorgenson/REM system to argue that a nuclear moratorium would cause a movement to node 4 because none of the higher fuel prices and capital costs were likely either in and of themselves or as a consequence of the nuclear moratorium. In this case, the results at node 4 should be compared with the results at node 8 in computing the economic costs of a nuclear moratorium which then become $PV_8(GNP) - PV_4(GNP)$.

Note that the modeler is not forced to adopt an advocacy position in this debate but, by running all the cases associated with the decision tree, he has provided information to both debaters. The debate can then focus on which of nodes 1 through 4 is likely to be reached if there is a nuclear moratorium and which of nodes 5 through 8 is likely to be reached if there is no moratorium.

A NUCLEAR RESEARCH AND DEVELOPMENT STRATEGY

The discussion of the Hudson-Jorgenson project showed how model builders could provide information to model users for a debate by running all the cases implied by a decision tree.

This approach has been extended by Alan Manne and Richard Richels [Manne and Richels, 1980]. In late 1977, Manne and Richels were invited to structure the economic analysis for the US government's Nonproliferation Alternative Systems Assessment Program (NASAP). Among other things, this group was evaluating the desirability of the US funding alternative advanced nuclear reactor concepts. The major contenders were the plutonium fueled fast breeder reactor (FBR) and an advanced converter reactor (ACR). The FBR produces more fissile material than it consumes and thus requires little or no input of natural uranium fuel; the FBR's disadvantage is the risk that weapons grade material may be diverted from the reactor itself or from the reprocessing facilities which convert used fuel into usable fuel. An ACR converts more of its fissile material into additional fuel than the currently available light water reactor (LWR); the ACR's disadvantages are that it does use significant amounts of natural uranium and, at high conversion efficiencies, a chemical reprocessing step would be needed and it might be possible to divert weapons grade material.

From previous cost-benefit analyses of the US breeder reactor program [Manne and Richels, 1978], the authors drew up a list of seven technoeconomic variables together with their assumed dates of resolution which would be im-

portant in determining the desirability of an FBR and an ACR. The first variable was the elasticity of substitution between energy and other factors of production; this is an important determinant of both the rate of electricity and total energy demand growth. The second variable was the cost of a new technology producing nonelectric energy which would be introduced in the year 2000; this also is an important determinant of the demand growth of electricity. The third variable was a limit on US coal production and consumption; a low limit makes nuclear-generated electricity more attractive than coal-generated electricity. The fourth variable was the number of light water reactors that there would be in the year 2000; this will both determine the rate at which we exhaust our uranium resource base and serve as a measure of the acceptability of nuclear power in general. The fifth variable was what would be the annualized uranium requirement for the ACR; a lower requirement of uranium makes the ACR more attractive as an alternative to the FBR. The sixth variable was the size of the uranium resource base available to the US; the lower the resource base, the more attractive are both the ACR and FBR. The seventh variable was the cost of a new technology producing electric energy which would be introduced in 2010; a low cost for such a technology would make both the ACR and FBR less attractive.

In addition to the technoeconomic uncertainties, Manne and Richels added two variables which addressed the question of the proliferation and diversion risks of alternative fuel cycles. There is considerable public debate about whether a decision by the United States to proceed with a breeder reactor program would prove stabilizing or destabilizing in the international arena; stabilizing because a decision by the US to forfeit the breeder option would set an example to countries without an existing capacity to manufacture nuclear weapons; destabilizing because a decision by the US to forego the breeder would tighten the competition between nations for a dwindling energy supply and lead to international conflict. These uncertainties were captured by an eighth variable. A ninth variable represented the uncertainty as to whether an ACR would be significantly more proliferation/ diversion proof than an FBR.

In addition to providing the major technoeconomic and political uncertainties surrounding the FBR and ACR development, Manne and Richels summarized five alternatives for reactor and fuel cycle development in the US together with their research, development, and demonstration costs; these are shown in Figure 2. To read Figure 2, suppose that we decide "today" to pursue both the FBR and ACR demonstration route (FBR and ACR demo). Then in 1990, we may make a decision to proceed with commercialization of the breeder reactor so as

to have the first generation available in 2000 (CBR-1 in 2000). Alternatively, we may decide to proceed with commercialization of the advanced converter reactor so as to have the first generation available in 2000 (ACR-1 in 2000) with either high uranium requirement (type A) or low uranium requirement (type B). Finally, we may decide to stop and not commercialize either the FBR or the ACR. Figure 2, in combination with the technoeconomic and political uncertainties, defines a (very large) decision tree. Using the Eta-Macro model [Manne, 1978], the net discounted benefits of each case implied by the tree were computed.

The set of decisions and associated uncertainties is much larger in the Manne-Richels analysis than in that carried out by Hudson-Jor-

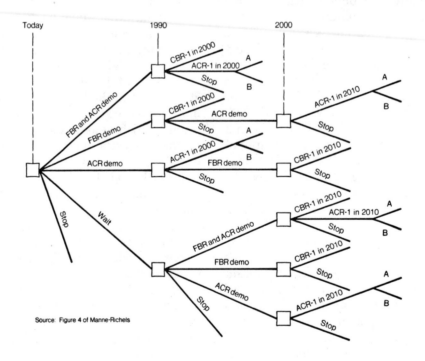

Source: Figure 4 of Manne-Richels

Figure 2. *Alternative Research, Demonstration, and Commercialization Plans. ACR is the Advanced Converter Reactor, FBR is the Plutonium-Fueled Fast Breeder Reactor, CBR is the Commercial Breeder Reactor, and A represents the high, B, the lower, Uranium Requirement*

Communicating Model Based Information for Energy Debates

genson. For instance, between today and 1990, if the choice is made to pursue the FBR and ACR demonstration route, there are 3×2^5 or 96 different cases. It becomes necessary therefore to summarize the information for the model user. This may be done by introducing two additional pieces of information into the analysis. The first is an assessment of the user's subjective probabilities of all relevant future events (the seven technoeconomic uncertainties plus the two proliferation/diversion uncertainties in this case); for instance, each user would be asked for his probability assessments that the uranium resource base would be high, medium, or low. The second is an assumption that the user is prepared to make a decision on the basis of maximum expected net discounted dollar benefits.

With this additional information a computer program may be written which starts at the latest decision to be made (2000 in this case), and computes the expected net discounted benefit of each decision by multiplying the net discounted benefit of each case for a given decision by its associated probability and summing over all relevant cases. That decision with a maximum expected net discounted benefit is the optimal decision. Having chosen all the conditional optimal decisions in 2000, the program then moves back to 1990 to compute the conditional optimal decisions and ultimately moves back to compute today's optimal decision.

By August 1978, Manne and Richels had made the ETA-Macro runs and an interactive computer program had been written which would enable an analyst to input a set of probabilities into the program and make a computer run with an almost instantaneous turnaround. In mid-August 1978, 16 individuals' probability assessments were polled at a NASAP seminar and the results were presented to the participants.

In a subsequent analysis Manne and Richels discovered that there were significant correlations in the probability assessments of the 16 respondents. They stated their conclusions as follows [Manne and Richels, 1980]:

If one is for or against plutonium fuel cycles, one tends to adopt arguments on uranium, on demand growth, etc., which also support one or the other position. In debates such as this one, we do not believe that unbiased scientific judgments are likely to emerge from expert working groups.

The wording of this paragraph seems to imply that the respondents had previously decided on their conclusions and chose the probability distributions for the nine variables to validate their conclusions. An alternative interpretation is that a disinterested scientist has previously thought through the determinants of breeder desirability and, because he believes that uranium is in short supply, that demand growth is likely to be high, etc., he becomes a breeder advocate. The converse is true for a breeder opponent. Thus any scientist sufficiently interested to participate in the breeder debate would be likely to have correlated probability assessments. It is obviously difficult to distinguish between these two interpretations.

Whichever interpretation is accepted, decision analysis combined with an energy systems model can provide major insight into complicated issues of public policy. An interactive computer program such as was developed in the NASAP study can provide a decision maker with insight into how sensitive the optimal decision is to changes in his probability assessments. It can also lead respondents to reexamine their initial premises.

ENDNOTES

Dale W. Jorgenson Associates, 1979, *Industry and Economic Impacts of Restrictions on Generating Capacity,* Electric Power Research Institute, Palo Alto.

Greenberger, M., Crenson, M.A., and Crissey, B.L., 1976, *Models in the Policy Process,* Russell Sage Foundation, New York.

Hudson, E.A. and Jorgenson, D.W., 1974, "US Energy Growth and Economic Policy," *Bell Journal of Economics and Management Science* Vol. 5, pp. 461–514.

Joskow, P.L. and Baughman, M.L., 1976, "The Future of the US Electric Utility Industry," *The Bell Journal of Economics* Vol. 7, pp. 3–32.

Manne, A.S., 1978, "ETA-Macro: A Model of Energy-Economy Interactions," in C.J. Hitch, ed., *Modeling Energy-Economy Interactions: Five Approaches,* Resources for the Future, Washington.

Manne, A.S. and Richels, R.G., 1980, "Evaluating Nuclear Fuel Cycles," *Energy Policy,* March.

Manne, A.S. and Richels, R.G., 1978, "A Decision Analysis of the US Breeder Reactor Program," *Energy* Vol. 3, pp. 747–768.

DISCUSSION QUESTIONS

1. What is a decision tree? How can it be useful in helping policy makers debate energy alternatives?

2. Of what benefit is a computer programmed analysis of the decision tree?

3. Why is probability assessment of outcomes a difficult part of decision tree analysis?

Inventory Modeling

Representing as much as 40 percent of the total invested capital in an organization, inventory is one of the most expensive and important assets that must be effectively and efficiently managed. Like other quantitative analysis techniques, a critical balance must be maintained in establishing inventory level policies. On the one hand, a firm can try to reduce its inventory holding and carrying cost by reducing inventory levels. On the other hand, customers may become dissatisfied with frequent inventory shortages. Thus, when inventory levels are high, a significant amount of a company's assets are tied up, and the cost of holding inventory, obsolescence, theft, etc., can be staggering. Likewise, when inventory levels are kept low, stockouts can occur and the number of orders per year, and thus ordering costs per year, increase. Again, like other quantitative analysis techniques, inventory level policies are established that seek to minimize total inventory costs.

Inventory also provides many useful functions to the organization. Inventory can decouple manufacturing processes. When inventory levels are kept between manufacturing units, a breakdown in one manufacturing unit does not cause the entire operation to shut down because stored inventory can be used to keep the manufacturing process going. Inventory can also be used as a hedge against inflation when the cost of inventory is going up at a faster rate than the cost of other items and goods. Inventory policy can be used to buffer irregular supply and demand, take advantage of quantity discounts, and avoid stockouts and shortages, and thus customer dissatisfaction.

The two major decisions that must be made by any inventory system are 1) how much to order and 2) when to order. This assumes that the organization has already established what inventory items are needed. As mentioned previously, one of the major objectives in controlling inventory levels is to minimize total inventory costs. The most significant inventory costs are

1. the cost of the items
2. the cost of ordering
3. the cost of carrying or holding inventory
4. the cost of safety stock, and
5. the cost of stockouts in terms of lost sales and customer dissatisfaction.

Most inventory models attempt to establish how much to order and when to order while minimizing these various cost factors.

An Application of ABC Analysis to Control Imported Material
When a large number of inventory items are involved and the total dollar amount is high, applying rigorous inventory control techniques to all items can be difficult. The overall purpose of ABC Analysis is to divide inventory into three classes, where the A classification refers to those inventory items that make up a large percentage of the total cost of inventory. This was the case of a manufacturing firm described in this article by Canen and Galvão.

The firm described by Canen and Galvão is a Brazilian affiliate of a USA-based company. In Brazil, importers like the firm described in this article must deposit a substantial amount of the total value of imported goods with the state-owned Banco de Brazil. These deposits, which have a duration of one year, do not earn interest, and because of Brazil's high inflation rate, these deposits are extemely costly. As the result of ABC Analysis, the firm was able to realize a reduction of almost 30 percent in inventory-related costs.

Project EOQ: A Success Story in Implementing Academic Research
The article by Larry Austin describes the successful implementation of an EOQ project. The actual project was undertaken by students in a graduate-level

course in Logistics Management at the Airforce Academy. The overall objective of the research project was to modernize the existing EOQ system to include price discount solicitation and other factors which would result in a lowering of total inventory costs. For this study, the Airforce business research management center agreed to help in gathering the necessary data and information that would be required.

The inventory items investigated included approximately 250,000 items that represented a value of approximately $400 million. In order to investigate the inventory system, four groups of five students each were assembled. The first group was responsible for computer model building; the second group was responsible for an analysis of holding costs; the third group was responsible for demand, prediction, and safety stock analysis; and the fourth group was responsible for an analysis of price discounts and ordering costs. After each group completed its analysis separately, the members of the groups were integrated into one team that investigated the entire inventory situation. Using a number of cost-saving techniques, including computer simulation and forecasting, the key recommendations resulted in a forecasted savings of approximately seven million dollars.

An Application of ABC Analysis to Control Imported Material

Alberto Gabbay Canen
Roberto D. Galvão

4

Successful operation of a manufacturing firm depends to a large extent on an adequate inventory balance of raw materials and components. Excess inventory means a high amount of tied-up capital; a low inventory can produce interruption in the production flow. Appropriate inventory levels become even more crucial when part of the material is imported. Long lead times add to the uncertainty of demand between replenishments; in addition, import restriction laws issued by foreign countries where affiliates of multinational companies are located must also be taken into consideration.

In the case of Brazil importers must deposit a high percentage of the total value of the import license (FOB value) with the state-owned Banco do Brasil. The deposit is for a period of one year, and besides being devaluated due to inflation in the period (the inflation rate in Brazil was forecast at 45% for 1979), no interest is paid on the tied-up capital. The compulsory deposit and other charges more than double the FOB value of an imported item before it can be used in the manufacturing process (for details see example in the Appendix).

Reprinted by permission of Alberto Gabbay Canen and Roberto D. Galvão, "An Application of ABC Analysis to Control Imported Material," *Interfaces*, Vol. 10, No. 4, August, 1980, Copyright 1980 The Institute of Management Sciences.

The situation described above was a source of considerable financial difficulty for one of the Brazilian affiliates of a USA-based company. The company management needed a quick improvement in its financial position and there was little time for a sophisticated study of its inventory policy. An ABC analysis provided a good insight into the situation and enabled a considerable improvement in the company's performance.

ABC ANALYSIS

In December 1977 the company had a total inventory of US$ 1 million and the compulsory deposit due to imported material was approximately US$ 400,000. A complete bill of materials was developed to determine the source and the corresponding percentage of components held in inventory. Table 1 provides this information. The ABC classification of these items is given in Table 2, and the distribution of the class A items is shown in Table 3.

As it can be seen, 23.54% of the total annual usage is imported from the USA, and this corresponds to only 12 items. The items imported from Argentina were of no immediate concern since the Brazilian government exempts imported material from the Latin American Free Trade Association (LAFTA) counties from paying the compulsory deposit. Rigorous control was applied to the 12 items imported from the USA. As a consequence, in a period of one year (December 1977 to December 1978) the contri-

Table 1. *Source of Items*

Source of Items	No. of Items	Percentage
Locally produced	230	52.8%
Bought in Argentina	137	31.4%
Bought in the USA	62	14.2%
Bought in other countries	7	1.6%
Total	436	100.0%

Table 2. *ABC Classification*

Class	% of Annual Usage Costs (US$)	No. of Items
A	75.34%	36
B	20.00%	105
C	4.66%	295
Total	100.00%	436

Table 3. *Distribution of the Class A Items*

	Source of Item			
	Locally Produced	Bought in the USA	Bought in Argentina	Total
No. of Items	21	12	3	36
% of annual usage cost (US$)	48.74%	23.54%	3.06%	75.34%

bution to costs of inventory-related costs dropped from US$ 0.15 per US dollar of sales to US$ 0.11 per US dollar. The financial position of the company has improved and time can now be dedicated to implementing a more encompassing inventory control system for the other items.

CONCLUSIONS

The ABC analysis enabled a reduction of almost 30% in inventory-related costs. In addition, the study showed very clearly that there exist in Brazil strong incentives to procure locally as much as possible of one's own needs.

APPENDIX

The example below shows the unit cost of a typical imported item before it can be used by the company, as compared to its FOB value.

FOB value	US$ 0.653
Freight + Insurance	0.062
Subtotal: Cost, Insurance, and Freight value	0.715
Local Duties	0.560
Total: Unit Cost in Brazil	US$ 1.275

The example shows that the unit of the item for the company usage is approximately twice its FOB value. If, as it is the practice of most manufacturers in Brazil, the costs due to the compulsory deposit are added to the total above, the final unit cost approaches 2.5 times the item's FOB value.

Author's Note Added in Proof. The inflation rate during 1979 in Brazil was between 75% and 80%. Since this paper was accepted for publication, Brazilian laws relating to imported material have gone through some changes.

DISCUSSION QUESTIONS

1. In general, why is ABC analysis a useful technique in controlling inventory?

2. Why was ABC analysis particularly important in this situation?

3. Briefly describe how ABC analysis was used and the cost savings that resulted.

4. Describe three companies or industries for which a technique like ABC analysis would be useful.

"Project EOQ": A Success Story in Implementing Academic Research

Larry M. Austin

5

INTRODUCTION

Inventory theory was one of the earliest, and certainly one of the most successful, operations research techniques to be applied in business, industry and the public sector. As early as 1952, the United States Air Force had developed and implemented a simple economic ordering quantity (EOQ) system for repetitive purchases of expendable (nonreparable) weapon system spares [4], and in 1958 the Department of Defense directed the use of basic EOQ principles by all defense procurement and logistics agencies [5]. Although many changes were made over the years, as late as 1973 Air Force Logistics Command (AFLC) was still using a variation of the basic Wilson model [8] to determine optimal ordering quantities for its 250,000-item active inventory of expendable spares. Annual procurement costs total approximately \$350–\$400 million, and AFLC managers wanted to explore the possibility of installing a price discount capability in its bid solicitation system.

Since price discount solicitations are common in commercial procurement, and since the mathematical theory involving optimization of total acquisition cost is simple and well known (e.g., [8]), implementation of such a capability by AFLC would appear to have been a trivial undertaking. However, as is so often the case, the complex constraints and requirements of the "real-world" system did not coincide with theoretical models. This paper reports on the frustrating, but highly successful, research and implementation effort which came to be known as "Project EOQ."[1]

ORGANIZATION OF THE RESEARCH EFFORT

At the Air Force Academy, a graduate-level course in logistics management was taken each year by certain academically gifted seniors in their final semester. In the past, the course had been taught in a seminar format using case studies. Meanwhile, in the spring of 1974, AFLC requested the assistance of the Academy in modernizing its EOQ system to include a price discount solicitation capability, and several faculty members with appropriate academic training and experience had expressed an interest in the proposed research. The Air Force Business Research Management Center had agreed to assist in obtaining the required data and background material, with the Air Force Procurement Research Office acting as on-site project manager. It subsequently occurred to the faculty members involved that this project could provide a unique opportunity for the cadets who would be enrolled in the logistics management course to tackle a "real-world" problem—complete with massive amounts of data and "messy" constraints—rather than a set of neat, well-structured case studies. The nineteen cadets, whose majors were in computer science, economics,

management and mathematics, were enthusiastic about the idea. Both the sponsor and the Academy approved the experiment, and "Project EOQ" was initiated in January, 1974.

It became apparent early in the game that opportunities for improvement in AFLC's EOQ system were not limited to installation of a price discount capability. First, the system currently used an eight-quarter moving average to predict demand for each of the 250,000 items in inventory, and it was felt that more sophisticated techniques might significantly improve the accuracy of demand forecasting. Second, AFLC was currently using a holding charge of 32% of average on-hand inventory,[2] which was applied to every item regardless of cost or classification. This factor was thought to be excessively high, as well as inappropriate for application to every item in the inventory. Third, AFLC was currently using a safety stock of one month's demand, undifferentiated as to dollar value or utilization rate, and the team believed that a better fill-rate (the ratio of orders filled from stock to orders received) and lower cost could be attained by developing a more sophisticated approach in this area. Fourth, AFLC was not satisfied with its ordering cost parameters ($142 per order for orders under $2500; $424 per order for larger orders), and research into this facet of the system was indicated.

Finally, many studies had previously been done on AFLC's EOQ system, with very little actual improvement resulting. All parties agreed from the start that "Project EOQ" would not end up as just another theoretical probe resulting in a final report and little else. It was decided, therefore, to build a simulation model using actual data in order to test the effects of recommended changes to the system.

As a result of this preliminary analysis, the research team was subdivided into four opera-

---

1. Details of the various topics discussed herein may be found in [1].

2. The 32% charge was composed of: 10% opportunity cost; 1% handling and storage; and 21% obsolescence cost.

tional groups, each composed of four or five students and a faculty member, as follows:

Group 1: computer model-building;
Group 2: holding cost analysis;
Group 3: demand prediction and safety stock analysis;
Group 4: price discount and ordering cost analysis.

The four teams worked independently during the first phase of the research effort, but the results of their efforts were later integrated into a set of prioritized recommendations. Implementation of these recommendations, in various combinations, was simulated to produce prospective annual cost savings for AFLC. The effect of total implementation of the team's recommendations is given in Table 1.

Table 1. *(Projected net annual savings)*

Average Price Discount	Net Annual Savings ($ millions)
3%	21.5
5%	39.6
8%	68.2

PRICE DISCOUNTS

One critical assumption of simple economic ordering quantity models is that the price per unit is constant regardless of order size. In effect, these models attempt to minimize purely *internal* costs (e.g., ordering, holding, backordering, and stockout), while ignoring the supplier's economic *production* quantity (EPQ). Since most expendable weapon system spares have no commercial application, suppliers must incur a setup cost for producing each order obtained. Thus, without an opportunity to quote decreased unit prices for larger order quantities, a match between the buyer's EOQ and the supplier's EPQ is purely a matter of serendipity.

In commerical procurement transactions, solicitation of price discounts is a simple matter: the buyer merely asks for price quotes based upon the supplier's preferred quantities—perhaps within some feasible range. The award is then made to the competing supplier whose bid results in the lowest total annualized cost (all other things being equal), regardless of quantity or price. Either "all-units" or "incremental" discounts may be accepted at the option of the buyer, or offered at the option of the seller.

In defense procurement, however, the situation is much more complex. First, the Armed Services Procurement Regulations (ASPR) prescribe competitive (advertised) procurement in all cases in which such an approach is feasible. Furthermore, competing suppliers must be given the opportunity to bid on the same quantities, which effectively negates the possiblity of allowing suppliers to quote prices based upon their individual EPQ's. Since purchase solicitation quantities must therefore be determined by the government in advance, "incremental" discounts are ruled out immediately.[3] The alternative is to solicit "all-units" discounts based upon predetermined solicitation quantities.

Even in the case of "all-units" price discounts, the situation is not straightforward. First, the differential ordering costs mentioned above form a step-function, and are based upon simplified buying procedures which are permitted for small purchases (under $2500),[4] as opposed to more paperwork and higher approval levels for purchases above this amount. This discontinuity in the cost function is tricky to handle, since it is based upon order quantity rather than annual demand. Second, the Department of Defense had directed [6] that no less than a three-month supply, and no more than a three-

---

3. This is true because, when soliciting "incremental" discounts, the order quantity can be any number of units and is determined by the combination of prices quoted for the various increments. Thus, order quantity is determined by the supplier, not the buyer.
4. This figure has recently been raised to $10,000.

year supply, of any item be purchased at one time. These artificial constraints on order quantities have several interesting effects: elevating the holding costs on high value, frequently ordered items; and raising the ordering costs on numerous low value, infrequently ordered items. (In fact, the ordering cost for low value items frequently exceeds the cost of the units themselves.) The net effect of these constraints is to complicate the determination of solicitation quantities for price discount purposes.

The most frustrating constraint of all, however, and the one that presented the most serious barrier to implementation of a price discount capability in AFLC, was the fiscal restriction. Funds to purchase expendable spares are allocated separately by Congress on a year by year basis, and exceeding a given fiscal year allocation—even to save considerable money in the long run—is not permissible under federal law. In addition to legal restrictions, AFLC had further imposed quarterly administrative restrictions on expenditures by its five Air Logistics Centers. The impact of these fiscal constraints was expressed by one senior AFLC manager in the following (seemingly paradoxical) comment following a briefing by the research team: "Your recommendations make sense, and I agree that soliciting price discounts would probably save a lot of money, but we simply can't afford to do it."

The recommended price discount solicitation system

A thorough study of laws and regulations covering fiscal year obligation authority revealed no feasible way to implement an across-the-board price discount solicitation capability for all of AFLC's 250,000 inventory items. However, since expendable weapon system spares exhibit strong Pareto ("ABC" rule) characteristics, a workable transition scheme was developed by the team. Beginning with the first day of a new fiscal year, it was recommended that all items which would normally be purchased two or more times per year (EOQ ≤ half of annual demand) be identified for price discount solicitation, which effectively limited the set of applicable items to those which would have been purchased more than once within current-year obligation authority. While this approach limited application to about 4% of the items, it included almost two-thirds of the dollar value of purchases. Recommended price discount solicitation quantities for the transition year are given in Table 2.

In order to test the actual effect of price discount solicitation, a test, using the approach in Table 2, was initiated at the Ogden Air Logistics Center in April 1974, when actual price discount solicitations were attached to Purchase Requests (PR's). The form was structured in such a way that the lowest quantity solicited was the PR quantity as stated in the usual manner,

Table 2. *(Solicitation quantities for transition year)*

Normal Line Item Value for the Solicitation	Price Discount Solicitation quantities
Annual Demand (AD)/4[a]	AD/4, AD/2, 3 · AD/4, AD
Between AD/4 & AD/2	EOQ, (EOQ + AD)/2, AD
Between $2500 & AD/2	EOQ, AD, 2 · AD[b]
< $2500	Do not solicit price discounts; use small purchase procedures

[a] Under DOD restrictions, purchase quantity may not be less than three months' supply.
[b] For items in the lower end of the dollar value range, it was decided that the one year demand rule could be relaxed without serious risk of over-obligation of current-year funds.

Table 3. *("Steady state" solicitation quantities)*

Major Category	Subcategories	Price Discount Solicitation Quantities
I AD ⩾ $10,000 or EOQ > $2500	EOQ < 3 · AD/4	EOQ, 2 · EOQ, 3 · EOQ, 4 · EOQ
	3 · AD/4 ⩽ EOQ < AD	EOQ, 2 · EOQ, 3 · EOQ
	AD ⩽ EOQ < 3 · AD/2	EOQ, 2 · EOQ
	EOQ ⩾ 3 · AD/2	EOQ, 3 · AD
II $2000 ⩽ AD < $10,000 and EOQ ⩽ $2500	Option of buyer: remain within small purchase limits	EOQ, any quantity up to $2499
	Option of buyer: exceed small purchase limits	Same quantities as in Major Category I above
III $833 ⩽ AD < $2000	EOQ > $2000	EOQ, $2499
	EOQ ⩽ $2000	EOQ, (EOQ + $2499)/2, $2499
IV $300 ⩽ AD < $833	———	EOQ, 3 · AD
V AD < $300	———	Do not solicit price discounts

so that prospective suppliers could ignore the price discount form and still be responsive to the PR. The results of the 2½-month test were better than expected, with 70% of the PR's being returned with price discounts quoted, and with discounts averaging 4½% being offered by suppliers.[5] On the basis of this successful experience, the test at Ogden ALC was indefinitely extended, and the quarterly internal fiscal constraints were relaxed for this purpose.[6]

The solicitation system for the transition period obviously did not take advantage of all possible savings to be realized through price discounts, since the experiment was artifically limited to large (over $2500) purchases. The "steady state" price discount solicitation system recommended by the research team is outlined in Table 3.

Since the computation of these price discount solicitation quantities is obviously complicated, a brief explanation of the logic used to derive Table 3 is in order. Four criteria were used: (1) the DOD constraint on ordering more than a three-year supply of an item must be observed; (2) the effect of the ordering cost step-function between large and small purchases must be taken into account; (3) the order quantities in each case must be sufficiently far apart in magnitude to allow a supplier to differentiate between them as to price discounts; and (4) the DOD constraint on ordering less than a three-month supply of an item must be observed. The effect of criterion (1) is seen in the computation

5. Price discounts were calculated on a "cascading" basis in order to derive a conservative estimate. That is, if three prices $(P_1 > P_2 > P_3)$ were quoted on three increasingly larger quantities $(0 < Q_1 < Q_2 < Q_3)$, then the price discounts (PD_i) were individually computed as follows: $PD_1 = (P_1 - P_2)/P_1$; $PD_2 = (P_2 - P_3)/P_2$. The 4½% average discussed above is the arithmetic mean of all discounts treated separately.
6. Subsequent to the completion of "Project EOQ," a special revolving fund was set up at Ogden ALC for a purpose of validating savings achieved through price discounts.

of solicitation quantities in Categories IV and V. Categories II and III are driven by criterion (2), and criterion (4) affects only Category I. Criterion (3) was the most troublesome, and it affects solicitation quantities in Categories I, II, and III, as well as the determination of the cut-off point between Categories IV and V.

The most interesting situation displayed in Table 3 arises as a result of the large purchase/small purchase dichotomy. A legal interpretation of this ASPR provision was obtained from experts in procurement law, and the upshot is that the determination of large vs. small purchase would depend upon the maximum quantity solicited. That is, a particular PR (within a certain range) could be kept within small purchase limits by soliciting bids on a maximum quantity of $2499, or deliberately moved into the large purchase range by soliciting at least one quantity above $2499. Note that the *solicitation, not the final award*, determines the purchase category. For this reason, it was recommended that this option (Category II) be left to the experienced judgment of the buyer. A simple computer program was written to assist buyers in these cases; the program computes the price discount which would have to be obtained in order to cover the additional ordering cost generated by moving to a large purchase situation.

The price discount simulation model

Complete information on each of the 250,000 active inventory items was maintained on 26 magnetic tapes. Rather than attempt to simulate the entire inventory (a formidable and very expensive task!), a stratified random sample of 9,767 items was selected. The simulation runs were made on the sample, and the results were then projected to the entire inventory. A description of the sample is given in Table 4. Standard random selection procedures were used to select individual inventory items within each dollar category.

Note that, while the sample contained only about 4% of the inventory items, over 40% of the total dollar value (in terms of annual demand) was represented. The sample records were loaded on a single magnetic tape, which made extensive experimentation and sensitivity analysis possible.

In deciding upon appropriate average price discounts for the simulations, little empirical evidence was available to guide the team. A recent test by the General Accounting Office [7] at one Air Logistics Center evoked price discount quotes from suppliers ranging from 1% to 31%, with the average being about 7%. To assure conservative results, simulations were run with all possible combinations of three average discounts (3%, 5%, 8%) and three maximum discounts (10%, 15%, 20%). Due to the conservative nature of the assumed distribution of price discounts,[7] it was found that the maximum allowable discount made almost no difference in the overall results, so subsequent runs were made using a maximum discount of 20%. The results of these simulation runs, with all but price discounts remaining unchanged in the EOQ system, are presented in Table 5.

An interesting thing occurred while the cadets were making the computer simulation runs. Although they were well aware of the Central Limit Theorem and understood its implications for the simulation model, they nevertheless wanted to be *sure*. Therefore they ran the simulation 25 times on the Academy's B-6700 computer. As could have been predicted, the total annual costs generated varied by only about ½ of 1% from maximum to minimum. That they were impressed by this result is a decided understatement! The moral here is clear: it is one thing to establish the validity of a powerful theoretical result by a formal mathematical proof; *it is quite another—and more convincing—thing to allow students to demonstrate the result for themselves.*

---

7. The Appendix contains an expanded discussion of the simulation model.

Table 4.   *(Composition of stratified random sample)*

Annual Demand in Dollars	% of Total Items in Sample	Dollar Value in Sample ($000's)	Number of Items in Sample
< $25	1%	5	628
$25–$500	2%	311	2,305
$501–$2500	5%	2,201	2,201
$2501–$10,000	10%	6,986	1,613
$10,001–$45,000	33%	31,325	1,851
> $45,000	100%	124,942	1,169
Totals		165,770	9,767

Table 5.   *(Projected net annual savings from price discount solicitation)*

Average Price Discount	Gross Savings in Annual Acquisition Cost ($ Millions)	Net Savings in[a] Total Annual Cost ($ Millions)
3%	19.6	10.3
5%	39.9	25.9
8%	67.2	50.7

[a] Adjusted for net increase in ordering/holding cost caused by higher average inventories.

ADDITIONAL RESEARCH RESULTS

While the research and recommendations with respect to solicitation of price discounts were the most successful part of "Project EOQ," the other areas of investigation also generated potentially profitable recommendations. These areas are discussed briefly below.

Demand prediction

The current AFLC demand prediction technique (an eight-quarter moving average) was tested against four more sophisticated techniques[8] for forecasting accuracy. In each case, the most current eight quarters of demand for approximately 6,000 randomly selected items were forecast with predictors constructed from demand in the previous eight quarters. Four

criteria were used to compare the results: mean absolute deviation; weighted mean absolute deviation; sum of squared deviations; and weighted sum of squared deviations [2]. Single exponential smoothing, with a smoothing constant of $\alpha = 0.1$, was approximately three times as accurate as the next most accurate of the predictors tested,[9] and was twice as accurate as measured by the most conservative criterion (weighted sum of squared deviations). Differential treatment for different categories of demand was also recommended, as outlined in Table 6.

In addition to the overall demand prediction analysis, a special analysis of the 250 highest dollar-demand items was undertaken. Most of these items are aircraft spares, so a multiple linear regression model was constructed using numbers of aircraft, sorties flown, and flying

8. Single, double and triple exponential smoothing (three different weights for each) and simple linear regression.

9. $D_t = \alpha \cdot d_{t-1} + (1 - \alpha) D_{t-1}$, where: D_t = forecast demand for period t; d_t = actual demand for period t; α = smoothing constant.

Table 6. *(Demand predicition recommendations)*

Item Category	% of Items in Category	Recommendation
Low Demand Items (less than three quarters of positive demand history in the last eight qtrs.	44%	Item Manager reviews all field demands for appropriateness (management by exception)
Erratic Demand Items (at least three quarters of positive demand history in last eight quarters, but with demand standard deviation greater than average demand)	21%	Use single exponential smoothing with tracking signal to indicate a shift in demand pattern
"Normal" Demand Items	35%	Use single exponential smoothing with $\alpha = 0.1$

hours for each aircraft type as the independent variables, and demand for each part as the dependent variable in each case [3]. The coefficients of determination (R^2) for the individual spare parts models varied from 0.13 to 0.75, with an average R^2 of 0.47. Introduction of a one quarter time lag between the data for the independent and dependent variables resulted in a slight improvement in the R^2 (average) to 0.52. The team concluded that the results of this investigation were not convincing enough to recommend implementation of this approach, but did suggest further research in this area.

Holding cost

In June 1973, AFLC had decreased its holding cost parameter from 39% to 32%, based upon a downward revision of the obsolescence component from 28% to 21%. Partially as a result of evidence generated by "Project EOQ," the obsolescence component was further decreased in April 1974 to 13%, resulting in a holding parameter of 24%. (The 10% opportunity cost and 1% handling and storage cost components,

which were established originally by the Department of Defense, were unchanged.) While the research team believed this to be a move in the right direction, there was still concern about the efficacy of the practice of applying an undifferentiated obsolescence to all items in the inventory. In an effort to refine this process, a variable obsolescence approach was investigated. Each item in the inventory is classified in two mutually exclusive and exhaustive ways—by one of 341 System Management Codes (SMC's) which identifies the item with a particular weapon system, and by one of 311 Federal Supply Class Codes (FSCC's) which identifies the item by general type. A computer scan of the inventory tapes revealed that only 634 of the SMC/FSCC pairs contained obsolescent items (while there are technically 106,051 possible SMC/FSCC combinations, most are infeasible). The actual obsolescence percentages ranged, as expected, from 0–100%, with most in the 1–2% category.

The variable obsolescence parameters were input into the simulation model, substituting the actual obsolescence rate for the current parameter, and the rather startling results are exhibited in Table 7 (compare with Table 5).

Table 7. *(Projected net annual savings from use of variable obsolescence)*

Average Price Discount	Gross Savings in Annual Acquisition Cost ($ Millions)	Net Savings in Total Annual Cost ($ Millions)
No Price Discount	7.8[a]	7.8
3%	23.4	17.4
5%	43.0	35.6
8%	69.2	61.8

[a] Note that lower holding costs in certain cases caused price discounts to be economically advantageous that were not so under a constant holding cost situation.

Safety stock analysis

Although a concerted attempt was made, the team was unable to develop a satisfactory method for determining stockout cost for expendable weapon system spares. "Time-weighted mission essentiality" is the criterion preferred by the Department of Defense [6], but no economic surrogate for this operational criterion could be identified. A secondary objective—to minimize total investment in safety stock for a given overall fillrate—was analyzed, but the results were inconclusive. Basically, the optimization of this objective involves high safety stock levels for low cost items, and low (or zero) safety stock levels for high cost items, which totally ignores mission essentiality. Further research was recommended in this area.

Miscellaneous areas of investigation

During the course of this research effort, AFLC readjusted its ordering cost parameters to $444 (from $424) per order for large purchases, and to $149 (from $142) per order for small purchases. The combined effect of this change and the previously mentioned downward revision in the holding cost parameter was to decrease the total number of annual purchase actions by approximately 12%. While these changes caused many more small dollar actions to be affected by the three-year buy constraint on one hand,

they had the salutory effect of moving large dollar actions affected by the three-month buy constraint closer to the true economic order quantities. Even more important, the reduced volume of PR's allowed experienced, highly trained buyers more time to do a better job on the remaining actions, and made implementation of a price discount solicitation capability more manageable.

Finally, AFLC had long employed the practice of using a "standard price" 15% higher than the unit price in its EOQ computations, on the theory that AFLC is acting as a wholesaler. The 15% add-on was viewed as a service charge to its customers. The research team noted that the only real effect of this practice was to cause the EOQ (in units) to be artificially understated by about 7%, and AFLC discontinued this practice prior to the termination of "Project EOQ."

CONCLUSIONS

"Project EOQ" was successful in two distinct ways. First, and most obvious, implementation of key recommendations resulted in savings of $7 million *forecasted* for the first (transition) year—the figure stated in the citation which accompanied the Air Force Business and Procurement Research Award for 1975 to each member of the research team. Full implementation of a price discount capability at all five Air Logistics Centers will soon be a reality, and AFLC subsequently sponsored additional research in all peripheral areas discussed in this paper.

Second, and perhaps even more personally gratifying, was the success achieved in orienting an academic course to the solution of a real problem. As a result, there are nineteen Air Force lieutenants who are convinced of the power and usefulness of management science—not because they heard about it in a classroom, but because they did it themselves.

REFERENCES

1. Austin, L. M., Anselmi, M. S., Carlburg, R. E. and Clark, H. A., "Project EOQ: Feasibility of Price Discounts in Procurement of Non-reparable Spares," Technical Report No. 74-18, USAF Academy, Colorado (Sept. 1974).

2. Brown, R. G., *Smoothing, Forecasting, and Prediction of Discrete Time Series*, Prentice-Hall, Englewood Cliffs, N.J. (1964).

3. Chou, Y. L., *Statistical Analysis*, Holt, Rinehart, & Winston, New York (1969).

4. Coile, J. T. and Dickens, D. D., "History and Evaluation of the Air Force Depot Level EOQ Inventory Model," unpublished Master's thesis, Air Force Institute of Technology, Dayton, Ohio (1974).

5. Department of Defense Instruction No. 4140.31 (June 1958).

6. Department of Defense Instruction No. 4140.39 (July 1970).

7. Private communication, working papers supplied by the Kansas City Regional Office of the General Accounting Office (Mar. 1974).

8. Whitin, T. and Hadley, G., *Analysis of Inventory Systems*, Prentice-Hall, Englewood Cliffs, N.J. (1963).

DISCUSSION QUESTIONS

1. What were the major objectives of this investigation into inventory control policy?

2. Would the results of this research into existing inventory policy be applicable to inventory policies that exist for companies that specialize in manufacturing?

3. Would a technique such as ABC analysis be appropriate for the inventory items discussed in this article?

4. How is demand currently being predicted and what techniques were investigated during the research project?

5. Describe the major components of the holding cost parameter and briefly discuss the recommendation of the research team concerning the holding cost parameter.

6. What technique was used to analyze the price discount solicitation system?

Mathematical Programming

Many management decisions involve making the most effective use of an organization's resources. These resources might be people, raw materials, advertising budgets, machines, or space. They are used to produce products such as trucks or transistors, or services such as education, medical care, or account auditing. *Mathematical programming* is a widely used quantitative analysis technique designed to help managers in making resource allocation decisions. In the past 30 years, it has been applied to military, industrial, financial, marketing, accounting, and agricultural problems, among many others.

A few specific examples of problems in which mathematical programming has been successful are:

1. Development of a production schedule that will satisfy future demand for a firm's product and at the same time *minimize* total production and inventory costs.
2. Establishment of an investment portfolio from a variety of stocks or bonds that will *maximize* a company's return on investment.
3. Allocation of a limited advertising budget among radio, TV, and newspaper spots in order to *maximize* advertising effectiveness.
4. Selection of a product mix in a factory to make best use of machine and work hours available while *maximizing* the firm's profit.

All mathematical programming problems, as you can see above, seek to maximize or minimize some quantity (usually profit or cost). This is called the *objective* of a programming problem.

The second property that mathematical programming problems have in common is the presence of restrictions, or *constraints,* that limit the degree to which management can pursue its objective. We want, therefore, to maximize or minimize a quantity (the objective function) subject to limited resources (the constraints).

Mathematical programming encompasses the areas of linear programming, integer programming, non-linear programming, and goal programming. *Linear programming* (LP), the most common, deals with problems in which the objective function and constraints can be described by linear equations. *Integer programming* is an extension of LP in which all decision variables must have whole (or integer) solution values. *Non-linear Programming,* much more complex mathematically, applies when either the constraints or objective function are non-linear in form. Finally, *goal programming* deals with situations in which more than one goal or objective is to be attained.

An L.P. Model for Work Force Scheduling for Banks
The first article, "An L. P. Model for Work Force Scheduling for Banks," provides a brief but realistic example of the use of linear programming in employee scheduling. The concept can be and has been used in restaurants, factories, hospitals, and department stores, as well as in banks. Mr. Moondra describes how Chase Manhattan Bank schedules part-time and full-time employees to meet peak period demands every day. Actual input and output data are provided to illustrate the model's assumptions.

LP Applications in Scottish Agriculture
Ian Balms non-mathematical article, "LP Applications in Scottish Agriculture," discusses the work of a Scottish college in helping advance the efficiency and profitability of farms in Scotland. Four general types of applications are noted; they range from (1) deciding what crops to grow each year, (2) modeling the

management of a whole farm, (3) conducting economic analyses for various national/local crop policies, and (4) providing least cost diet plans for feeding the farm stock. The author discusses the successes, failures, opportunities, and difficulties in implementing the college's outreach program for farmers and agricultural advisors.

A Linear Programming Salary Evaluation Model for High School Personnel

Next, Fabozzi and Daddio's article, "A Linear Programming Salary Evaluation Model for High School Personnel," describes how one high school was able to use LP to help set equitable salary levels. The new approach overcomes criticism to the "fixed step salary method" in which only years of college and experience account for salary levels of teachers and administrators. The particular school in this paper had a goal of maximizing the salary of the most highly qualified teachers and retaining them. Variables such as class make-up, subjects taught, supervisory responsibility, education, experience, and non-classroom workload were all considered. The concept behind the model is of broader interest, for it extends beyond high schools to all organizational compensation programs, and can hence be used in any field.

Use of the Transportation Method of L.P. in Production Planning

C. D. Sadleir's article, "Use of the Transportation Method of L. P. in Production Planning," describes the application of LP to a production problem facing a large English shoe manufacturer. The firm's decision, *where to produce* each style, model, and size of shoe, is an example of the general category of mathematical programming problems called the *transportation problem*. Transportation problems, which can be solved by either LP or a special transportation algorithm, are often used in deciding when to locate a new factory, which factories in a large firm should supply each regional warehouse, and how to allocate production resources among various plants. The latter is the example detailed in this article, where the goal is to minimize total cost subject to overall demand and to capacity constraints at each plant.

Application of Linear Programming vs. Goal Programming to Assignment Problem

Another popular application of LP has been to a category of administrative problems called the "assignment problem." Examples in management and marketing include assigning jobs to machines, workers to tasks, and salespeople to sales territories. Mehta and Rifai's article, "Application of Linear Programming vs. Goal Programming to Assignment Problem," first illustrates the assignment of a firm's project leaders to clients, with the goal of minimizing total project costs. The article then introduces goal programming. Goal programming is a modification and extension of LP that allows simultaneous solution of a series of sometimes conflicting management goals. In this case, management recognizes *seven* goals it would like to obtain, including the cost minimization objective.

An Application of Goal Programming at Lord Corporation

A second article dealing with goal programming, by Salvia and Ludwig, is called "An Application of Goal Programming at Lord Corporation." In this brief paper, the authors describe the model that was developed and used at Lord Corporation to assist top management in the problem of allocating funds to competing research and development projects. Ten goals were established, and 25 projects were considered. The goals and program results are presented.

An L.P. Model for Work Force Scheduling for Banks

Shyam L. Moondra

6

FORMULATION OF PROBLEM

The workload in many areas of bank operations has the characteristics of a non-uniform distribution with respect to time of day. For example, at Chase Manhattan Bank, the number of domestic money transfer requests received from customers, if plotted against time of day, would appear to have the shape of an inverted-U curve with the peak reached around 1 p.m. For efficient use of the resources, the manpower available, should, therefore, also vary correspondingly. Figure 1 shows a typical workload curve and the corresponding manpower requirement at different hours of the day.

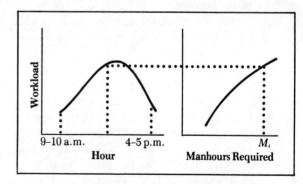

Figure 1. *Workload Curve*

Reprinted with permission of the *Journal of Bank Research*, published by Bank Administration Institute, Winter, 1976.

A variable capacity can effectively be achieved by employing part-time personnel. Since part-timers are not entitled to all the fringe benefits, they are often more economical than full-time employees. However, other considerations may limit the extent to which part-time people can be hired in a given operating department. The problem is to find an optimum work-force schedule that would meet manpower requirements at any given time and also be economical.

THE L.P. MODEL

We will make the following assumptions partly to simulate the real situation and partly to simplify the problem. It should be emphasized that these assumptions are not required in their strictest sense, and can very easily be modified as needed. For simplicity's sake all the parameters are assumed to be deterministic.

1. By corporate policy, part-time man-hours are limited to a maximum of $a\%$ of the day's total requirement.
2. Full-time employees work for eight hours (one hour for lunch included) per day. Thus a full-timer's productive time is 35 hours per week.
3. Part-timers work for at least four hours but less than eight hours and are not allowed any lunch break.
4. 50% of the full-timers go out to lunch between 11 a.m. and 12 noon and the remaining 50% between 12 noon and 1 p.m. The model can be modified very easily for any other situation.
5. The shift starts at 9 a.m. and ends at 7 p.m. (i.e., overtime limited to two hours). For a given situation, if this assumption does not hold, two alternatives are: 1) The work left over at 7 p.m. should be considered as hold-over for the next day, or 2) the model should be extended for the time periods

beyond 7 p.m. (This will necessitate the introduction of additional variables.)
6. A full-time employee is not allowed to work more than five hours overtime per week (so he is paid at the normal rate for overtime hours and not at one-and-a-half times the normal rate applicable to hours in excess of 40 per week). The fringe benefits are not applied to the overtime hours.

Notations: The following notations are used.

x = Average cost per full-time man-hours (fringe benefits included).
y = Average cost per overtime man-hour for full-timers (straight rate excluding fringe benefits, cf. assumption 6)
r = Average cost per part-time man-hour
M_i = Man-hours required for the ith hour $i = 1, 2, \ldots\ldots\ldots\ldots, 9, 10$ (9 a.m. to 7 p.m.)
F_1 = Number of full-time employees
F_2 = Number of full-time employees working overtime between 5 p.m. and 6 p.m.
F_3 = Number of full-time employees working overtime between 6 p.m. and 7 p.m.
P_i = Number of part-time employees starting at the beginning of the ith hour ($i = 1, \ldots\ldots, 7$, since no part-timer can start after 3 p.m., cf. assumption 3)
Q_i = Number of part-time employees leaving at the end of the ith hour ($i = 4, \ldots, 10$, cf. assumption 3)

Objective Function: We want to minimize the total manpower cost given by
$$(1)\ Z = x \times F_1 + y\,(F_2 + F_3) + r(10P_1 + 9P_2 + 8P_3 + 7P_4 + 6P_5 + 5P_6 + 4P_7 - 6Q_4 - 5Q_5 - 4Q_6 - 3Q_7 - 2Q_8 - Q_9)$$

Constraints: For a given hour, the available man-hours should be at least equal to the required man-hours. Therefore, we have:

(2) $F_1 + P_1$ $\geq M_1$

(3) $F_1 + P_1 + P_2$ $\geq M_2$

(4) $\tfrac{1}{2}F_1* + P_1 + P_2 + P_3$ $\geq M_3$

(5) $\tfrac{1}{2}F_1* + P_1 + P_2 + P_3 + P_4$ $\geq M_4$

(6) $F_1 + P_1 + P_2 + P_3 + P_4 + P_5 \quad\quad -Q_4$ $\geq M_5$

(7) $F_1 + P_1 + P_2 + P_3 + P_4 + P_5 + P_6 \quad -Q_4 - Q_5$ $\geq M_6$

(8) $F_1 + P_1 + P_2 + P_3 + P_4 + P_5 + P_6 + P_7 - Q_4 - Q_5 - Q_6$ $\geq M_7$

(9) $F_1 + P_1 + P_2 + P_3 + P_4 + P_5 + P_6 + P_7 - Q_4 - Q_5 - Q_6 - Q_7$ $\geq M_8$

(10) $F_2 + P_1 + P_2 + P_3 + P_4 + P_5 + P_6 + P_7 - Q_4 - Q_5 - Q_6 - Q_7 - Q_8$ $\geq M_9$

(11) $F_3 + P_1 + P_2 + P_3 + P_4 + P_5 + P_6 + P_7 - Q_4 - Q_5 - Q_6 - Q_7 - Q_8 - Q_9$ $\geq M_{10}$

* cf. assumption 4

The part-timers work for at least four hours (cf. assumption 3). Therefore we have:

(12) $Q_4 \leq P_1$

(13) $Q_5 \leq P_1 + P_2 - Q_4$

(14) $Q_6 \leq P_1 + P_2 + P_3 - Q_4 - Q_5$

(15) $Q_7 \leq P_1 + P_2 + P_3 + P_4 - Q_4 - Q_5 - Q_6$

(16) $Q_8 \leq P_1 + P_2 + P_3 + P_4 + P_5 - Q_4 - Q_5 - Q_6 - Q_7$

(17) $Q_9 \leq P_1 + P_2 + P_3 + P_4 + P_5 + P_6 - Q_4 - Q_5 - Q_6 - Q_7 - Q_8$

Since part-timers work for less than eight hours (cf. assumption 3), we have:

(18) $Q_4 + Q_5 + Q_6 + Q_7 \geq P_1$

(19) $Q_4 + Q_5 + Q_6 + Q_7 + Q_8 \geq P_1 + P_2$

(20) $Q_4 + Q_5 + Q_6 + Q_6 + Q_7 + Q_8 + Q_9 \geq P_1 + P_2 + P_3$

Total part-time man-hours cannot exceed the given limit (cf. assumption 1), therefore we have:

(21) $10P_1 + 9P_2 + 8P_3 + 7P_4 + 6P_5 + 5P_6 + 4P_7 - 6Q_4 - 5Q_5 - 4Q_6 - 3Q_7 - 2Q_8 - Q_9 \leq a(\Sigma M_i) / 100$

We can now formally state our problem as:

Minimize Z given by (1), subject to (2) through (21) and
$F_1, F_2, F_3, P_1, P_2, P_3, P_4, P_5, P_6, P_7, Q_4, Q_5, Q_6, Q_7, Q_8, Q_9 \geq 0$

An L.P. Model for Work Force Scheduling for Banks

Example
The use of the above L.P. Model is illustrated in the following example.

Input:
x = \$5.053
y = \$4.04
r = \$3.912
a = 40%
M_i = 14,25,26,38,55,60,51,29,14,9
for i = 1, 2, ... , 10

Output: Using the two phase method as described in Hadley, the following results are obtained.

SUMMARY

Since the number of employees cannot be fractional, the use of linear programming is only an approximation. For truly optimum results, this problem should be formulated as an integer programming problem.

The man-hours required for each hour of the day were assumed to be deterministic. In a real situation, it would be found that there is a wide fluctuation in these man-hours from day to day. To account for this variability, one should revert to stochastic linear programming.

The results of the example given in Figure 2 show that the optimum workforce schedule

Figure 2. Work-Force Schedule

Time Period	Number of Persons Required	Number of Persons Available		
		Full-time	Part-time	Total
9–10 a.m.	14	29	—	29
10–11	25	29	—	29
11–12	26	15	11	26
12–1	38	14	26	40
1–2	55	29	26	55
2–3	60	29	31	60
3–4	51	29	22	51
4–5	29	29	5	34
5–6	14	9	5	14
6–7 p.m.	9	9	0	9

Figure 3. Time Schedules

Full-Time Employees

Number of Employees	Starting Time	Number of Employees	Lunch Period	Number of Employees	Leaving Time
29	9 a.m.	14	11–12	20	5 p.m.
		15	12–1	9	7 p.m.

Part-Time Employees

Number of Employees	Starting Time	Number of Employees	Leaving Time
11	11 a.m.	9	3 p.m.
		2	4 p.m.
15	12 Noon	15	4 p.m.
5	2 p.m.	5	6 p.m.

allows for an idle time of 26 man-hours in the entire day. Part of this idle time in the optimum solution is due to the restriction that an employee can start only at the beginning of an hour (or leave at the end of an hour). If we reduce our time period from one hour to half-an-hour (or even better to 15 minutes), the optimum results would show a markedly improved schedule with lesser idle time. This would, however, increase the number of variables and, therefore, the cost of computation.

REFERENCE

Hadley, G., "Linear Programming," Addison-Wesley, Reading, Massachusetts, 1962.

DISCUSSION QUESTIONS

1. Explain in your own words what this model is trying to do and how it works.

2. To make sure you understand how the L. P. model is formulated, use the article's example data and insert them into the constraints and objective function. Your new formulation should be complete enough to solve by computer should your instructor request that you do so.

3. If full-time employees were paid double their normal hourly salary for working overtime, how would the objective function change?

4. Why shouldn't the bank use all part-time employees (currently they are limited to $a = 40\%$ of daily man-hours)?

5. What are the limitations in using this model?

LP Applications in Scottish Agriculture

Ian R. Balm

7

BACKGROUND INFORMATION

The West of Scotland Agricultural College is one of 3 Colleges in Scotland (East and North are the other two). The Colleges provide the agricultural advisory service in Scotland as well as undertaking teaching, research and development. One of the functions of the Economics Division in the West College is to provide information and farm management aids to help the farm and horticultural adviser both in general and on specific farms. The LP work fits into this framework through its use as an individual farm advisory aid and also as a research and development tool, as the description of the applications will try to show.

LINEAR PROGRAMMING APPLICATIONS

The present applications of LP in Scotland could be split into four main categories, each with differing requirements on the structure of the LP Matrix and on the means by which information is entered into and taken from the LP package.

Reprinted with permission from *Operational Research Quarterly*, Vol. 31, No. 5, by Ian R. Balm, "LP Applications in Scottish Agriculture," Copyright 1980, Pergamon Press, Ltd.

(a) Farm planning

The use of LP to determine the profit maximising farm plan[6, 7] is the most obvious application. It is also the application on which the reputation of LP mainly rests in agriculture, but the degree of success has been mixed, depending to some extent on the type of farm on which it has been used.

Very broadly, farm types can be split into two categories—arable or grassland. Arable farms grow mainly cereals, potatoes and other crops requiring annual cultivation and seed sowing. These farms have a relatively wide choice of crops to grow, and may make a cropping policy decision each year. The arable farm offers scope for LP use because of this decision problem, the various on farm restrictions [*sic*], and the fact that the input/output relationships are reasonably well established. In practice, however, farmers do tend to stick to similar plans each year.

Grassland farms, as might be expected, use livestock to process grass and other feeds into a saleable form—milk, meat or wool. Livestock farming tends to be a longer term process, with several years elapsing between the start of a programme of change and its completion. Also, the relationships are not at all well established and this can severely affect the reliability of an LP model. Adjustments to a farm plan tend to be made gradually and a partial budget is sometimes more appropriate than an LP solution. In these cases it is the use of a sledgehammer (LP) to crack a nut, and it may not even crack it properly because of the poor definition and reliability of the technical relationships referred to earlier.

There have been attempts at routine farm planning by LP, for example, ICI's MASCOT[3] with its matrix generator and report writer, and the English Agricultural Development and Advisory Service's "typical farm type" matrices.[2] When used on arable farms these tools have been successful not only in helping to shape new plans, but also in identifying bottlenecks. However, their value for planning grassland farm is more dubious.

In Scotland, the East of Scotland Agricultural College provide[s] a farm planning service for the upland, grassland, farm with a matrix generator and report writer. It is based on a relatively small matrix, which could make it difficult to represent an actual on-farm situation adequately. But its use is slowly growing as advisers become more familiar with the concept and value of LP.

In general, LP for farm planning on nonarable farms has not been notably successful. Even on arable farms its use is relatively uncommon. Apart from the information problem and the low year-to-year flexibility of a farm plan, other difficulties include the fact that few farmers have the single objective of profit maximisation, and the construction of an adequate matrix for representing any farm is very time consuming. This often means that a poor model is built, the results are not satisfactory to the practical farmer and so the reputation of LP in agriculture has become a little tarnished. This has not been helped by the use of LP in recent years as a source of papers for academic journals when, in some cases, the need for some practical value has been lost sight of.

(b) Whole farm modelling for economic and technical research purposes

Whole farm application of LP in the West of Scotland Agricultural College has been orientated away from a farm planning service, and towards the use of LP as a research tool for looking at the best structure and management of a "representative" dairy farm. The objective of this is to able to pinpoint, under various economic, environmental and technological conditions, the 'ideal' management strategy for a dairy farm. Factors taken into consideration include best calving pattern for the herd, best grazing and grass conservation management policy, which feeds should be bought and which home grown, and which enterprises can complement or even replace the dairy herd.

The structural requirements of the LP Matrix for this exercise are different from those in the farm planning situation. The model has to be expanded so that each of the constituent elements of, for example, keeping a cow can be examined and manipulated. This means that instead of an activity "cows" there are many—silage quality (silage is grass cut in the summer and conserved for winter feeding), grazing options, alternative yields and calving months and so on. Hence the management of the dairy cow is not predetermined, the model is used to derive it and examine its response to technical changes or different prices.

The model can also be used to look at the impact a new technique might have on a dairy farm, assuming that the technique is compatible with the farming system being modelled.

The model can be used in general advisory work to farmers. The results are made known to College advisers who can then choose to pass on relevant information to farmers.

The question of whether to specialize in winter or in summer milk production can be used as an example of the use of the model. Cows yield more milk soon after calving and yields decline gradually thereafter. The milk is sold through a cooperative milk marketing board which has traditionally set higher prices for milk in winter than in summer. This has encouraged most farms to aim at producing most of their milk in the winter from cows calving in the autumn. Winter milk production means heavy purchased feed costs because the feed requirements of cows are high in early lactation. Summer milk production, on the other hand, has the advantage that the feed requirements of cows more or less match the seasonal grass growth quite closely. Now, with costs rising, the summer/winter differential in milk price closing and a milk levy on every litre produced, the case for high input winter milk production is marginal, and the model itself is moving away from recommending autumn calving.

(c) Economic evaluation of research information

The College undertakes a fair amount of trials works on crops, grassland, animals and horticulture. The results of these trials have to be evaluated economically to assess their value to the farmer. This evaluation can be done by LP, when a model is built representing the system into which the various trials can be included. An example of this is the evaluation of tomato trials carried out at the Glasshouse Investigation Unit for Scotland, which is located at the West of Scotland Agricultural College.

The College provides advice to the horticulturalists in the area, especially the Clyde Valley tomato growers.[5] Scotland is not an ideal place to grow tomatoes with cold windy winters and poor light, but there is a premium paid in Scottish markets for "Scotch" tomatoes. Growers have been increasingly pressurised by rising costs, notably oil which can cost over £20,000 per acre of glass. They were, therefore, facing the problems of how to maintain yield and revenue while reducing costs. The Glasshouse Investigation Unit for Scotland has done trials over the years to assess yield response to various treatments. To try to give guidance to growers on the best action to take, information was taken from trials assessing the effects of different sowing dates, temperatures, plant spacings, etc. on yield and seasonality of tomato production. Sowing later, in January rather than December, and lowering temperature could both save oil, but over the season, revenue might also fall.

All the different treatments were included in a model glasshouse of varying size and labour availability.

The objective was to simulate the impact the trials could have in an economic sense, so that growers could be shown which tomato growing techniques might prove more profitable in their own situation.

Example results from the model are:

(a) The crop grown at a low night temperature

of 13°C compared with the recommended standard of 15°C, was, in general, most profitable;

(b) Wider plant spacing and later sowing, both fuel saving measures, were only worthwhile when there was a shortage of labour;

(c) Continuing the crop beyond mid-October was not justified.

Obviously these results alter as new trials are carried out and costs change, so the model is regularly updated and rerun, to show the best response to changes. At the time of writing (June 1979) the model was being used to look at the possible effects of oil rationing on the best cropping policy for growers.

Information is passed out to growers in reports and via the College's horticultural advisers. This work has been well received by researchers and, more importantly, by growers and the industry in general.

(d) Least cost ration formulation

Least cost rationing is one of the most successful applications of LP in agriculture and has been taken up by several firms supplying feedingstuffs to farmers.

In dairy herds in the West of Scotland the average cost of purchased feed over the winter of 1978–79 was around £180 per cow. Obviously in a 100 cow herd this represents a heavy expenditure, and a small per cow reduction through improved ration management can save the farmer a substantial amount of money.

Try[ing] to encourage more efficient feeding the College provides a winter rationing service for individual farms, based on LP and using the results of chemical analyses of conserved feeds, carried out by the College. The service must conform to practical problems of feeding dairy cows, one of which is that the daily yield varies according to a fairly predictable curve for 9–10 months after calving. Since nutritional re-

quirements vary with the daily milk yield, a series of rations are required for the period from one calving to the next. The rationing package produces rations for up to 9 different daily yield levels, and feeds are allocated across the nine groups so that nutritional requirements are met, but limited supplies of feeds are not exceeded. Cheaper home grown, conserved, feeds are used in such a way that as little expensive purchased feed as possible is required.

The farmer or adviser completes a questionnaire which collects basic information such as feeds available and their qualities and quantities, prices of purchased feeds, details of the herd feeding management etc. This information is then combined with standard data on nutritive values and fed into a matrix generator which sets up the LP matrix unique to the individual farm. Output from the LP package is then translated into a report suitable for use by adviser or farmer by a report writing program.

The rationing LP matrix itself is a conventional least-cost matrix, although integer programming is used to ensure that only one silage type is included in any one ration. This is done because the farmer will usually only wish (or be able) to feed one silage type to any particular group of cows.

So it can be seen that the rationing LP has been tailored towards practical requirements. These are minimum information input requirements from the farmer, an easily read and concise report, and orientation of the structure of the matrix towards practical/managerial needs of farmers.

To sum up, firstly the various applications demand that different emphasis is put on the structure of input to and output from the LP package. Routine individual farm use requires that at least as much effort is put into the means of obtaining and entering information to the LP package and presenting the results that go into the construction of the matrix itself. This is illustrated in the ration formulation programme, and the more successful farm planning LP's. Secondly the matrix itself must be designed so that it is oriented towards the application, and what that application demands in terms of results from the LP.

DIFFICULTIES OF USING LP IN AGRICULTURE

The main problem with agricultural applications is that the process being modelled is living.[4,6–8] There are, therefore, many unknown or poorly defined biological relationships which can influence the system. This presents more of a problem in some areas than others. Perhaps the worst is grassland with variables which include—seasonal growth patterns, response to fertiliser and annual weather conditions, nutritional use by livestock and so on—indeed, many of the specific relationships cannot be closely defined at all. This is even true of crops grown in heated glasshouses, where differences in sunlight between years affect results, and therefore could affect the best course of action.

Thus the modelling of a farm, especially a grassland based farm, is a process where the builder has firstly to try to extract from the relevant specialists and the farmer the basic input/output relationships in the living chain from fertiliser bag to milk sales. Next a preliminary model is built and run. Results are then taken back to the specialists so that constraints and coefficients can be redefined if necessary. This process continues until a satisfactory model is obtained.

The more often quoted difficulties of LP application (if indeed they still are difficulties when IP is available[1]) such as linearity, single solutions, non integer results, single objective—can become less significant and more easily got around than the basic problem of a lack of reliable, repeatable relationships to form the core of the model.

The problems of year-to-year variations in responses could be considered under the heading of risk, suggesting Quadratic programming. There are however two main difficulties here—one is the lack of an accessible and tested QP package. The second problem is that the necessary variance/covariance information cannot be obtained. Another option, which also helps to overcome the profit maximisation problem, is to develop some sort of multiple state and multiple goal objective. In this case a series of objectives could be set up ranging from profit to risk levels and personal preferences. The farmer is then asked to give a subjective measure of an enterprise's contribution to each non quantifiable goal, and also the relative weighting of the goals themselves so that a "utility" maximising solution is produced. However there are likely to be weighting problems, and the solution may not always move in the direction intended following a restatement of the objective weights. The technique does not overcome the basic problems of poor data availability, but it could be used to steer the results away from the riskier enterprises.

There is also the problem that an actual farm starts from a given position of livestock numbers, area of grass, buildings, etc. If an optimal farm plan is produced it may be far from optimal when the cost and time required to move from the present position to the optimal is considered. The plan may not be optimal if and when it is eventually achieved, or it may not be optimal if heavy livestock investment is required. This suggests the need for whole farm models to be multi-period models, with a series of years represented, starting from the present position, so that the optimal path of change is determined. Of course this would become a never ending process as prices and technology change and the model updated and rerun. The farmer would always be moving towards an optimum but possibly never reaching one. This does not answer the question whether the farmer is better to follow such a course or to adjust his present system slowly in response to change. Clearly this would depend on the farmer's abilities. However it would be better to have this smooth progress, then attempt to jump to a series of isolated plans over the years.

With the development of faster, more efficient codes for linear programming this type of large problem can be handled, even on so-called mini computers.

OPPORTUNITIES AND BENEFITS FOR LP IN AGRICULTURE

On the more positive side, the use of LP even in the poorly defined area of agriculture does have advantages for the researcher and farm adviser.

One of the main benefits is that farmers, advisers and specialists are made to think about the system and this can reveal areas of particular lack of knowledge. The actual optimal LP solution itself may not necessarily allow easier decision making for the farmer but there is a large amount of ancillary information which can be very useful. It seems that there is a need to educate the end-users (advisers) that there is more to an LP run than the optimal solution. What *does not* come into the solution can provide as much information as what *does* come in. It could be cost or price, poor yields, or any one of a number of limited farm resources such as lack of specific machinery, building space, or labour. Price sensitivity reveals information about competiveness of enterprises, whether enterprises subject to price fluctuations are risky or not, and so on.

Bottlenecks holding back farm profitability can be identified, and the implications of relaxing these limitations assessed. All these factors can be picked out and the adviser or farmer must subjectively weigh up the information and decide how much of an optimal plan can be implemented depending on the farmers attitude to risk, his expectations and preferences.

This is where the LP model builder must bring himself to the practical level, discuss these points with the adviser, decide changes and re-run the model. In this way the end user can gain far more from the LP run than simply a list of the sizes of the best enterprises.

In conclusion, it is vital that LP model building and its interpretation is carried out in such a way that useful information is given, and the optimal solution is also managerially realistic and sensible. If the solution does not stand up, the credibility is lost and new critics of LP and computers are born. This, at least, is the case in agriculture.

ENDNOTES

1. K. Butterworth (1972) Practical application of integer programming to farm planning, *J. Farm Mgmt Ass.* **2,** 151–157.
2. P. J. James (1972) Computerised farm planning, *J. Farm Mgmt Ass.* **2,** 78–84.
3. R. Bond, P. G. Carter and J. F. Crozier (1970) Computerised farm planning—MASCOT. *J. Farm Mgmt Ass.* **1,** 17–23.
4. K. J. Thompson and A. E. Buckwell (1979) A micro-economic agricultural supply model. *J. Agric. Econ.* **30,** 1–11.
5. I. R. Balm and A. S. Horsburgh (1978) *More Profitable Tomato Production Based on Scottish Research Information.* West of Scotland Agricultural College, Research and Development Publication No. 3.
6. G. E. Dalton (Ed.) (1975) *Study of Agricultural Systems.* Applied Science, London.
7. J. S. Nix (1979) Farm management: the state of the art (or science). *Proceedings of the 1979 Agricultural Economics Society Conference,* April, 1979.
8. J. R. Moneypenny (1975) Aggregative programming model of Australian agriculture. Report No. 7, University of New England, Armidale.

DISCUSSION QUESTIONS

1. What are the four major applications that Professor Balm describes? Provide an example of each.

2. Why hasn't L.P. been more successfully applied in farm planning?

3. Why do you think least cost rationing has been more widely accepted by farmers than other L.P. applications?

4. If you were building a quantitative model to minimize feed costs, what variables would you include?

5. Could these models be transferred and used in U.S. and Canadian farming as well? What factors need to be considered?

A Linear Programming Salary Evaluation Model for High School Personnel

Frank J. Fabozzi
Richard Daddio

8

INTRODUCTION

The fixed step salary schedule is the most widely utilized method of salary evaluation for school district personnel in the U.S.A. Under the fixed step schedule, salary increments are associated exclusively with increases in the number of years of experience and the amount of formal training as measured by the number of credits completed or the highest degree earned. Bruno,[1] however, has indicated a number of serious problems that have resulted from the rigidity of this approach to salary evaluation.

First, neither logic nor internal consistency generally prevail in a fixed step salary schedule. Although minimum and maximum salaries are determined through salary negotiations with teacher bargaining units, Benson[2] points out that intermediate salaries are often calculated by simple rule of thumb. The internal inconsistency then generated within the salary structure means that each member of the school district will often not receive a fair and adequate compensation vis-à-vis every other member.

Reprinted with permission from *Operational Research Quarterly*, Vol. 28, No. 2, by Frank J. Fabozzi and Richard Daddio, "A Linear Programming Salary Evaluation Model for High School Personnel," Copyright 1977, Pergamon Press, Ltd.

Second, in some parts of the U.S., the inability of the fixed step schedule to provide a salary differential for work in more difficult teaching environments has resulted in a serious decline in teacher quality in ghetto areas where it should be the highest.

Third, the fixed step approach economically discriminates against the highly qualified and experienced teacher who opts to remain in the classroom rather than make the transition to an administrative position. Additional compensation for administrators for added workload and responsibility is obviously economically justified; however, it does not follow that low qualified administrators should receive a higher salary than the most qualified teacher. To the extent that the fixed step salary schedule motivates the most qualified teacher to leave the classroom, it fails to provide an economic incentive for good teaching.

Fourth, the lack of recognition of certain specialized skills which are in relative short supply has placed some school districts at a competitive disadvantage compared with other school districts as well as with industry.

Finally, the development of a fixed step salary schedule does not consider the resources of the school district or the established school district priorities and policy objectives. For example, the question: "How can additional funds which are made available to support salaries be incorporated into the salary structure in a logical and consistent way?" is not answered.

One alternative system of salary evaluation which is strongly opposed by teacher bargaining units, is based on "merit schemes." Under the "merit pay" or "pay for performance" approach, increments are based on a set of objectives reviewed by the administration. Although this principle appears to be equitable it assumes that an administrator is capable of making objective and valid distinctions between the performance of school district personnel under his or her supervision. Meyer[3] argues that most salary administrators will admit that it is very difficult to administer a merit pay plan properly, particularly since there is no generally accepted method of measuring a teacher's effectiveness in the classroom. Without such a measure of performance which can be agreed upon by all parties and suitable controls, the merit approach will generate internally inconsistent rewards, leading to a decrease in teacher morale.

Bruno[1] has developed an alternative salary evaluation model based upon linear programming which overcomes these drawbacks. This approach generates an internally consistent salary structure after considering imposed hierarchial and budgetary conditions as well as the two factors found in the fixed step approach, and the established school district priorities and objectives.

Charnes, Cooper and Ferguson[4] and Rehmus and Wagner[5] have suggested the application of linear programming to determine executive compensation. The advantage of the present model is that it considers the resources made available by the organization to support the salary structure, permits overlaps in salary between the different job functions of the organization, and allows the salary structure to reflect school district objectives.

The purpose of this study is to apply the linear programming approach to a high school within a district rather than an entire school district. The particular school district has been exploring the possibility of formulating a separate salary structure for each school level (high, junior high and elementary).

JOB FUNCTIONS, FACTORS AND RELATIVE WEIGHTS

The high school under consideration has a full-time professional staff of 79 individuals of whom there are four administrators, a Principal, two Assistant Principals, and a Dean of Students.

The remaining 75 members comprise 13 department heads and 65 teachers.

Job functions
The only three organizational functions considered were, in order of decreasing responsibility and salary,

1. School Administrators (principal, assistant principal, Dean of Students),
2. Department Heads,
3. Teachers.

In this study, the school district requested that only these three classifications should be considered, but others such as teacher aides, school business manager, counselors, school nurses could be included by making adjustments.

Factors considered in salary evaluation
The fixed step salary schedule considers only two factors in salary evaluation: the number of years of teaching experience and educational attainment. Four other factors will be considered in the linear programming model and two factors have been substituted for the present one for formal educational attainment. They are not exhaustive, and other factors can be incorporated, depending on the objectives of the school district and the compromise agreements with the teacher bargaining unit. The flexibility of linear programming allows an almost unlimited number of factors to be incorporated. The factors used in this application are:

1. The individual academic class make-up as measured by the standard student tracking systems (X_1).
2. The relative demand for the subject matter taught as measured by the total enrollment for the department relative to the total enrollment for the school. For an administrator, the factor represents the special skills possessed (X_2).
3. Supervisory responsibility in terms of areas or scope of responsibility (X_3).
4. The highest academic degree obtained (X_4).
5. Total work experience including district and non-district experience (X_5).
6. The number of college credits above the highest degree, plus in-service hours (X_6).
7. The relative additional workload corresponding to the job function (X_7).

The optimal solution to the linear programming model will specify the value to be assigned to each factor.

Specification of the relative weights
A relative rating scheme which represents the relative importance of each factor within a job function must be developed. The contribution of a factor to the salary of each individual will be equal to the product of the value assigned to the factor in the optimal solution and the relative weight assigned to the respective factor in the job function. An individual's salary will then be the sum of each factor contribution.

The relative weights in this application were arbitrarily selected. However, as Bruno[1] notes:

'Since the real issue, from a salary standpoint, is the product of the factor weight as determined by the model and the relative weight, it is felt that the arbitrary assignment of relative weights is not a serious limitation. The model considers these relative weights as well as other constraints in determining the actual weight for each factor.'

The final relative weight scheme and the characteristics associated with each factor are presented in Table 1.

The individual class make-up factor (X_1) was assigned three characteristics: easy, medium and difficult. The characteristics were determined by first ranking the standard student tracks by de-

Table 1. *Factors Included in the Application Model with Relative Weights, Characteristics, and Number of School Personnel Possessing Each Characteristic*

Factor	Variable	Relative rating and characteristic	Number of employees possessing characteristic	Weighted total for each characteristic
Academic class make-up	X_1	3 Difficult	8	24
		2 Medium	54	108
		1 Easy	17	17
				149
Subject matter or special skill	X_2	3 High demand	44	132
		2 Medium demand	20	40
		1 Low demand	15	15
				187
Supervisory responsibility	X_3	5 District wide 1	1	5
		4 District wide 2	1	4
		3 School wide	3	9
		2 Department wide	16	32
		2 Class wide	58	116
				166
Highest academic degree attained	X_1	4 Ph.D. or Ed.D.	0	0
		3 M.A.	62	186
		2 M.Ed.	0	0
		1 B.A.	17	17
				203
Total work experience	X_5	7 15 years	36	252
		6 12–14 years	10	60
		5 9–11 years	3	15
		4 6–8 years	13	52
		3 3–5 years	10	30
		2 1–2 years	7	14
		1 0 years	0	0
				423
College credits beyond highest degree	X_6	5 MA plus 60 or Ph.D. plus 15	16	80
		4 MA plus 45 or Ph.D.	10	40
		3 MA plus 30	13	39
		2 BA plus 45 or MA plus 15	16	32
		1 BA plus 0–30 or MA	24	24
				215
Relative additional workload	X_7	5 District wide 1	1	5
		4 District wide 2	2	8
		3 School	3	9
		2 Department	16	32
		1 Class	57	57
				111

clining relative teaching difficulty (D-Track = 1, C-Track = 2, B-Track = 3, and A-Track = 4). The tracks represent a classification of student groups by academic ability. Next, the sum of the rankings for the five classes taught by each teacher was computed. If the sum computed is less than six it is characterized as difficult, greater than six but less than twelve it is characterized as medium, and finally, greater than twelve it is characterized as easy. Administrators and department heads are assumed to be difficult situations due to the nature of their job functions[*sic*].

Three characteristics are used for the subject matter area factor (X_2): high, average and low demand. Demand was determined by the total enrollment for the department relative to total enrollment for the school. For supervisory responsibility (X_3) five characteristics are employed. District wide 1 and 2 represent joint district responsibility and single district responsibility respectively.

The characteristics associated with the work experience factor (X_5) and credits earned factor (X_6) correspond to the present characteristics established by the school district.

The relative additional workload factor (X_7) represents outside duties such as curriculum committees, disciplinary committees, general counsels, etc., and responsibilities associated with each. Five characteristics are used for this factor. The characteristics are similar to the supervisory responsibility factor (X_3).

MATHEMATICAL SPECIFICATION OF THE SALARY STRUCTURE

A description of the salary structure requires a specification of five constraint sets which indicate: (1) the salary of the theoretically highest and lowest qualified person for each job function, (2) the minimum money spread between the highest salary for each job function (e.g. the money spread between the theoretically most highly qualified department head and teacher), (3) the maximum percentage salary spread within each job function (e.g. the percentage spread between the theoretically most highly qualified administrator and lowest qualified administrator), (4) the minimum percentage salary overlap between job functions (e.g. the percentage overlap of the salary of the theoretically lowest qualified department head to that of the theoretically highest qualified teacher), and (5) the maximum and minimum money values for each factor.

Each constraint set is mathematically expressed below in its generalized form and for the school under examination.

Specification of maximum and minimum salary for each job function

For each job function the salary of the theoretically most highly qualified and lowest qualified person must be formulated. Letting

a_{ij} = the highest rated relevant characteristic associated with factor i for job function j in the school,

b_{ij} = the lowest rated relevant characteristic associated with factor i for job function j in the school,

X_i = the factors considered in the salary evaluation model,

λ_j = the theoretically highest or maximum salary for job function j,

σ_j = the theoretically lowest or minimum salary for job function j, and

n = the number of factors considered in the salary evaluation model,

then the theoretically highest salary for job function j can be expressed as:

$$a_{1j} X_1 + a_{2j} X_2 + \ldots + a_{nj} X_n = \lambda_j$$

while the theoretically lowest salary for job function j can be expressed as:

$$b_{1j} X_1 + b_{2j} X_2 + \ldots + b_{nj} X_n = \sigma_j.$$

In the present application there are three job functions; therefore, there will be six constraints representing the salaries of the theoretically highest and lowest qualified personnel.

Present district policies were used to determine relevant factors and characteristics for each job function. Further refinements were supplied by the pertinent State certification laws. For example, the State requires that department heads and administrators must possess a minimum of a Master's degree and three years of experience. The salary for the theoretically highest and lowest qualified person for each job function follows:

Administrator ($j = 1$):

(1) $3X_1 + 3X_2 + 5X_3 + 4X_4$
$+ 7X_5 + 5X_6 + 5X_7 = \lambda_1$ Highest

(2) $3X_1 + X_2 + 3X_3 + 2X_4$
$+ 3X_5 + 2X_6 + 4X_7 = \sigma_1$ Lowest

Department Head ($j = 2$):

(3) $3X_1 + 3X_2 + 2X_3 + 4X_4$
$+ 7X_5 + 5X_6 + 3X_7 = \lambda_2$ Highest

(4) $3X_1 + X_2 + 2X_3 + 2X_4$
$+ 3X_5 + 2X_6 + 2X_7 = \sigma_2$ Lowest

Teacher ($j = 3$):

(5) $3X_1 + 3X_2 + 2X_3 + 4X_4$
$+ 7X_5 + 5X_6 + 2X_7 = \lambda_3$ Highest

(6) $X_1 + X_2 + 2X_3 + X_4$
$+ 2X_5 + X_6 + X_7 = \sigma_3.$ Lowest

Minimum money spread between the highest salary for each job function
Letting
λ_j = the theoretically highest salary in job function j,

λ_{j+1} = the theoretically highest salary in the next lower job function $j + 1$, and

δ = the desired money difference in salary.

then the minimum money difference between the highest salary for each job function can be expressed as:

$$\lambda_j - \lambda_{j+1} \geq \delta.$$

In the present application, the minimum money spread was set at $1,500 between all job functions. In other applications, the differential need not be the same between job functions. The two constraints in this application can therefore be expressed by:

(7) $\lambda_1 - \lambda_2 \geq 1500$
and
(8) $\lambda_2 - \lambda_3 \geq 1500.$

Maximum percentage salary spread within each job function
To control the salary spread between the most highly qualified and lowest qualified person for a given job function, the following constraint must be imposed for each:

$$\sigma_j \geq \gamma\lambda_j, \ \gamma \geq 0,$$

where γ = the maximum percentage spread in salary for job function j.

In the present application, γ was selected to be 45% for each job function. Hence, the three constraints imposed to control the salary spread within a job function in the present application can be expressed by:

(9) $\sigma_1 \geq 0.45 \ \lambda_1;$
(10) $\sigma_2 \geq 0.45 \ \lambda_2;$
and
(11) $\sigma_3 \geq 0.45 \ \lambda_3.$

Minimum percentage salary overlap between job functions

The minimum percentage salary overlap between the lowest qualified person in a job function to that of the highest qualified person in the next lower job function must be included in the salary structure. The general expression for this constraint is:

$$\lambda_{j+1} \geq \omega\sigma_j,$$

where ω = the specified minimum overlap in salary between job functions j and $j + 1$.

Since there are three job functions in the present application, two constraints are needed. The minimum percentage overlap in salary in both instances is specified at 5% (i.e. = 1.05). The two constraints are then:

(12) $\lambda_2 \geq 1.05\ \sigma_1$; and   (13) $\lambda_3 \geq 1.05\ \sigma_2$.

Maximum and minimum boundaries for each factor

The setting of upper and lower boundaries is a crucial step in the design of the salary structure. By the limiting of each factor's monetary range, we can ensure that the salary scheme is not dominated by any single factor.

The determination of such bounds will be the product of negotiations with the teacher bargaining unit, the Parent–Teacher's Association and other concerned groups. The lower bound represents the minimum monetary worth for each factor and the upper limit represents the maximum monetary worth. The bounds for each factor were selected in this application after discussions with concerned groups. The bounds are:

(14) $100 \leq X_1 \leq 500$ (18) $1{,}000 \leq X_5 \leq 2{,}000$
(15) $100 \leq X_2 \leq 500$ (19) $\ \ 200 \leq X_6 \leq 1{,}000$
(16) $100 \leq X_3 \leq 2{,}000$ (20) $\ \ 100 \leq X_7 \leq 2{,}500$
(17) $100 \leq X_4 \leq 1{,}000$

BUDGETARY CONSTRAINTS

The budgetary constraint represents the total amount of district funds available for support of the salary structure. This constraint can be expressed by:

$$\sum_i \sum_k p_{ik}\, r_{ik}\, X_i = \Theta,$$

where

p_{ik} = the number of employees in the school having characteristic k of factor i,

r_{ik} = the relative rating assigned to characteristic k of factor i,

X_i = factor i used in the model, and

Θ = the total amount of resources available to support salaries in the school.

In the present application, salaries for the high school were isolated from the total school district salary funds. The amount of $1,338,835 was determined to be available to support salaries for the high school. Table 1 provides the necessary data for the product of p_{ik} and r_{ik}. The budgetary constraint is therefore:

(21) $149\ X_1 + 187\ X_2 + 166\ X_3 + 203\ X_4$
$+\ 423\ X_5 + 215\ X_6 + 111\ X_7 =$
$1{,}338{,}835.$

SPECIFICATION OF THE OBJECTIVE FUNCTION

The objective function must reflect the established school district priorities and policy objectives. For example, if the objective is to retain teaching staff and minimize teacher turnover, the maximization of the salary of the most highly qualified teacher, λ_3, would be the appropriate objective function. *Per contra*, if the district desires to attract young, inexperienced teachers, the maximization of σ_3, the salary of the lowest qualified teacher, would be the appropriate objective function.

If the school district desires to establish different salary schedules for the three different grade schools, as the school district under examination has been considering, the district might specify a different objective function for the salary evaluation model for each grade school. For example, in the elementary and junior high school, the objective might be to attract young, inexperienced teachers; while, for the high school, the objective might be to retain its teaching staff and minimize teacher turnover. The advantage of the linear programming model is that it permits the school district to select one of several alternative objective functions which best meets its established objectives.

The objective of the school district under examination is to retain its teaching staff and minimize teacher turnover. Hence, the objective function is the maximization of the salary of the most highly qualified teacher, λ_3. The linear programming model to evaluate the salary of those high school personnel under consideration is then:

maximize: $3X_1 + 3X_2 + 2X_3 + 4X_4 + 7X_5 + 5X_6 + 2X_7$

subject to the constraints (1)–(21).

RESULTS OF THE STUDY

Table 2 presents the optimal value for each of the seven factors considered in the salary evaluation model and provides a feasible range for each. This range indicates the extent to which the solution for the factor can vary before violating a constraint, i.e. the solution becomes infeasible.

The highest and lowest salary for each job function is presented in Table 3 along with the ranging analysis. Here the maximum and minimum salary for each job function derived from

the linear programming model are greater than the respective salaries provided by the present contract, but if it had not been, then appropriate constraints would have had to be introduced for the period of the transition.

Of course, not all salaries can be simultaneously increased during the transition period without violating the budgetary constraint. The salary of some individuals will increase or decrease depending on the characteristics possessed by the individual. For example, under the present fixed step salary schedule, a teacher with a Master of Arts degree plus fifteen credits and with four years of teaching experience would earn $12,600. However, using the linear programming model, the same teacher with a Master of Arts degree ($3X_4$) plus fifteen credits ($2X_6$), four years teaching experience ($3X_5$), a medium class load make-up ($2X_1$), a medium demand subject matter ($2X_2$), classwide supervisory responsibility ($2X_3$), and a relative additional workload which is department wide ($2X_7$) will have a salary of:

$$2X_1 + 2X_2 + 2X_3 + 3X_4 + 3X_5 + 2X_6 + 2X_7$$

$$= 2(500) + 2(250.75) + 2(2,000) + 3(100) + 3(1,000) + 2(765.91) + 2(2,500)$$
$$= \$15,784.07.$$

This salary is greater than that indicated by the present salary schedule. On the other hand, had the teacher possessed a Master of Arts ($3X_4$) plus fifteen credits ($2X_6$), four years teaching experience ($3X_5$), an easy class load make-up (X_1), a low demand subject matter (X_2), classwide supervisory responsibility ($2X_3$), and no relative additional workload (X_7), that teacher's salary would be $12,082.57 (less than at present).

Similarly, the intermediate salaries for department heads will deviate above and below the present salaries specified depending on the individual characteristics possessed. Under the present contract, the salary for administrators

Table 2. *Optimal Factor Values and Ranging Analysis*

Factor	Description	Optimal value ($)	Range *($)
	Objective function: maximize highest teacher salary (λ_3)		
X_1	Academic class make-up	$500.00	$144–715
X_2	Subject matter or special skill	250.75	−213–530
X_3	Supervisory responsibility	2,000.00	1,911–2,053
X_1	Highest academic degree attained	100.00	−372–392
X_5	Total work experience	1,000.00	859–1,084
X_6	College credits beyond highest degree	765.91	—
X_7	Relative additonal workload	2,500.00	2,253–2,649

* The range in which the factor value can vary before a constraint is violated, i.e. an infeasible solution is reached. (Excluding the boundary and non-negativity constraint imposed on the factor.)

Table 3. *Optimal Salary Schedule*

Job Function	Description	Optimal salary ($)	Range * ($)
	Objective function: maximize highest teacher salary (λ_3)		
1 Highest	Administrators	$35,981.80	$35,048–35,982
Lowest		22,482.54	21,566–22,626
2 Highest	Department Heads	24,981.80	24,542–24,982
Lowest		15,482.57	14,724–15,626
3 Highest	Teachers	22,481.80	—
Lowest		10,116.6	10,040–10,149

* The range in which the salary can vary before a constraint is violated, i.e., an infeasible solution is reached.

specifies only the maximum and minimum. All intermediate salaries are presently negotiated individually. The school district has been considering developing a schedule for administrators. The linear programming salary evaluation model provides intermediate administrative salaries which depend on the characteristics of the administrator. The adherence to the salaries generated from the model will ensure internal consistency in the compensation of all school district personnel under consideration.

The salary structure generated was based on a budget of $1,338,835. If additional funds were made available to support high school personnel salaries, a new salary schedule would be generated. Table 4 provides the optimal salary structure if the budget is increased by $75,000 and $150,000.

SALARY STRUCTURE USING ALTERNATIVE OBJECTIVE FUNCTIONS

As mentioned above, the maximization of the most highly qualified teacher is only one of several possible objectives. Other objective functions were used in order to compare salary structures. The two other objective functions considered were (1) maximization of beginning teacher's salary (σ_3) and (2) minimization of the budget (θ).

A Linear Programming Salary Evaluation Model for High School Personnel

Table 4. *Alternative Optimal Salary Schedule for Budget Increments of $75,000*

| | | *Objective function: maximize highest teacher salary (λ_3)* | | |
| | | *Optimal salary ($) with a budget of:* | | |
Job function	*Description*	$1,338,835	$1,413,835	$1,488,835
1 Highest	Administrators	$35,982	$36,911	$37,645
Lowest		22,483	23,070	23,215
2 Highest	Department Heads	24,982	25,911	26,645
Lowest		15,483	16,070	16,215
3 Highest	Teachers	22,482	23,411	24,145
Lowest		10,117	10,535	10,865

The optimal value for each factor for the alternative objective functions is presented in Table 5. Maximum and minimum salaries for each job function for alternative objective functions are presented in Table 6.

SUMMARY

The linear programming approach to salary evaluation permits a consideration of a virtually unlimited number of pertinent factors for a job function, the financial resources available to the school district, and the established objectives of the school district in constructing a salary schedule. The salary schedule generated overcomes the criticisms of the rigid fixed step salary approach presently employed. In this paper, the linear programming model was applied to a high school in a school district. The optimal salary schedule for the theoretically highest and lowest qualified person for each job function derived from the optimal value for each factor was greater than the corresponding salary under the present salary compromise. Intermediate salaries, however, vary depending on the characteristics possessed by the individual. A comparison of alternative salary schedules when different objective functions were used is also presented.

Moreover, by parameterizing the bounds for the factor values, the school district can determine alternative salary schedules and corresponding required budgets. This information would be most valuable to a school district in analyzing the cost of demands made by the teacher bargaining unit.

Table 5. *Optimal Factor Values and Ranging Analysis for Alternative Objective Functions*

| | *Objective function* | | | | | |
| | *Maximize beginning teacher salary (σ_3)* | | *minimize the budget (θ)* | | *Maximize highest teacher salary (λ_3)* | |
Factor	*Value ($)*	*Range ($)*	*Value ($)*	*Range ($)*	*Value ($)*	*Range ($)*
X_1	$500.00	−$223–1,004	$186.91	$50–976	$500.00	$144–715
X_2	500.00	−76–902	363.10	−642–450	250.75	−213–530
X_3	2,000.00	1,815–2,341	2,000.00	1,870–2,036	2,000.00	1,911–2,053
X_1	469.63	−1,614–838	100.00	−40–369	100.00	−372–392
X_5	1,000.00	757–1,177	1,000.00	931–1,033	1,000.00	859–1,084
X_6	200.00	−301–549	200.00	106–381	765.91	—
X_7	2,500.00	1,897–2,912	2,500.00	2,291–2,558	2,500.00	2,253–2,649

A Linear Programming Salary Evaluation Model for High School Personnel

Table 6. *Optimal Salary Structure and Ranging Analysis for Alternative Objective Function*

| | Maximize beginning teacher salary (σ_3) | | Objective Function Minimize the budget (θ)* | | Maximize highest teacher salary (λ_3) | |
Job function	Salary ($)	Range ($)	Salary ($)	Range ($)	Salary ($)	Range ($)
1 Highest	35,379	35,142–35,645	32,550	32,133–32,912	35,982	35,048–35,982
Lowest	22,339	22,132–22,676	20,524	20,350–20,869	22,483	21,566–22,626
2 Highest	24,379	24,142–24,645	21,550	21,550–21,912	24,982	24,542–24,982
Lowest	15,339	15,132–15,676	13,524	13,350–13,869	15,483	14,724–15,626
3 Highest	21,879	21,642–22,145	19,050	19,050–19,412	22,482	—
Lowest	10,170		9,350	9,256–9,687	10,117	10,040–10,149

* The optimal value for the budget is $1,191,547.62. In this model, the following constraint was added: $\sigma_3 \geq \$9,350$. That is, a minimum value was imposed on the salary of the lowest qualified teacher.

ENDNOTES

1. James E. Bruno (1971) Compensation of school district personnel. *Mgmt Sci.* **17**, 569–587.
2. Charles S. Benson (1968) *The Economics of Public Education.* Houghton-Mifflin Company, Boston.
3. Herbert H. Meyer (1975) The pay–for–performance dilemma. *Organizational Dynamics* **5**, 56.
4. A. Charnes, W. W. Cooper, and R. O. Ferguson (1955). Optimal estimation of executive compensation by linear programming. *Mgmt Sci.* **1**, 138–151.
5. Frederick P. Rehmus and Harvey M. Wagner (1963) Applying linear programming to your pay structure. *Business Horizons* **4**, 89–98.

DISCUSSION QUESTIONS

1. Why is the fixed step salary system a poor policy in many schools?
2. What factors do the authors suggest be included in the L.P. model? What additional factors do you think could also be included?
3. If you were applying this model in a large state university, what other variables would you want to include?
4. How can "ranging" (or sensitivity analysis) be useful in the application described?
5. What are the alternative objective functions that the model might use?

Use of the Transportation Method of Linear Programming in Production Planning: A Case Study

C. David Sadleir

9

INTRODUCTION

Background to the study

This paper describes part of a study relating to a multi-plant, multi-product production planning problem in the context of a particular shoe-manufacturing enterprise. The company had no prior experience of operational research techniques and none of the existing staff were formally trained in operational research. Coincident with the start of the study, the company had decided to install a small digital computer with initial emphasis on computerizing existing systems.

Nature of the problem

The total problem studied was one of making macro-decisions with respect to when and where to "make" the shoes, for each of the two making seasons, in order to provide production schedulers with a guide for use in the preparation of detailed schedules. "Make" in this context has a special meaning; it is the process of joining the upper leather to the sole material. The variations in the making process can be usefully categorized by types called *constructions*. Although styling changes are frequent, the basic constructions remain operative for several seasons.

In general, advance orders are obtained for most styles offered in a season. Some of these styles will be continued from previous seasons. A selection of styles is supported by warehouse stock throughout the season and may be re-ordered.

The cost of meeting the demand for one unit, that is one pair, is a function of the time at which the unit is made relative to the selling date, the stock support policy and the technology of the particular plant where it is made. Constraints exist on the distribution of spare capacity, the percentage of the total capacity of some plants utilized by certain construction types and the relative amounts of certain constructions which can be allocated between two particular plants. In addition, there are technological preferences for the mix of constructions allocated to certain plants.

APPROACH

Factors affecting the choice

Apart from the terms of reference imposed by the company, several factors contributed to the choice of approach. In particular, there were three major considerations. It was a major concern that the procedures resulting from the study should be implementable. Since the company was preparing for the installation of its first computer, the general level of data-processing sophistication was not particularly advanced. In addition, there were no operational research personnel on the staff to maintain a new system which might represent significant relative sophistication. The potential computing capacity was not large but the use of bureau machines for such planning work was not precluded.

The complexity of the problem from a computational viewpoint is dependent on the number of styles, plants, constructions, stocking policies, sales groups and planning periods. In a typical season, there may be over 130 different styles to be allocated among 8 plants. From a production viewpoint, this represents from 10 to 18 construction types. From a marketing viewpoint these styles are categorized in a number of sales groups which is usually of the order of 10. In the practical context, with a planning horizon involving 24 half-monthly periods, these factors combine to create a problem of significant size and complexity.

As in many such situations, necessary data were sparse or impossible to extract economically or in a reasonable length of time. The usual problems of collecting production cost data were aggravated by the recent acquisition of an additional plant with an "incompatible" accounting system and by a shortage of available personnel to carry out the investigations.

Adopted approach

In the light of these considerations, it was decided to treat aggregate demand and capacity data as given and attempt to find acceptable linear approximations to the relevant cost functions. The overall strategy employed was that of dividing the problem into sub-problems which were initially considered as independent. Solutions to these sub-problems were obtained using optimizing techniques where possible.

The two major sub-problems examined were those of "when to make?" and "where to make?" Each was formulated as a separate transportation-type problem using ideas suggested by Bowman[1] and discussed by Hanssmann[2]. A third sub-problem of style allocation was also explored and heuristic rules were developed to aid in the decision process. The implications of this sub-optimal approach were then considered along with various methods of combining the models.

The remainder of this paper focuses attention on the sub-problem of "where to make?" The mathematical details of the model are included in the appendix for interested practitioners.

THE SUB-PROBLEM OF "WHERE TO MAKE?"

Irrespective of when shoes are made, there are several constraints on where they can be made. Every shoe can be categorized according to a specific construction and not every plant can make every construction. Where a construction can be made on more than one plant, it is not necessarily true that costs are the same at each plant. The problem is to allocate constructions to plants so as to minimize total cost subject to the basic demand and capacity constraints as well as certain special constraints on construction mix and spare capacity distribution.

The special constraints were evolved in co-operation with the director of production as a result of careful examination of several solutions to various interim models. They are as follows:

1. Construction mix within plants. If certain combinations of constructions are allocated to a particular plant, there is a maximum acceptable allocation of a construction or combinations of constructions which may be allocated. For example, the combined total pairage of construction types A and B allocated to a particular plant may not exceed 50 percent of the total capacity available at that plant.

2. Spare capacity. The spare capacity on any plant is to be within plus or minus a given proportion of the total spare capacity available at all plants (expressed as a percentage of the total capacity). For example, if the total spare capacity is 8 percent of the total available capacity, then on any particular plant, the spare capacity must

be within the range 5–11 percent of that plant's total capacity.

3. Construction mix between plants. If an allocation of certain construction types is made at all to either one of two particular plants, then there is a requirement that some pairage having these constructions be allocated to both plants.

The first two constraints can be incorporated directly into the transportation-type model. The second constraint is really a special case of the first. The third constraint cannot be incorporated directly into such a model since it presupposes a solution. However, this constraint can be satisfied by a simple algebraic procedure, given an initial solution.

DATA REQUIREMENTS AND THEIR IMPLICATIONS

Table 1 outlines the data required to solve the sub-problem of "where to make?" and identifies the source of the data. Although the model described in the appendix would be considered relatively simple, if not naïve, by many operational researchers, it is interesting to examine the potential difficulties imposed by these data requirements.

The concept of construction type was well known to production personnel prior to this study but no attempt had been made to recognize it explicitly in the planning process. For the model, however, an estimate of demand by construction type is an essential element of data. Once the construction types had been identified and their explicit definitions agreed, a preliminary analysis was performed to determine if such estimates could be generated directly from historical sales patterns. The available historical sales data by construction revealed little hope for such a system at least in the short term. Furthermore, the sales estimating experience and expertise were intimately related to sales groups

Table 1. Data Requirements vs. Source

Data	Source
1. The *Planning Interval* to be considered	Management judgement or the solution to the "when to make?" sub-problem
2. Definition of the shoe *Construction Types* to be allocated	Styles selected by marketing are categorized by production personnel
3. Identification of the "making" *Plants*	Production management
4. Identification of all *Feasible Allocation* spaces	Production management
5. Total estimated *Demand* by construction type	Marketers provide style estimates which imply construction estimates
6. Total available production *Capacity*	Production management
7. *Unit Cost*	Management judgement and/or accounting records and/or operational research
8. Bounds on *Spare Capacity* by plant	Management judgement supported by sensitivity analysis
9. Bounds on *Construction Mix* within plants	Management judgement supported by sensitivity analysis
10. Bounds on *Construction Mix* between plants	Management judgement supported by sensitivity analysis

(a marketing concept) rather than construction type (a production concept) and these do not match. The necessary demand data were eventually obtained by aggregation of the total season estimates for individual styles. Fortunately, each style has a unique construction characteristic. This process required explicit coding of the style specification to reflect the construction type and to facilitate automatic data processing.

Actual cost data were available only for those locations at which a particular construction had been made previously. There was some initial reluctance on the part of production management to consider the possibility of "making" particular constructions at locations which had previously not been used. In addition, accounting systems were undergoing a process of redefinition and appropriate personnel were not available to study costs likely to be encountered by allocating particular constructions to "new" locations. Since the cost of using one location

relative to the other is the important factor and since the addition of a constant to all cost cells in any row or column of the transportation matrix does not affect the allocation generated by the model, the use of relative costs based on subjective estimates was proposed. The production director agreed to this and felt confident about identifying the "ideal" location(s) at which to make a particular construction and reasonably able to estimate the increased cost of deviating from the ideal to some other location.

A sample of the set of subjective estimates was scrutinized by the accounting department. Eventually, all parties concerned agreed that they would be willing to make decisions based on these estimated costs. In making the estimates, the director considered the direct labour cost, various overheads related to departments, specific technology and particular plants. In addition, some account was taken of the interaction of certain making plants with other stages in the manufacturing process. "Ideal" locations were assigned a cost of zero and other feasible locations were given an appropriate incremental value. Impossible allocations were assigned a prohibitively large cost to force their exclusion from the solution.

In the context of the overall planning process, it is important to recognize that the model described in the appendix does not contain an explicit consideration of time. Once the planning interval is selected, the solution is time-independent. Selection of the planning interval obviously affects the demand and capacity data and the consistency of the overall planning procedures.

This problem was considered separately as the sub-problem of "when to make?" and the resulting solution was allowed to dominate. Heuristic procedures were developed to reconcile the two solutions.

Existing procedures for selection of the planning interval were largely based on management judgement and experience and were marketing-oriented rather than production-oriented. Furthermore, the nature of the planning process was such that the question of "when to make?" could be more readily answered first on a basis related to broad marketing categorizations. Demand data were available in the form of sales estimates which were more in the nature of targets. Thus, given these targets, a rational time-dependent plan could be evolved and within this framework the question of "where to make?" could be answered in an "optimal" manner. The answer to this question is based on detailed knowledge of styles to be offered for sale and this detail is not available for all styles at the same time. The selection process involves the participation of various field personnel who view many styles over a period of time and "vote" on the selection.

One advantage of the explicit formulation of the "where to make?" question is that the computation can be left to the last possible moment and/or alternative allocations can be rapidly computed as the selection process proceeds. In practice, this is facilitated somewhat by the fact that most construction types include many styles. Thus, a particular style may be replaced during selection with little or no effect on the allocation if the style is of the same construction and has approximately the same estimated potential market. Such a situation is not uncommon.

It should be clear from the above that, despite the apparent simplicity of the model, its use is very dependent on effective co-operation and communication between marketing and production management. The necessary interaction in an organization of even modest size implies the explicit definition of the areas of responsibility involved and the recognition of the importance of accurately and quickly communicating and interpreting marketing decisions into the production environment. This characteristic is not, of course, exclusively related to the application outlined here.

RESULTS

Analytic results vs. management judgement

Table 2 gives a sample solution matrix for a particular season. Besides being tested with various sets of historical data, the model was used to reach a parallel decision for a current season. This provided insight into the practical data-collection problems and a comparison with decisions taken in the usual manner by production management. The resulting comparison is summarized in Table 3. Each plan was evaluated using the same set of subjective cost estimates.

Considered in isolation, the allocation determined by the model represents a saving of £12,000 or 36 per cent of the total relative making cost for the season. It will be noted that the model utilizes 19 making locations as opposed

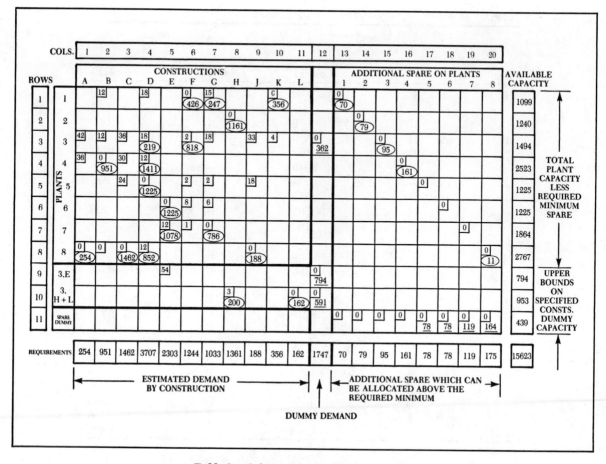

Table 2. *Solution Matrix (Pairage in 100's)*

to 21 actually used by management. The same constructions appear on 5 of the 8 plants in both allocations, that is, plants 2, 4, 5, 6 and 8. Major differences occur on plant 3 where the "optimal" solution has only 4 allocations, one of which was not considered by management. Minor differences occur on plants 1 and 7.

Senior management and operating personnel considered the solution and the operational procedures associated with it to be practicable. The production director particularly welcomed the results as a basis for comparison with his subjective decisions.

Sensitivity analysis

The following are representative of the various sensitivity analyses. For the data of Table 2, a change in the range of spare capacity distribution from "unrestricted" to ±3 per cent generated a cost change from £17,750 to £20,820 and the percentage of production allocated to "ideal" locations changed from 69.4 to 63.0 per cent respectively. The cost penalty for a tighter range of spare capacity distribution was considered negligible by management; particularly, in relation to the flexibility associated with spreading the spare capacity over all plants.

Table 3. *Management Judgement vs. Analytic Solution*

Plant	Management judgement		Analytic solution	
	Const.	*Cost (£)*	*Const.*	*Cost (£)*
1	F	0	F	0
	—	—	G	1544
	K	0	K	0
2	H	0	H	0
3	D	1162	D	1642
	E	7040	—	—
	—	—	F	682
	G	2982	—	—
	H	83	H	250
	K	162	—	—
	L	0	L	0
4	B	0	B	0
	D	8460	D	8925
5	D	0	D	0
6	E	0	E	0
7	E	8270	E	5390
	F	54	—	—
	G	0	G	0
8	A	0	A	0
	B	0	B	0
	C	0	C	0
	D	4630	D	2390
	J	0	J	0
Total		32,843		20,823

Much of the resulting cost reduction obtained by the model relative to the actual base case arises from the exclusion of construction type E from plant 3 (see Table 2). For the particular season, management would have been reluctant to implement this decision for various reasons associated with the labour force and plant technology.

CONCLUSIONS

The transportation-type formulation proved to be practicable. The simplicity of the model, particularly its tabular representation, provided a readily explained and easily understood framework for discussions with senior management. The resulting solutions did not represent disturbing changes to production management and did indicate that significant direct savings could be made.

The model facilitated the generation of demonstrable results in a reasonable time. The process of formulating and testing the model in close co-operation with senior management led to the development of explicit and immediately useful production categorizations and highlighted a number of areas that would be enhanced by the formulation of more explicit policy decisions. Certain special constraints which previously had been considered in an *ad hoc* manner were recognized, formulated explicitly and "costed".

The simplicity of the computations associated with the transportation formulation make the approach equally viable by completely manual methods. This characteristic was particularly useful in demonstrating the practicability of implementing the procedures. A member of the company's staff, initially unfamiliar with the procedure, was able to solve the problem manually in a reasonable time.

There is, of course, a significant difference in the operational feasibility of using such a model on a once-off basis as compared with imbedding it in a repetitive planning sytem. The latter is more difficult largely because of the data-gathering problems and the need for disciplined and timely communication among the essential participants. This characteristic is usually present for any quantified decision-making procedure. The model discussed here provides one useful structure for purposes of systematizing the data-collection procedures. Since the necessary data has other uses, particularly in the raw materials planning problem, the development of such procedures is further encouraged.

The model can easily be used as a basis of comparison for judgemental decisions made by management. Since there are numerous software packages available for computerized solution of the transportation problem, such a use is relatively straightforward either in-house or on a bureau computer.

ENDNOTES

1. E. H. Bowman (1956) Production scheduling by the transportation method of linear programming. *Ops. Res.* **4,** 100.
2. F. Hanssmann (1962) *Operations Research in Production and Inventory Control,* p. 114. John Wiley, New York.

APPENDIX

"Where to Make?"

Let

x_{ij} be the pairage of construction j allocated to plant i;

y_i be the additional spare above the required minimum allocated to plant i;

c_{ij} be the cost per pair of making construction j at plant i;

c_i be the cost per pair of additional spare capacity at plant i;

A_i be the total capacity available at plant i;

B_j be the total demand for construction j;

Y_i be the maximum additional spare above the required minimum at plant i;

m be the number of plants;

n be the number of constructions;

r be the number of special row constraints;

$L1, L2$ be the lower and upper limits respectively on the range of spare capacity.

Then the problem is to find a set of $x_{ij} \geq 0$, $y_i \geq 0$ such that:

$$\sum_i \sum_j c_{ij} \, x_{ij} + \sum_i c_i \, y_i \text{ is minimized subject to}$$

Row equations:

$$\sum_j x_{ij} + y_i = a_i,$$

$$j = 1, 2, \ldots, n,$$
$$a_i = (1 - L_1) \, A_i,$$

$$\sum_k x_{ik} \leq p_i \, a_i, \quad p_i < 1.0, \quad k \in j.$$

Column equations:

$$\sum_i x_{ij} = B_j, \quad i = 1, 2, \ldots, m, m + 1, \ldots, m + r,$$

$$y_i \leq Y_i, \quad i = 1, 2, \ldots, m,$$

and such that:

$$\sum_j B_j + \sum_i Y_i = \sum_i a_i + \sum_i p_i a_i.$$

Note that:

$$Y_i = ((L_2 - L_1)/(1 - L_1))\, a_i$$

and once a solution is obtained, the total spare capacity allocated to a particular plant i, s_i, is obtained from $s_i = y_i + L_1 A_i$.

DISCUSSION QUESTIONS

1. What is the shoe manufacturer's objective in using L. P.? Within what constraints must it operate?

2. What data are needed to develop the decision model? Where do they come from?

3. Compare the results of the L. P. model with the decision that managers would have made without L. P. What is the advantage of making such a comparison?

4. This model appears to have been successfully adopted and implemented. Why do you think this is so?

Application of Linear Programming vs. Goal Programming to Assignment Problem

Anal J. Mehta
Ahmed K. Rifai

10

The assignment model is a linear programming model that has been applied to a variety of administrative problems in manufacturing and marketing. Examples of assigning include: jobs to machine centers or plants, workers to tasks, and salesmen to sales territories. These are only a few of numerous cases in which this technique may be applied. Major contributions to the assignment problems have been made by P. S. Dwyer,[1] M. M. Flood,[2] D. F. Votaw and A. Orden,[3] and H. W. Kuhn.[4] Specialized algorithms have been developed for solving the assignment problems. The assignment technique can be illustrated by the following example.

ILLUSTRATIONS OF THE ASSIGNMENT TECHNIQUE

Assume that the XYZ Marketing Company has just received requests for market research studies from five clients. Currently, four project leaders are relatively free and are available for the assignments. They are all capable of handling each assignment of the five clients. Management

Reprinted by permission of *Akron Business and Economic Review*, Winter, 1976, pp. 52–55.

Table 1. *Commission Cost for each Leader-Client Combinations*

Leaders	Clients 1	2	3	4	5
1	$X_{11}(\$300)$	$X_{12}(\$290)$	$X_{13}(\$280)$	$X_{14}(\$290)$	$X_{15}(\$210)$
2	$X_{21}(\$250)$	$X_{22}(\$310)$	$X_{23}(\$290)$	$X_{21}(\$300)$	$X_{25}(\$200)$
3	$X_{31}(\$180)$	$X_{32}(\$190)$	$X_{33}(\$300)$	$X_{31}(\$190)$	$X_{35}(\$180)$
4	$X_{41}(\$320)$	$X_{42}(\$180)$	$X_{13}(\$190)$	$X_{44}(\$240)$	$X_{45}(\$170)$

realizes that the time and cost to complete the assignments will depend upon the skill, experience, and attitude of each of the project leaders. Management has evaluated these three factors through survey and past experience. The project commission cost for each leader-client combinations is shown in Table 1.

Project leaders are on a fixed salary plus a 1% commission based on the cost of the project. For example, if project leader number 1 is assigned to client number 3, his commission will be $280 ($X_{13}$ = $280) and the total cost will be $28,000. Different cost combinations reflect a different level of expertise and experience of project leaders.

The assignment technique is based on a one to one allocation, i.e., assigning exclusively one salesman to one territory, one project leader to one client, or one production worker to one machine—etc., with the objective of minimizing cost or maximizing profit.

According to the above requirement, it is obvious that in order to solve the problem on hand we must have five project leaders to serve the five clients. To satisfy this requirement (matching the total number of project leaders

with the total number of clients) an additional imaginary project leader can be added. Logically, the assignment cost of this imaginary project leader will be zero (see Table 2). In the final solution the demand of one of the five clients will not be satisfied. This will be the client who is assigned to the imaginary project leader.

Mathematically, the above problem is expressed in linear programming form as follows:

$$\text{Minimize:} \quad \sum_{j=ii=1}^{n}\sum^{m}C_{ij}\,X_{ij}$$

$$\text{s.t. } X_{ij} = \begin{cases} 1 \text{ if project leader i is assigned to} \\ \quad \text{client j} \\ 0 \text{ otherwise} \end{cases}$$

$$i = 1, 2, 3, 4, 5 \text{ and}$$
$$j = 1, 2, 3, 4, 5$$

For instance, in Table 1 the assignment costs (C_{ij}) are shown in parenthesis and the decision variables (project leaders and their corresponding customers) are denoted by X_{ij}. The above problem was solved by computer and the solution was to assign:

Table 2. *The New Revised Commission Cost*

Leaders	Clients 1	2	3	4	5
1	$X_{11}(\$300)$	$X_{12}(\$290)$	$X_{13}(\$280)$	$X_{11}(\$290)$	$X_{15}(\$210)$
2	$X_{21}(\$250)$	$X_{22}(\$310)$	$X_{23}(\$290)$	$X_{21}(\$300)$	$X_{25}(\$200)$
3	$X_{31}(\$180)$	$X_{32}(\$190)$	$X_{33}(\$300)$	$X_{31}(\$190)$	$X_{33}(\$180)$
4	$X_{41}(\$320)$	$X_{42}(\$180)$	$X_{13}(\$190)$	$X_{11}(\$240)$	$X_{15}(\$170)$
5	$X_{51}(\$\ 0)$	$X_{52}(\$\ 0)$	$X_{53}(\$\ 0)$	$X_{51}(\$\ 0)$	$X_{55}(\$\ 0)$

$X_{15} = 1$; project leader number 1 to client number 5, commission $210
$X_{21} = 1$; project leader number 2 to client number 1, commission $250
$X_{34} = 1$; project leader number 3 to client number 4, commission $190
$X_{42} = 1$; project leader number 4 to client number 2, commission $180
$X_{53} = 1$; project leader number 5 to client number 3, commission $\underline{\$\quad 0}$
$\$830$

Since the commission was 1% of the total project cost, the total project cost would be $83,000 (830.00/0.01). From the above solution it can be noticed that the demand of client 3 was not satisfied since the imaginary project leader (number 5) was assigned to him.

So far, we have presented an assignment problem with one objective (minimization of cost) where linear programming was used. Now it is time to present an assignment problem with multiple objectives where goal programming is to be used.

Goal programming is a modification and extension of linear programming that allows a simultaneous solution of a system of complex conflicting objectives rather than a single simple objective. Thus, goal programming is a way of handling previously unsolvable linear programming problems. A problem may be unsolvable because the conflicting goals make it impossible to achieve one goal without sacrificing another or because the goals are simply set at a level unattainable within the limits of available resources. This setting of unattainable goals may be done to motivate or to reflect long-run objectives. In 1965, Ijiri[5] made the first attempt to apply goal programming to management control problems. He suggested a method for treating multiple goals according to their importance. More recently, extension and application of goal programming have been diligently explored by S. M. Lee.[6]

APPLICATION OF GOAL PROGRAMMING

Let us assume that the optimal solution of the previous problem is not acceptable by the president of the XYZ Marketing Company since he has reservation[s] about neglecting the demand of client number 3 who has been a major customer. Further, the marketing manager has guaranteed project leader number 3 a minimum commission of $190 per assignment. From the past experience, the president knows that project leader number 1 and client number 5 do not get along well. Also client number 1 is a fairly new customer whereas client number 2 has been with the company for a long time. In terms of importance, client number 2 is twice as important as client number 1. Management also wishes to minimize the total costs of all projects while considering the above different goals.

According to the new assumptions the assignment technique of linear programming will no longer be applicable because it can handle only one objective, whereas now we have multiple objectives to satisfy. This deficiency of linear programming can be tackled by using a goal programming model.

The above revised problems and its goals, with their associated rank order priorities (P_1 = highest rank), are formulated in a goal programming form as follows:

P_1: Use all four project leaders
P_2: Meet demand of client number 3
P_3: Meet demand of client number 2 and number 1. Client number 2 is twice as important as client number 1
P_4: Project leader number 3 should make at least $190 in commission
P_5: Avoid assignment of project leader number 1 to client number 5
P_6: Minimize underachievement of meeting demand
P_7: Minimize total costs

MODEL CONSTRAINTS

The goal programming constraints are formulated as follows:

(1) *Clients Demand*

$$X_{11} + X_{21} + X_{31} + X_{41} + d_1^- = 1$$
$$X_{12} + X_{22} + X_{32} + X_{42} + d_2^- = 1$$
$$X_{13} + X_{23} + X_{33} + X_{43} + d_3^- = 1$$
$$X_{14} + X_{24} + X_{34} + X_{44} + d_4^- = 1$$
$$X_{15} + X_{25} + X_{35} + X_{45} + d_5^- = 1$$

Since we assume that one project leader can work for only one client, positive deviational variables (d^+) indicating more than one assignment per project leader are excluded.

(2) *Project Leaders*

$$X_{11} + X_{12} + X_{13} + X_{14} + X_{15} + d_6^- - d_6^+ = 1$$
$$X_{21} + X_{22} + X_{23} + X_{24} + X_{25} + d_7^- - d_7^+ = 1$$
$$X_{31} + X_{32} + X_{33} + X_{34} + X_{35} + d_8^- - d_8^+ = 1$$
$$X_{41} + X_{42} + X_{43} + X_{44} + X_{45} + d_9^- - d_9^+ = 1$$

Since we wish to assign four project leaders to four clients and the number of clients exceeds the number of project leaders, we will minimize both positive and negative deviational variables (d^+, d^-).

(3) *Project Leader Number 3*

$$5j = 1_{\Sigma} C_{3j} X_{3j} + d_{10}^- - d_{10}^+ = 190$$

We wish that project leader number 3 makes at least \$190 in commission. d_{10}^- represents underachievement of this goal, while d_{10}^+ represents the overachievement.

(4) *Project Leader Number 1*

$$X_{15} - d_{11}^+ = 0$$

We wish to avoid assigning project leader number 1 to client number 5. The d_{11}^+ represents deviation from this goal. If the model succeeds in driving the value of d_{11}^+ to zero, project leader number 1 will not be assigned to client number 5.

(5) *Total Costs*

$$\sum_{j=1}^{5} \sum_{i=1}^{4} (C_{ij} X_{ij}) - d_{12}^+ = 0$$

C_{ij}'s are represented in parentheses in Table 1. We wish to minimize total cost and tentatively have set a goal of zero. The d_{12}^+ represents the deviation from this goal.

The complete goal programming model for the problem will be as follows:

Complete Goal Programming Model

$$\begin{aligned}
\text{Min } Z = \; & P_1 \, (d_6^- + d_6^+ + d_7^- + d_7^+ + d_8^- + d_8^+ + d_9^- \\
& + d_9^+) + P_2 \, d_3^- + P_3(2d_2^- + d_1^-) + P_4 \, (d_{10}^-) \\
& + P_5 \, d_{11}^+ + P_6 \, (d_1^- + d_2^- + d_3^- + d_4^- + d_5^-) \\
& + P_7 d_{12}^+
\end{aligned}$$

$$X_{11} + X_{21} + X_{31} + X_{41} + d_1^- = 1 \tag{1}$$
$$X_{12} + X_{22} + X_{32} + X_{42} + d_2^- = 1 \tag{2}$$
$$X_{13} + X_{23} + X_{33} + X_{43} + d_3^- = 1 \tag{3}$$
$$X_{14} + X_{24} + X_{34} + X_{44} + d_4^- = 1 \tag{4}$$
$$X_{15} + X_{25} + X_{35} + X_{45} + d_5^- = 1 \tag{5}$$
$$X_{11} + X_{12} + X_{13} + X_{14} + X_{15} + d_6^- - d_6^+ = 1 \tag{6}$$
$$X_{21} + X_{22} + X_{23} + X_{24} + X_{25} + d_7^- - d_7^+ = 1 \tag{7}$$
$$X_{31} + X_{32} + X_{33} + X_{34} + X_{35} + d_8^- - d_8^+ = 1 \tag{8}$$
$$X_{41} + X_{42} + X_{43} + X_{44} + X_{45} + d_9^- - d_9^+ = 1 \tag{9}$$

$$\sum_{j=1}^{5} C_{3j} X_{3j} + d_{10}^- - d_{10}^+ = 190 \tag{10}$$

$$X_{15} - d_{11}^+ = 0 \tag{11}$$

$$\sum_{j=1}^{5} \sum_{i=1}^{4} C_{ij} X_{ij} - d_{12}^+ = 0 \tag{12}$$

GOAL PROGRAMMING SOLUTION

The above Goal Programming problem was solved by computer program developed by S. Lee,[7] yielding the following assignments and commission costs:

$X_{13} = 1$; project leader number 1 to client number 3, commission $280

$X_{21} = 1$; project leader number 2 to client number 1, commission $250

$X_{32} = 1$; project leader number 3 to client number 2, commission $190

$X_{44} = 1$; project leader number 4 to client number 4, commission $240

d_{12}^+ = total commission costs = $960   960

The remaining variables in the solution stub had zero values.

The following observations were made regarding the achievement of goals:

P_1 achieved: All four project leaders were assigned and each was assigned to one separate client.

P_2 achieved: The demand of client number 3 was met.

P_3 achieved: The demands of clients number 2 and 1 were met.

P_4 achieved: The fourth goal of at least $190 in commission for project leader number 3 was achieved.

P_5 achieved: Project leader number 1 was not assigned to client number 5 since $X_{15} = 0$.

P_6 not achieved: The demands of all five clients were not achieved as there were only four project leaders. $d_5^- = 1$ indicates that the demand of client number 5 was not satisfied.

P_7 not achieved: This goal to achieve zero assignment commission cost was impossible. The total assignment commission cost was $960 ($d_{12}^+$ = $960). Since the commission rate was 1%, the total project cost was $96,000 (960.00/.01).

SUMMARY AND CONCLUSION

We have presented two cases of an assignment situation. The first case had one single objective to achieve where linear programming was used. The second case had multiple objectives where goal programming was used. The mathematical formulation of the two models (linear and goal programming) was presented in detail. Now, it is time to evaluate the results of the two models to gain more insight about them.

In comparing the results of the two models it can be noticed that the total project cost for [the] goal programming problem is $13,000 ($96,000 − $83,000) higher than that of [the] linear programming problem. This is due to the introduction of multiple conflicting goals. For instance, the following two priorities, in the goal programming problem, are contradicting each other: priority goal number 4 tends to maximize cost by assigning project leader number 3 to a costly assignment since we have guaranteed him at least $190 in commission. On the other hand, priority goal number 7 is striving to minimize total costs of assignment. This kind of formulation leads to a solution which is not necessarily the minimum cost solution for the given priority goals. However, if we revise goal number 4 from at least $190 commission so that it can be compatible with goal 7, we get the minimum cost solution. Thus, we changed goal number 4 from at least $190 in commission to exactly $190 in commission for project leader number 3.

The above example was presented to introduce the reader to the potential application of the goal programming model to more sophisticated problems. Computer goal programming can become one of the most useful tools in the area of decision making. The delay in its application has been partly due to the fact that most research papers are oriented toward the mathematical aspect of the model rather than the application aspect. Of course, the goal programming model is not a panacea. It is nothing more than a method which provides the most satisfying solution under the given constraints and priority factors. Its successful application depends entirely upon the capability of the decision maker in defining and ranking the objectives.

ENDNOTES

1. P. S. Dwyer, *The Solution of Hitchcock Transportation Problem With a Method of Reduced Matrices*, (Ann Arbor, Mich.: University of Michigan Statistical Laboratory, December, 1955).
2. M. M. Flood, "On the Hitchcock Distribution Problem," *Pacific Journal of Mathematics*, No. 2, (June, 1953).
3. D. F. Votaw and A. Orden, "The Personnel Assignment Problem," in Orden and Goldstein, L. (eds), *Symposium of Linear Inequalities and Programming*, Project Scoop (U.S. Air Force, 1952).
4. H. W. Kuhn, "The Hungarian Method for the Assignment Problem," *Naval Reserve Logistics Quarterly*, 2 (March–June, 1955).
5. Y. Ijiri, *Management Goals and Accounting for Control*, (Amsterdam: North-Holland Company, 1965).
6. S. M. Lee, *Goal Programming for Decision Analysis*, (Philadelphia: Auerbach Publishing Company, 1973).
7. *Ibid.*, pp. 126–160.

DISCUSSION QUESTIONS

1. What is meant by "assignment problem"?

2. What are the weaknesses of solving an assignment problem using linear programming?

3. What goals are more important to the XYZ Company than minimizing total costs?

4. Explain the concept of goal programming in your own words.

5. Why did total project cost using goal programming exceed the cost with L. P. model?

An Application of Goal Programming at Lord Corporation

Anthony A. Salvia
William R. Ludwig

11

INTRODUCTION

In nearly all theories and studies of management, the key responsibility of the manager is that of guiding his organization from its present state to a desired future state by controlling the allocation of resources. In this paper we focus on the allocation of funds to competing research and development projects. The approach we take utilizes the technique of goal programming.

According to Lee [1], ". . . goal programming is a technique that is capable of handling . . . multiple goals with multiple subgoals. In addition, the objective function . . . may be composed of nonhomogeneous units of measure." These two capabilities of the technique provided the impetus for its implementation at Lord Corporation.

The objective function in a goal program is not constructed of choice variables, but rather consists of deviational variables for each goal. These variables are minimized, starting with the highest priority goal and proceeding in priority order through the set of goals. In the next sec-

Reprinted with permission of Anthony A. Salvia and William R. Ludwig, "An Application of Goal Programming at Lord Corporation," *Interfaces*, Vol. 9, No. 4, August, 1979, Copyright 1979 The Institute of Management Sciences.

tion we see how the priority ordering directly affects project selection.

RESEARCH AND DEVELOPMENT GOALS

In beginning the decision process, Lord established a list of 10 goals as follows:

1. No program may consume more than 10% of the resources.
2. Sales growth should exceed 15% per year.
3. Discounted cash flow rate of return should exceed 30%.
4. Projects have five-year capital limits.
5. Projects promote constructive change in the industry.
6. Company develops leadership role.
7. Company develops new technology.
8. Advanced technology is interrelated.
9. Project provides diversification of product and market.
10. Current balance of allocations between units is to be maintained.

Note that these goals represent a wide variety of desiderata on the corporation's list: 1 represents a kind of insurance against a disastrous project; 2–4 are essentially financial; 5–9 relate to corporate purpose and image; and 10 prevents severe dislocations of competent technical personnel. Twenty-five competing projects were included in the program. Four separate runs of the goal programming algorithm were produced under the following conditions:

Run 1—priorities as above, no uncertainty.
Run 2—priorities as above, financial inputs discounted to allow for uncertainty.
Run 3—priorities rearranged (corporate purpose goals higher), no discounting.
Run 4—priorities rearranged, discounting.

Table 1 indicates the allocations made in each of the four runs, and Table 2 displays the extent to which goals were achieved.

The entries in Table 2 are taken directly from the four computer runs. In every case, a positive entry indicates that the given goal was exceeded, while a negative entry indicates a shortfall. Thus, for example, in the first run, the discounted cash flow rate of return was 51.8%, exceeding its goal [goal (3), 30%] by 21.8. At the same time, the allocations indicated in Run 1 do not quite achieve goals (6) through (9).

The deviations for the nonfinancial goals, (5) through (9), were determined in the following way. Prior to any of the runs, management assessed each project's probable impact on each nonfinancial goal, using a scale of 0 to 10; 0 represented an adverse impact, 10 extremely favorable. An overall target of 8.0 for each nonfinancial goal was established. The entries for each run in Table 2 represent the sum of the deviations from 8.0 for the set of projects selected by that run; thus, the 12 projects selected in Run 3, for example, deviated a total of -15.5 units with respect to goal (8). (Note that the actual average achievement of the 12 projects relative to goal (8) is $(12 \times 8.0 - 15.5)/12 = 6.7$.)

DISCUSSION

A number of conclusions may be gleaned from the two tables below. (a) Discounting increases by a small amount the number of projects required to achieve the financial goals. Note that Run 3 (undiscounted) involves 12 projects, but Run 4 (discounted) requires 14 projects to achieve generally the same results. The difference may be attributed to a deflation of cash flows produced by the discounting. (b) The results generally are quite typical of mathematical programming solutions in general, in that each run produced several zero allocations (in the language of linear programming we would call

Table 1. *Percent Resource Allocation By Project.*

Project	Run 1	Run 2	Run 3	Run 4
1	10	10	10	10
2	10	10	10	10
3	10	10	10	10
4	10	10		2
5	8			
6		4	10	10
7		6	10	8
8	2			
9				
10	10	10	10	10
11	10	4		1
12	10	10	10	10
13				2
14		3	5	
15				
16	3	10	10	10
17	2	10	10	6
18	10	7	3	10
19			10	
20				
21				
22	5			1
23				
24				
25				
TOTAL	100	104	108	100

Table 2. *Goal Attainment.*

Goal	Run 1	Run 2	Run 3	Run 4
(1)	Yes	Yes	Yes	Yes
(2)	0	0	0	0
(3)	+21.8	0	0	0
(4)	0	0	0	0
(5)	0	0	+ 0.2	0
(6)	− 0.9	−0.3	0	+ 0.3
(7)	− 0.8	−0.5	0	Large
(8)	− 0.6	−0.5	− 15.5	− 12.7
(9)	− 0.2	−0.1	Large	− 8.2
(10)	Yes	Yes	Yes	Yes

these nonbasic variables). (c) It is instructive to compare the candidate lists for Runs 1 and 2, or Runs 3 and 4, to assess the impact of uncertainty upon the decision process. Examining, for instance, projects 5–8, Run 1 selects 5 and 8 to a total of 10% of available resources. That same 10% goes to 6 and 7 when uncertainty enters; clearly 6 and 7 are lower in "yield" with respect to the financial goals, but also lower in risk. (d) Even more interesting are the contrasts in allocations when goal priorities are adjusted. If we contrast Runs 1 and 3, a very marked change in the composition of the candidate list is evident. Those projects appearing in 1 but not in 3 (projects 5, 8, 11, and 22) provide good sales growth, cash flow, and short investment horizons, but little or no impact on the less tangible goals of leadership, technological advancement, etc. The diametrically opposite statement may be made about those projects selected in Run 3 but not in Run 1. (e) A few projects appear in all candidate lists. Undoubtedly (at least to the accuracy of our data and the extent of our belief in our priorities) these projects ought to be undertaken. (f) Finally, note that two of the Runs (2 and 3) exceeded 100% allocation. This is an indication that the goal programming algorithm will violate constraints, if need be, to satisfy the user's priorities. In those two runs the extent of violation is not considered serious, and the results could be prorated to achieve 100%.

MANAGEMENT INVOLVEMENT

Lord Corporation management was involved in all the phases of this program in a very integral way. The establishment of the goal list was their task, and the nonfinancial goals in particular are essentially a paraphrasing of the corporation's statement of purpose. The notion of discounting was introduced to satisfy the key decision maker, who had expressed doubt over the corporation's

ability to perform as well as Run 1 indicated with so few projects. The trade-off of priorities among the two types of goals was also a deliberate choice to do some introspection.

A second approach to this same problem was also made via integer programming to permit management to contrast the results; the integer program solution was not nearly so satisfactory as described above.

Of the list of projects finally selected, 15 projects were chosen which appeared on an average of 3.2 candidate lists; only two projects which appeared on any of the lists were discarded; three others, which appeared on no lists, were added by management. Two of those three were part of the integer programming solution, however.

CONCLUSION

The use of goal programming was of considerable benefit to Lord Corporation in its problem of resource allocation to research and development projects. It appears to offer significant advantages over integer programming or other mathematical programming techniques, primarily because of the way in which a variety of variable types can be accommodated.

Perhaps of equal or greater benefit, the exercise provided the opportunity for management to assess the nature of the conflict between financial goals and goals relating to corporate purpose. It has become incumbent on that management to seek to describe and judge the impact of all business development programs on the nonfinancial goals of the company. We observe that most managers do this implicitly, but seldom are those deliberations explicit and communicable.

Considerable further detail, about both Lord Corporation and the decision environment, and about the mathematical details of the goal programming algorithm, are contained in reference 2, which in turn has a rather extensive bibliography.

ENDNOTES

1. Lee, Sang M., *Goal Programming for Decision Analysis*, Auerbach Publishers, Philadelphia, Pa., 1972.
2. Ludwig, W. R., The Selection of Research and Development Projects Through Goal Programming, 1974, Engineering Report, Behrend Graduate Center, Station Road, Erie, Pa., 16563.

DISCUSSION QUESTIONS

1. What are deviational variables and how are they used in goal programming?

2. Why were four separate computer runs contributed to the Lord problem? Explain the role of each run.

3. Comment on the authors' approach to handling deviations for non-financial goals.

Queuing Theory

Queuing theory is the study of waiting lines: people waiting for a ticket, haircut, etc.; airplanes in line for takeoff, machines in line for repair.

Queuing processes have three basic components: arrivals, service facilities, and the actual waiting line. Most queuing problems deal with the question of finding the ideal level of service a firm should provide. Service levels are characterized by such factors as service system's utilization rate, percentage of time idle, average time a customer spends waiting in the queue and in the system, and average number of customers in the queue and in the system.

The Great Gaspump Lineup

"The Great Gaspump Lineup" is an interesting article that relates queuing theory to the problems of gasoline shortages. Professors Lewison and English propose that the long lines we have seen on several occasions since 1973 are not caused by a shortage of gasoline, but rather by an increase in the arrival rate of customers. Their data show that refilling tanks more often ("topping off") can raise the expected waiting time in queues from six minutes to six hours.

A Queuing Case Study . . .

The second queuing article, "A Queuing Case Study of Drive-In Banking," by B. L. Foote, describes the efforts of two industrial engineering students at the University of Oklahoma to help a local bank decide how to expand its drive-in facilities. In examining the options available, arrival and service data had to be collected through observation and then tested to see if they fit the probability distributions commonly used in queuing models. Results of the study were accepted and implemented by the bank. The bank also reports that "the system is functioning well now, and less than five percent of our customers are having to wait more than five minutes on a weekly basis."

The Great Gaspump Line-Up: Consumer Psychology and the Vindication of Queuing Theory

Dale M. Lewison
Wilke English

12

In recent years "the great gaspump line-up" has become an all too common scenario in many parts of the United States. By now the events of this scenario are virtually standard fare. First, gasoline supplies start getting a little tight. Second, major suppliers respond to this tightness by cutting back slightly on deliveries to their dealers. Third, with reduced supplies, a few dealers actually run out of gas toward the end of their delivery period or start to cut back on operating hours. Fourth, almost without warning "the great gaspump line-up" occurs with motorists lining up for blocks, scrambling, scuffling, and even shooting to get the precious fluid. Fifth, almost as suddenly as the lines have formed, they dissipate as consumers become tired of the process and realize that there is no serious shortage. The final event in the scenario is to blame the oil companies for the "great gaspump line-up" by accusing them of creating a false shortage for the purpose of escalating prices.

Are the long lines at service stations a result of a real or a created gasoline shortage or are they the natural outcome of a "panicky" consumer psychology—the "topping-off syn-

Reprinted by permission of *Arkansas Business and Economic Review*, Vol. 12, No. 3, Fall, 1979, p. 16–20.

211

drome"? How can a minor shortfall in gasoline supplies (e.g. 5 or 10 percent) create four hour waiting lines at the pumps? There are statistical answers, or at least partial answers, to those questions. The answers come from a branch of operation research known as "queuing theory" or "waiting line models."

ENTER QUEUING THEORY

Queuing theory is a branch of mathematics that concerns itself with the movement of objects or persons through some type of service facility. As with most of the fields in operations research the serious study of service queues began during and shortly after World War II. Consequently, by now, an extensive body of theory has been developed with in-depth analysis having been applied to almost every conceivable type of servicing arrangement.

In actuality, the problem of cars waiting for gasoline is one of the more simple types of service facilities and represents one of the first applications of the queuing theory. Using only the rate of arrival and the rate of service as inputs, equations have been developed that can compute the expected length of the waiting line, the expected waiting time for an individual unit, the probability of no wait, and certain other statistics.

THE NATURE OF WAITING TIMES

The important thing to note about this body of theory is that the graph of waiting times (see Figure 1) shows a rather peculiar distribution. The shape of this distribution is more exaggerated than a simple exponential expansion, almost taking the appearance of a 90-degree, left-hand turn. In other words, moderate increases in the arrival rate have virtually no effect upon the service times; hence, the normal fluc-

tuations in gasoline consumption such as weekday vs. weekend, summer vs. winter, work-day vs. holiday, do not produce long lines. However, as the arrival times begin to approach the service times, the waiting time increases at an alarming rate. The end result of this process is shown in Figure 1: when the arrival time is equal to or exceeds the service time, then the length of the line goes to infinity—the waiting line will never be serviced.

To be explicit, the long lines at the gasoline station may not be caused by a shortage of gasoline, but rather may result from an increase in the rate of arrival of the customers. The explanation for this increase is evident upon inspection: consumers acting in the interest of their own protection by "topping-off," that is, by filling up more often. When supplies are tight, consumers strive to avoid getting caught with their tanks empty and stations closed. Possibly the consumers' only and certainly their best defense against being caught without gas is to keep their tanks as full as possible at all times. However, as they come in more often, the arrival rate is greatly increased. Even though they are technically the 'same' customers buying the same total amount of gas, they are arriving at the station more frequently.

For example, suppose that motorists who, previously, have been filling their tanks when the needle was almost on empty begin to fill up when they are down to half a tank. The result is a virtual doubling of the number of customers with little or no increase in consumption. Furthermore, if these same customers now decide to start refilling at the ¾ mark, there will be another doubling in the number of customers. Hence, if the fearful customers switch from refilling at empty to refilling every time they have used but ¼-tank, then the filling station will find itself besieged by four times as many customers as it previously served: a condition which is sure to swamp even the best managed station.

To better illustrate the tremendous impact that an increase in arrival times has upon the

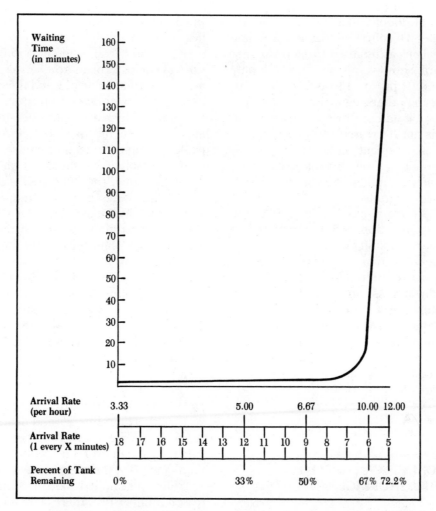

Figure 1. *The Relationship Between Waiting Time and Arrival Rate*

time which a unit must spend waiting in the input queue, consider the following hypothetical example.[1] Assuming that customers arrive exponentially at a rate of one every 18 minutes or 3.33 units per hour at a single facility which can service a unit in 5 minutes or at a service rate of 12 units per hour then, the expected waiting time is approximately one minute.[2] Assume that the arrival rate, above, represents motorists who are filling up when their tanks are virtually empty. Now, if those same motorists decide to fill up when their tanks are only half empty, the

1. While admittedly hypothetical, the above example is probably quite conservative in that it allows a rather substantial rate of increase before that increase begins to strain against capacity. Due to the pressure of competition which demands efficiency, our service stations probably do not have as much slack in them (under normal conditions) as this example would imply.

2. Using the formula: $E(Tw) = \dfrac{a}{2s(s-a)}$; the use of exponential arrival rates and constant service times is based upon actual studies of gasoline service stations as reported in the operations research literature.

arrival rate will double, that is, one customer every 9 minutes. Of course, it does take less time to pump 8 gallons as opposed to 16 (assuming a 16 gallon tank); however, pumping time is only a part of the total process of pulling into position, clearing the pump, removing the gas cap, paying for the gas and so forth. But overall, the service rate is not decreased to any significant degree by more frequent refills. With the new arrival rate resulting from ½-tank reservicing, the formula now computes an expected waiting time of around 3 minutes.

But the process is just beginning! As the arrival rates begin to approach the service time of 5 minutes, the waiting times increase dramatically. The calculations shown in Table 1 and illustrated in Figure 1 reflect how dramatic these increases really are. As can be seen in Table 1 the waiting time goes to infinity before the motorists reach the point where they fill up when their tanks are only ¼ empty. The California experience with all-day lines provides a good example of this process and a vindication of queuing theory.

FEAR OF SHORTAGE CAN HELP TO CREATE ACTUAL SHORTAGE

The foregoing discussion has tried to show that the mere fear of gasoline shortfalls may create the appearance of massive shortages. By refilling their tanks more often, motorists effectively increase the number of customers thereby increasing the arrival rate. As documented by queuing theory, the increase in the arrival rate has the odd property of first having little effect, only to later have a dramatic effect. Thus, to switch from refilling at empty to refilling at half a tank, a change of 50 percent, only increases the waiting time from 1 minute to 3 minutes. Yet, by increasing the frequency of fill up by refilling

whenever the tank level falls to 72 percent full instead of at the 66 percent level, the waiting time increases from 6 minutes to 6 hours. This example helps explain how service stations may operate normally one day and the very next day have to cope with lines 10 blocks long.

Since an increase in arrival rate is caused by more frequent fill up of old customers as opposed to some dramatic increase in new customers, gasoline consumption should remain about the same: the same customers buying in smaller quantities at more frequent intervals. Unfortunately, the perception of a shortage may also lead to certain types of activities which tend to exacerbate whatever real shortage there may actually be.

First, the motorists are forced to spend a long time waiting in line. Both the time spent waiting and the gasoline spent idling represent a diversion of resources into nonproductive areas. Gasoline that could have been used in moving from place-to-place is now wasted while idling in a slow-moving line.

Second, as everyone strives to fill up at the same time the normal timing of the market is destroyed. The refineries and dealers are structured to handle a relatively constant demand schedule. When everyone comes in for a fill up simultaneously, those capacities are over-taxed.

Third, as implied above and connected with reason number two, there is the problem of explicit hoarding. Every time there is a "gasoline shortage," there also appears a simultaneous "gasoline can shortage." Consumers, again acting in their own best interest, rush out to buy gasoline cans and to hoard gas for the future. Although this effect may seem minimal, it can nevertheless be quite severe in that it comes at such a bad time. It is like getting the hiccups while laboring with emphysema. At the time when the gasoline delivery system is struggling desperately to keep up with present demand, customers are coming in and demanding both present and future supplies.

Table 1. *A Hypothetical Example of Expected Waiting Times*

Arrival Rate (one every how many minutes)	Arrival Rate (per hour)	Percentage of Tank Remaining	Expected Waiting Time in Minutes
18	3.33/hour	0%(on empty)	.96 minutes or ≅ 1 min.
12	5.00/hour	33%(⅓ tank)	1.785 minutes or ≅ 2 min.
9	6.67/hour	50%(½ tank)	3.128 minutes or ≅ 3 min.
6	10.00/hour	66%	12.49 minutes or ≅ 12 min.
5:50	10.28/hour	67%	14.94 minutes or ≅ 15 min.
5:40	10.58/hour	68%	18.63 minutes or ≅ 19 min.
5:30	10.90/hour	69%	24.77 minutes or ≅ 25 min.
5:20	11.26/hour	70%	37.87 minutes or ≅ 38 min.
5:10	11.61/hour	71%	74.83 minutes or ≅ 75 min.
5:05	11.80/hour	71.7%	149.78 minutes or ≅ 2½ hours
5:04	11.84/hour	71.8%	187.33 minutes or ≅ 3 hours
5:03	11.89/hour	71.9%	249.60 minutes or ≅ 4 hours
5:02	11.92/hour	72.0%	372.48 minutes or ≅ 6 hours
5:01	11.96/hour	72.1%	747.49 minutes or ≅ 12½ hours
5:00:5	11.98/hour	72.17%	1497.48 minutes or ≅ 25 hours
5:00	12.00/hour	72.222%	infinity

LET THE MARKETING MECHANISM WORK

Most of the talk concerned with the gasoline shortage has centered around allocation and rationing schemes which would limit the amount which a customer could buy. Such rationing schemes are (a) generally ineffective in limiting demand; (b) quickly produce black markets and other 'illegal' plays for avoiding regulation thereby not only reducing the effectiveness of the rationing attempt but also helping to foster a general disrespect for the government and its laws; and (c) result in the channeling of productive resources into a non-productive bureaucracy.

The best solution is to let the market set both supply and demand through the pricing mechanism. And if the government feels that it must do something to end the panic, let it insist that reservicing with gasoline be limited to those vehicles whose fuel gauges before purchase show no more than ½-tank of fuel remaining; it should not encourage additional service station visits to "top-off" by trying to limit purchase quantities to relatively small amounts.

DISCUSSION QUESTIONS

1. What factors are responsible for rapid increases in the queue lengths at gasoline stations?

2. Explain the statistical relationship between "topping-off" and gaspump lines.

3. Explain the meaning of the graph in Figure 1.

4. What are the underlying assumptions of queuing theory that are employed in the calculations in Table 1? Are they reasonable in the case of a gas station?

A Queueing Case Study of Drive-In Banking

B. L. Foote

13

This case is a summary of the efforts of two students in an Applied Operations Research course taught in the University of Oklahoma School of Industrial Engineering in the fall of 1972. The case involved the effort of a local bank to expand their drive-in facilities. Two options were basically available: a "robo-window" system and a traditional expansion of the current system which involved teller stations approximately 8′ by 8′ stationed on a traffic lane. The robo system involved a small cube approximately three feet in each dimension which had a speaker system and a pneumatic tube to deliver cartridges back to a central location. Space was at a premium and expansion of the present system was limited to five teller stations (they now have three) whereas up to seven stations were available if the robo system was used. The robo station was, of course, much cheaper (by about ½) than an 8′ by 8′ room for a teller.

The bank was less concerned about the costs as the quality of customer service. Our team was called in to assess the two systems.

The first concern was finding a measure of effectiveness. Interviews with bank officials rap-

Reprinted by permission of B. L. Foote, "A Queueing Case Study of Drive–In Banking," *Interfaces*, Vol. 6, No. 4, August, 1976, Copyright 1976 The Institute of Management Sciences.

idly dismissed total costs as a consideration. The prime consideration was lost customers due to poor service. Bank officials then defined poor service as causing a customer to wait longer than five minutes. This choice was not as arbitrary as it sounds, as further questions showed that customers base their impatience on the movement of the minute hand between two marks, which on most watches represents five minutes. Bank officials then set four minutes as the maximum waiting time. The team then suggested a risk level of approximately .05 and this was agreed to.

The team also suggested that the cost criterion should be evaluated as a back up piece of information, and suggested that for any design the imputed cost of waiting should be determined and submitted to bank officials for their judgement. This was agreed to. The team cheerfully set to work with a set of formulas from Taha's *Introduction to Operations Research*. Time studies were immediately taken using two observers to facilitate data collection. Initial tests disclosed that observing the cars, operating the watch and reordering were too much for one student to do without substantial error. Table 1 and similar tables were computed for various days and time intervals. (See Appendix equation 1.)

The expected frequency computations assumed that interarrival times were distributed exponentially. Since $\chi^2_{.01}$ with five degrees of freedom is 15.086, this looked like a good fit. (See Appendix equation 2.)

Other tables had similar results. A plot of the arrival rates in Figure 1 gave rise to some second thoughts. The queue was obviously always in a state of flux and the theory of the transient behavior of queues was probably needed. A look at some basic references was discouraging. The formulas were so complex that elaborate programming or simulation seemed to be called for in order to compute the probability of waiting in the system longer than four minutes. Further, the team could find no solid information on how long the "transient" state of a queue lasted. Someone remembered reading something about four hours. References were examined with no solid information found.

The bank operated by adding tellers as the waiting line grew. When about four were waiting another window opened up. This rule of thumb would be used in the new system, so the team thought perhaps that this might "smooth out" the transient behavior and perhaps some simple formulas could still be used.

The team next studied the service time. Since waiting times can be lessened either by adding servers or decreasing service times, the layout of the work station was studied and service times during busy periods were taken. No improvements in layout or work methods could be seen. Further, service times also were text book fits of the χ^2 distribution. However, a for-

Table 1. *(Friday 2:15–6:30)*

Interval (sec.)	Obs. freq.	Exp. freq.	Chi Square ($\lambda = .03$ arrivals/sec.)
0–19	208	206	.019
20–39	109	113	.142
40–59	64	62	.016
60–79	33	34	.029
80–99	19	19	0
100–119	13	10	.9
120 +	10	12	.333
	456	456	1.439

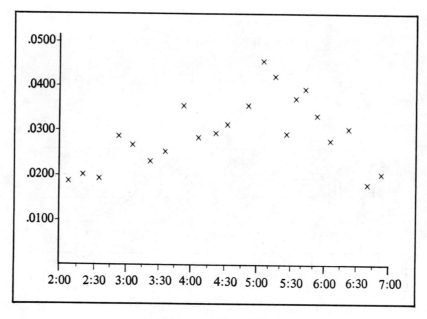

Figure 1. *Arrival Rates*

tunate observation was made. The service time of the system and the service time of the teller were two different times. The service time of the system consisted of the following events: realizing the car in front had moved, move to the teller window, give the teller instructions or requests plus material items, teller actions, move out. On three of these actions the teller was forcibly idle. The total of the five actions the team called block time. The block time was 72 seconds and service time was 48 seconds. These were average figures, of course. A little machine interference speculation was conducted. Perhaps two tellers could serve three lanes. Two tellers could sit in a teller station and serve the station lane and two "robo" lanes.

Figure 2 shows a sample of the machine interference diagramming done. The conclusion was that this assignment was a possibility. Of course the diagram was idealized based on averages, but it was felt that short service times would balance out in this case. When the time line was extended the waiting times vanished.

The time of vanishing of waiting time (115 sec.) was used as an estimate of transient state time. The relationship between 72 and 48 was too good to be true, but rechecks verified the figures.

The team then began calculations to see if the formulas in Taha could predict average waiting times. About two minutes after a window opened, observations were taken. One, two, and three server cases were observed. Table 2 gives the results.

Table 2 and tables like it were intriguing. The predictions seemed good except for one "outlier." Further the last calculation was *very* interesting. It seemed a variable teller window number policy could be approximated by formulas based on the maximum number of windows open at all times. Upon reflection this seemed very reasonable. The formulas used are reproduced in the Appendix equation 3 for the reader's convenience.

If we assume the cost of a server, c_j is constant (probably not true), Taha gives an inequality that can be used to estimate imputed cost of

A Queuing Case Study of Drive-In Banking

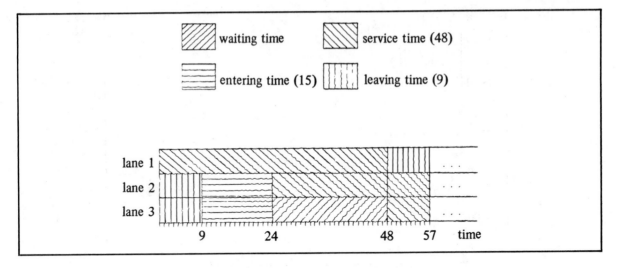

Figure 2. *Time Line Diagram*

waiting per hour, c_w. (Shown in the Appendix equation 4.)

These calculations showed the bank's current policy imputed customer waiting time at somewhere between 3 and 24 dollars per hour. These figures seemed acceptable to bank officials. The important calculation was still to come.

The use of the formulas were good for expected times, but what about the waiting time distribution? For the transient case the waiting time distribution is not known explicitly. For the steady state case, the distribution has the form of a gamma distribution. It was hoped that using steady state as an approximation would work

here also. Using Table 3 some empirical tests were made.

The gamma depends on two paramters α, β where $\alpha\beta$ = mean value.

For convenience α was chosen as 1, 2, 3, . . . since if α is noninteger we no longer have $(\alpha - 1)!$ in the function definition, but a very complicated evaluation. β was determined by $\alpha\beta$ = W. $\alpha = 2$ and $\alpha = 3$ are tested in Tables 4 and 5. $\chi^2_{.005}$ = 16.750. $\alpha = 2$ was chosen, of course.

The team then set to work. They calculated W, for various combinations of c; $1 \leq c \leq 7$. Using $\alpha\beta = W_s, \alpha = 2$, they computed $P(W_s \leq 4)$

Table 2. *(Predicted vs. Observed System Average Waiting Times)*

W, (Sec) Observed	W, (Sec) Predicted
89	85 (1 tellers, λ = .0214, μ = .0138)
106	86 (3 tellers, λ = .0216, μ = .0138)
100	174 (2 tellers, λ = .0211, μ = .0138)
90	94 (3 tellers, λ = .025, μ = .0138)
208	202 (3 tellers, λ = .0356, μ = .0138)
125*	124*(3 tellers, λ = .0305, μ = .0138)

λ = arrival rate (per sec.) μ = service rate (per sec.)
*Observed and expected values of W, for the entire period assuming three open windows at *all* times.

A Queuing Case Study of Drive-In Banking

Table 3. *(Observed System Waiting Times)*

Interval (Sec)		Obs. freq.
I	0–50	56
II	51–100	112
III	101–150	56
IV	151–200	24
V	201–250	13
VI	251–300	7
VII	300 +	8

by integration.

    These evaluations "showed" the new system could handle the projected arrival rates in the future with some room to spare. An expansion to five lanes with two "robos" added to the current three lanes was recommended with an assurance that adding a teller when the waiting line exceeded three or four would handle the projected volume and a customer would run less than a five percent chance of waiting more than four minutes.

Table 4. ($\alpha = 2$)

Interval	Obs. freq.	Exp. freq.	χ^2
I	56	67	1.81
II	112	88	6.55
III	56	66	1.52
IV	24	30	1.20
V	13	13	0
VI	7	8	.13
VII	8	4	4.00
Totals	276	276	15.21

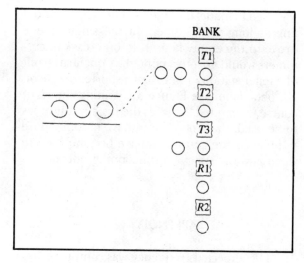

BANK

Figure 3. *Layout of Final System*

    The students happily handed in their report knowing they would be gone before the "robo" lanes would be built and the instructor waited for the results of the bank decision.

EPILOGUE

The "robo" lanes were built and worked as predicted. There was an exception. The phenomenon of jockeying is well known in queuing systems. Here we had a single lane that emptied into one or two car queues in front of each of the tellers. This was a departure from the basic single queue multi-channel service system which

Table 5. ($\alpha = 3$)

Interval	Obs. freq.	Exp. freq.	χ^2
I	56	48	1.33
II	112	105	.47
III	56	69	2.45
IV	24	37	4.57
V	13	9	1.78
VI	7	6	.17
VII	8	2	18.00
Totals	276	276	28.77

A Queuing Case Study of Drive-In Banking

was used to model the system. The sytem worked fine as long as customers in the single queue drove to the empty lane. But, on occasion, customers would go into a nonempty queue in front of a teller station rather than a shorter queue on a "robo" lane (see Figure 3). Waiting times, of course, expanded. Now, as the system continues to be used, the "robo" lanes have become more popular as the customers have become used to them and the system is functioning normally.

APPENDIX

1. The expected frequency was computed by the integral

$$\int_{t_1}^{t_2} .03e^{-.03t}.$$

2. $\chi^2_{(.01)}$ (called Chi Square) is a test number used to determine if a prediction is statistically acceptable. If the value computed in the table is less than this value we accept the prediction with a certainty of being wrong in rejecting one percent of the time.

3. $\rho = \lambda/\mu L_q$

$$= \frac{\rho^{c+1}}{(c-1)!}(c-\rho)^2 \left\{ \sum_{n=0}^{c-1} \frac{\rho^n}{n!} + \frac{\rho^c}{c!(1-/c)} \right\}^{-1} \rho/c<1$$

$W_s = L_q/\lambda + 1/\mu, \quad L_s = L_q + \rho, \quad W_q = L_q/\lambda$

where λ = arrival rate in arrivals per second
μ = busy period service rate (per second)
W_s = waiting time in the system (seconds)
c = number of servers
L_q = number expected in the queue
L_s = number expected in the system
W_q = waiting time in the queue.

4. $$\frac{c_j}{L_s(c)-L_s(c+1)} \geq c_w \geq \frac{c_j}{L_s(c-1)-L_s(c)}$$

DISCUSSION QUESTIONS

1. Describe and draw the service system being proposed.

2. What is a chi-square (χ^2) test and how can it be used in queuing theory?

3. What is the most time-consuming aspect of a case study like this?

4. If the data for arrivals and service times are not accurately portrayed by the common queuing theory probability distributions (such as Poisson, exponential, gamma, normal), how can a queuing analysis be conducted?

Simulation

Simulation is one of the most widely used quantitative analysis tools. The simulation approach involves building a mathematical model that attempts to describe a real-world situation. The model's goal is to include all important variables and their interactions, so that the effect of managerial changes on the whole system can be tested. Simulation has many advantages over other QA techniques, and is especially useful when a problem is too complex or difficult to solve by other means.

The Monte Carlo method of simulation is developed around the use of probability distributions and "random numbers." By generating a series of random numbers, the simulation procedure is conducted for many time periods. The results are then used to evaluate the long-term impact of each policy being studied and tested. Monte Carlo simulations can be conducted by hand for small problems or by computer for more complex ones. Four special purpose computer programming languages—GPSS, SIMSCRIPT, GASP, and DYNAMO—are commonly available and are efficient in handling simulation problems.

Hospital Admissions Systems: A Simulation Approach

The first article in this section, "Hospital Admissions Systems" by Lim, Uyeno, and Vertinsky, describes a simulation approach to admitting patients to the orthopedic ward of a Canadian hospital. The model's goal is to increase the effectiveness of a hospital operation by helping obtain a stable patient flow and an even hospital work-flow. A GPSS Computer program and a flow chart are illustrated, and validation statistics are presented.

A Simulation Model of the College Admissions Process

"A Simulation Model of the College Admissions Process" by Holzman and Johnson details a model developed to help a college admissions director evaluate policy decisions affecting freshman acceptances. Several factors that vary from year to year and can have a financial impact on the college are included in the interactive simulation model. Among them are total number of applications received, percent of freshmen accepted that actually enroll, and the "quality" (such as SAT scores) of the applications. The simulation was developed in modular form, consisting of ten subprograms and nine subroutines.

Simulation for Fire Department Deployment Analysis

The third paper describes the use of a SIMSCRIPT simulation to analyze alternative strategies for locating fire department companies in Denver, Colorado. The authors of "Simulation for Fire Department Deployment Analysis," Monarchi, Hendrick, and Plane, describe how they used travel time to measure fire suppression service. Along with travel time, they employed "heavy doses of judgment" to redesign the location of fire equipment. Their recommendation to city government projected a $23 million cost savings over a seven-year period.

Hospital Admissions Systems: A Simulation Approach

Timothy Lim
Dean Uyeno
Ilan Vertinsky

14

The level and variability of patient flows into the hospital play an important role in the determination of both level and stability of bed occupancy. Thus they act as a major determinant of the effectiveness of the hospital operation. Stability of patient flow may be achieved through centralized control in the health care delivery system or through an appropriate manipulation of backlog demands for elective hospital care.

An even work flow minimizes idleness and overtime. This does not necessarily imply 100% utilization of resources since slack must be allowed for emergency patients. Yet, if there is too much slack, waiting time for nonemergency patients rises unnecessarily.

A longer waiting list makes it easier to maintain a stable schedule. However, if the waiting time is too long, many patients will cancel. This causes an excessive and sometimes unsuccessful search for replacement patients. Similarly, the long waiting times may cause physicians to request admittance of patients to more than one hospital at a time. This phenomenon of multiple bookings allows the physician to choose the earliest possible admittance date at the cost of increasing uncertainties in hospital scheduling activities.

"Hospital Admission Systems: A Simulation Approach," by Timothy Lim and Dean Uyeno is reprinted from *Simulation and Games*, Vol. 6, No. 2 (June, 1975) pp. 188–201 by permission of the publisher, Sage Publications, Inc.

The waiting list of the hospital comprises a number of waiting sublists: one for each physician, one for each type of ward. Each physician may have any number of patients waiting for service at any one time without any institutional limits. The physician has control over the number of patients on his waiting lists through transfer of patients to other physicians and hospitals. There is a high degree of variability in "admission" habits among physicians. Some practitioners, by the very nature of their specialties, treat most patients in their office and admit only a small percentage of their patients. Others may have admitting privileges to more than one hospital and may distribute their patients among them.

A portion of the waiting lists of some physicians is composed of "urgent" patients, patients whose priority for care lies between that of emergency and elective patients. The hospital admitting staff continuously and actively seeks to schedule these patients for service before elective patients.

Since the ward is the basic unit of the hospital, scheduling of admissions must take account of the resources of wards. Patients must be chosen on the basis of physician demand, satisfying constraints of availability of appropriate bed space. To control hospital inflow effectively, the admission staff must estimate how many cancellations and postponements are going to take place in the near future and how many new patients can be notified for tentative entry.

After some discussion with the admissions supervisor of a local hosptial, it was decided to use an orthopedic ward as the unit of study. Since the ward is a fundamental subsystem of a hospital, the results of this study can probably be generalized to most other wards.

THE MODEL

A computerized model of the orthopedic ward was created. In this model it is possible to follow in a statistical sense the flow of patients through the hospital. The model was written in a widely used simulation language, GPSS. The program consists of over 300 blocks and over 170 functions. The project took about two years to complete.

In the model, requests for admission are created at the same rate as requests enter the actual hospital. This is done on the basis of 1971 data.

As the requests for admission enter the model, attributes such as priority, disease number, length of stay for that disease or condition, and physician number are assigned to the patient.

The likelihood of a patient request for admission being emergency, urgent surgical, urgent medical, or elective in nature reflects the proportions of these classes in actual data. Similarly, the lengths of stay of patients by disease category (an aggregation of the CPHA code [Commission on Professional and Hospital Activities, 1971]) were taken from actual hospital data. A chronological list in the model is used to determine when the simulated length of stay ends and the bed which the patient occupies is freed for someone else.

Patients are assigned to beds depending on the availability of appropriate space and the availability of surgery time. The order of admittance in the model is by priority with first priority for emergency patients, second for urgent, and third for electives. Emergency patients always get a bed and wait only if no doctor is available to operate immediately. In our model of the orthopedic ward, it is assumed that the emergency patient gets a bed in the ward. In actual fact, an emergency patient will be put, if necessary, in another ward or a hallway. If we had had sufficient financial resources to model the entire hospital, this could have been avoided. As in the actual hospital, urgent patients have a limited wait—at most seven days. To allow for urgent surgical cases about 10% to 20% of the surgical slate is left open.

The availability of physicians to do surgery

was based on an analysis of the times spent by the orthopedic surgeons and other surgeons at the hospital studied. The physicians had differing rates at which they did operations and had differing number of patients requiring hospitalization and surgery. There were four primary physicians. In the model no elective surgical patient was assigned to anyone other than his own surgeon. As in the real world, this meant that many patients had to remain on the waiting list

not only for bed availability and surgical room time, but also for the surgeon. In some cases it was even necessary to wait for the availability of a surgeon to assist in the operating room. A sample flow chart for urgent surgical patients is given in Figure 1.

Table 1 lists a partial GPSS program segment for urgent surgical patients who have waited less than seven days. The TRANSFER, WAIT command puts urgent surgical patients

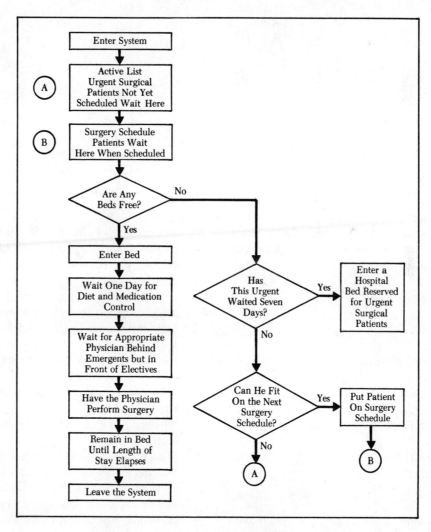

Figure 1. *Urgent Surgical Patient Flow in Model*

Hospital Admissions Systems: A Simulation Approach

Table 1. *Partial GPSS Program Segment for Urgent Surgical Patients*

UGOPS	QUEUE	15
	QUEUE	P5
UGOP	LINK	UROP,FIFO
NAH	LINK	XH100,FIFO
RPRIO	ASSIGN	2,0
	TRANSFER	,WAIT
SEE 1	TEST G	R$BED,O,PRO
	ENTER	BED
	DEPART	15
	DEPART	P5
	ADVANCE	1440
	PRIORITY	2
	QUEUE	18
	PREEMPT	V1
	SEIZE	P5
	RETURN	V1
	DEPART	18
	ADVANCE	P4
	RELEASE	P5
	TEST G	V$LEFT2,O,OUTT1
	ADVANCE	V$LEFT2
OUTT1	LEAVE	BED
FINIS	TERMINATE	O

in another program segment which checks to see when a bed may be entered. A standard run takes 20 seconds to assemble and 627 seconds to execute on an IBM 360/67.

MODEL VALIDATION

Before any simulation model can be confidently applied, it is necessary to show that the model accurately reflects real system behavior. Thus results of the hospital admissions model were compared with actual hospital data for the winter of 1971.

There are three ways in which the model could be validated (Naylor and Finger, 1967). These are:

1. Internal Consistency. For example, if 20% of the patients are assigned to physican A at the start of the model, then at the end of the model the output should show that 20% of the patients have completed treatment by physician A, subject to the variability introduced by the manner in which patients pass through the model.

2. Data generated by the model should agree with the data collected or agree with the information provided by hospital staff. For example, if patients have to wait due to unavailability of resources, then the waiting time should be similar to the waiting time gathered from the data or estimated by the staff.

3. Data fed in should produce results that can be checked with other data collected for validation. For example, the availability of operating room time should restrict the total number of patients that have operations per week.

In this study, one season was chosen for validation purposes. The validation statistics are gathered at the end of eight runs of the model for the season. The statistics gathered were the total number of surgeries performed by each physician, the length of the waiting list for orthopedics, and bed utilization. Because this is a simulation in which data are drawn from frequency distributions and the outcomes are not deterministic, the output should differ a little from run to run.

The average of the eight runs is taken and this is compared with the actual values extracted from analysis of operating room data (see Table 2). Most of the simulation results shown in Table 2 are very close to the actual values experienced. Unfortunately, it is difficult to verify the average number of admission requests in the hospital because of some missing data at the hospital. The average number of requests for all of 1971 in the model was 74.4. The hospital staff estimated the average number of requests to be about eighty for the 1972 season. We believe that the 74.4 value is fairly close to the actual value in the absence of 1971 data.

The bed utilization must be explained. The model showed an average of 80.4%. The hospital's figures are much higher than this for several reasons. Firstly, a bed in the hospital is considered to be occupied if a patient states his intention to enter the following day or the same afternoon in which he is notified of admission. In the model, a bed is not considered full until the simulated patient enters the hospital. If in real life a patient cancels out or does not show up, then the hospital has considered the bed occupied when in fact it was not. Secondly, the hospital considers a bed to be occupied if a patient does not leave until 5:00 to 6:00 p.m. At this time it is impossible to assign a new patient to that bed. So in reality the bed is empty for the night, but the bed is considered "occupied" in the daily statistics.

These two factors cause the hospital to report a higher occupancy rate than the ward actually accommodates. The nurses believe 85% to 90% is the occupancy rate of this ward; but in fact, due to the two factors mentioned, the rate is probably closer to 80%.

Based on these results, our model simulates

Table 2. *Results of Validation Runs*

Run	Physician No. 1	2	3	4	5	Average No. of Requests	Bed Utilization (%)
1	11.3	16.5	28.3	32.0	77.7	74.6	82.1
2	10.4	20.9	31.1	28.6	75.6	79.1	81.9
3	13.1	18.9	31.5	28.1	78.7	64.0	80.0
4	11.3	19.1	28.5	26.9	74.8	59.7	79.5
5	10.5	18.1	28.1	26.2	77.7	44.2	77.3
6	11.2	16.8	29.9	27.6	77.8	77.8	80.3
7	12.1	21.4	26.1	30.4	79.8	117.1	79.5
8	11.1	18.1	32.2	28.8	74.5	79.2	82.4
Average results from simulation	11.3	18.7	29.9	28.5	77.0	74.4	80.4
Actual Data	11.0	18.0	32.0	28.0	76.0	See Discussion	See Discussion

Hospital Admissions Systems: A Simulation Approach

the hospital features with which we are most concerned. Moreover, from a long sequence of experiments we believe that the hospital system responds isomorphically to the model for changes that affect the major features of the simulation model.

EXPERIMENTAL RESULTS

A series of experiments was performed to examine various policies. Since it was shown in the previous section that the model was a valid simulation of the parent hospital system, we infer that, if the following simulated policies were incorporated, the parent system would change in a similar manner. The simulated experiments were: (1) quickcalls, and (2) maximum queue length.

The results are summarized in Table 3. Also included in Table 3 for comparison purposes are the average results of the validation runs given in Table 2.

Quickcalls

Quickcalls are defined as elective patients willing to enter the hospital on very short notice—one day or less. That is to say, the admission date is not scheduled, but within a two-week period the

patient would be called and expected to enter in the next 24 hours. In this way, if anyone cancels, a quickcall could be brought in fairly quickly. This reduces the length of a possibly unfruitful search for a replacement; however, taken into consideration is the fact that a few persons may change their minds on being quickcalls when actually called. The incentive for a patient to become a quickcall is to keep his waiting time to a maximum of, in this case, two weeks. The present average waiting time at this hospital is approximately 4½ weeks.

In the simulation model, when a patient cancels, another patient will replace him from the quickcall list unless the quickcall list is empty. Since each physician still has the same number of patients, and the cancellation rate and the operating theater time allocation remain the same, the physician need not perform any more operations in the long term than in the normal nonreplacement case. The only effect would be that the simulated waiting list length would decrease dramatically from 74.4 to 53.6 requests. In actual practice, however, the physician would probably use the increased usable time available in the operating theater to perform more surgeries (up to 5% more in our experiments).

A comparison of the statistics from this experiment with the standard run statistics indi-

Table 3. *Summary of Experimental Results*

Exp. No.	Description	Total Number of Surgeries per Physician					Avg. Len. of Stay (days)	Bed Uti. (%)	Avg. Que. Len.	Avg. Wait Time Elect Surg. (days)	Comments
		1 1	*2* 2	*3* 3	*4* 4	*other* others					
—	Average Results from Simulation	11.3	18.7	29.9	28.5	77.0	11.7	80.4	74.4	31.4	Simulation of hosp. winter 1971 (Base for Comparisons)
1.	Quickcalls 7.5%	11.5	18.6	29.8	28.7	77.3	10.8	80.3	53.6	22.7	7.5% of elective pats are Quickcall
2.	Maximum Queue Length	11.9	19.9	31.9	29.0	77.7	11.1	83.1	49.5	20.3	The maximum no. of requests per physician on file

cates that all physicians operated at the same level as expected. Bed utilization and the average level of stay are very close. The only statistics that differ significantly are the length of the queue and the waiting time in the queue. The number of patients waiting for surgery decreases from 74.4 to 53.6, and the waiting time decreases from 31.4 to 22.7 days.

This is a substantial saving in waiting time. However, patients must be found who are willing to become quickcalls and who actually will show up when called. Furthermore, the hospital must accommodate those quickcalls who were not called during the two-week period, but have to be brought in because the maximum time limit has elapsed. This would possibly create some difficulty for other elective patients if the number of persons allowed to be quickcalls was inappropriately chosen and was too high. Quickcalls would not displace in any case urgent or emergency patients. In a questionnaire that was sent out to previous patients at this hospital, we found that more than one-third of the patients were willing to enter on a 24-hour on-call basis.

Maximum Queue

In this experiment the hospital retains all present procedures of selecting surgical patients and allocating beds, and each physician is allowed to submit only the number of elective admissions requests he needs on file to maintain his present level of service, for example, six. Only when some of the six have either been admitted or have canceled can the physician submit more requests. Urgent and emergency patients are given priority as before.

This requires that each physician check daily and submit admission requests as soon as any of his patients cancels or is admitted to the hospital. Clearly, because each physician has a different case mix, patient age mix, and working pace, the number of requests required for each physician need not necessarily be the same. To avoid disagreements, a common level for all physicians may be necessary.

Before doing this experiment, we performed a number of computer runs to determine the appropriate maximum queue length for each physician. In successive runs the maximum number of elective patients from which the admissions personnel could pick the admission slate was varied to determine the point at which the average number of operations the physician did was affected. The model showed that the maximum queue length for physicians 1,2,3, and 4 was 4,4,4, and 5, respectively. That is, if the physicians are to deliver the same level of service, they must maintain at least the mentioned maximum number of requests in the admittance office.

In the results for this experiment (Table 3), the average queue length or average number of requests for the ward is 49.5, which is much higher than the sum of the maximum number of elective requests for each physician. This is because urgent patients' requests are submitted regardless of the number of elective cases waiting for surgery. As in the previous experiment, the decrease in waiting time (from 31.4 to 20.3 days) is more apparent than real because now the request remains in the physician's office rather than in the hospital. The value of this experiment lies in the shift of responsibility for the determination of elective patient priority from the hospital admissions staff to the physician who knows the patient and his condition best. The experiment shows that this need not affect the number of patients the physician sees in the hospital. The hospital reduces its administrative workload also since this method tends to reduce the sheer volume of active requests for admission.

CONCLUSIONS

Based on the results shown in Table 3, two concepts which may help to facilitate hospital admissions systems emerge from this study. The concept of quickcall meets a practical need. While a physician is discussing the need for surgery with the patient, he could easily have the patient fill out a short form concerning the minimum notice he is willing to accept before entry to the hospital. In this way the physician could screen out cases which he would prefer not to handle without more advance planning. This would cost the physician very little extra time and effort and offers him greater flexibility in choice of patients to treat if a patient cancels. The quickcall system could result in a significant saving of hospital resources by reducing the search for substitute patients for cancellations.

The simulation showed that the quickcall system reduced the waiting time by approximately eight and one-half days at the hospital which was the site of the experiments. Since one of the main reasons for cancellations is long waiting times, the quickcall concept should tend to reduce the number of cancellations.

The maximum queue length concept is somewhat more difficult to implement. Physicians might not allow the hospital to restrict the number of elective requests each week (although a local hospital does this). It might be necessary to convince them of the usefulness of limiting the number of requests. From the physician's standpoint, since there is a limit to the number of cases he can submit under this concept, he could automatically screen and arrange them in order of his preference. At present he must rely on nonphysician admissions personnel at the hospital to give priority to the elective patients whose need is greatest. Another advantage is that the physician can use the queue to arrange his next few weeks of surgery to better suit his other time commitments.

In conclusion, the structure of this simulation model enables a wide variety of experiments to be run on the admissions system without the high cost and risk of actual pilot studies in the hospital.

The simulation model of the admissions process described in this paper not only demonstrated that a valid model of the admissions process can be obtained, but also showed the usefulness of the quickcall list and maximum waiting lists for patient surgical admission requests. It is recommended that these concepts be considered in the design or redesign of actual hospital admissions systems. The maximum waiting list concept could also be used for elective medical admission requests. Furthermore, this model could be extended to include the effect of added hours of operating room time for surgeons, assistants in surgery, and weekend or evening operating schedules, and to test and evaluate the efficiency and effectiveness of other changes in the hospital admissions systems.

ENDNOTES

Commission on Professional and Hospital Activities [CPHA] (1971) Length of Stay in PAS Hospitals, Canada 1970. Ann Arbor, Michigan, October.

NAYLOR, T. H. and J. M. FINGER (1967) "Verification of computer simulation models." Management Sci. 14, 2 (October).

DISCUSSION QUESTIONS

1. Why is a simulation model used in analyzing the hospital admissions system in this article?

2. Why is simulation considered a useful tool in general?

3. What are "quick calls" and why are they important in hospital admissions?

4. Describe the validation procedures used to test the simulation model.

5. What hospital wards resemble the orthopedic ward in the respect that this model could be easily extended? What ward would not be appropriate?

A Simulation Model of the College Admission Process

Albert G. Holzman
Donald B. Johnson

15

INTRODUCTION

When considering the implementation of a college admission policy, the complex interaction among restrictions must be recognized: from a financial standpoint, enrollment must be adequate to support dormitory and faculty operations, yet not so large as to cause overcrowding in the classrooms, laboratories, and residence halls; from an eductional viewpoint, the quality of instruction must not be sacrificed in order to fill classroom seats for efficient operation.

Choosing the best policy for a given situation has become a very intricate operation, particularly in light of considerable uncertainty existing throughout the admission process. In this article, the term college admission policy will refer to the process of accepting or rejecting freshman applicants for a given school year. The following factors, critical to the admission process, vary from year to year and result in considerable uncertainty about which applicants to accept or reject:

- the total number of applications to be received.
- the ratio of freshmen enrolling to accepted

Reprinted by permission of Albert G. Holzman and Donald B. Johnson, "A Simulation Model of the College Admission Process," *Interfaces*, Vol. 5, No. 3, May, 1975, Copyright 1975 The Institute of Management Sciences.

applicants. Since most prospective students apply to several schools, accepting an applicant does not always result in subsequent enrollment.

- The "quality" of the total population of applicants, as defined by some arbitrary measure, such as Scholastic Aptitude Tests (SAT) etc., scores, is not precisely known. The average total SAT score for all applicants may be 1150 one year and 1225 the next.
- Attempts to predict college success from the information gathered from tests and interviews yield correlation coefficients ranging from 0.4 to 0.7. Thus, the academic performance of individual applicants cannot be accurately predicted.

The problem in college admission decision making can be stated more specifically: What admission policy will minimize the adverse effect of the following factors?

- accepting a student who subsequently demonstrates the inability to do adequate college work;
- rejecting an applicant who had the potential to do adequate college work;
- accepting too few students such that the resultant enrollment is too low;
- accepting too many students such that the resultant enrollment is too high;
- accepting an applicant early in application processing which may result in denying admission to a better qualified applicant who applies at a late date.

The major concern in all admission policies is the criteria on which individual applicants are accepted or rejected. Although the admission decision relies on many, often subjective, bases, one of the major decision criteria is the predicted ability of the applicant to do college work. This ability to do college work is predicted primarily by high school grades and standardized aptitude tests and is closely tied to the college Grade Point Average (GPA).

The subjective bases, which include motivation to do college work and certain psychological factors, are evaluated by interviews, letters of recommendation and, to a much lesser extent, psychological tests. Considerable controversy exists over the applicability of intellectual predictive factors, e.g. Scholastic Aptitude Tests, high school grades, class rank, etc., in determining college admission. This controversy stems in part from the inability of these factors to predict college "success" as determined by college Grade Point Average. In addition controversy also exists over the relevance and desirability of the uncritical use of college GPA as a measure of success.

ALTERNATE APPROACHES FOR DECIDING UPON COLLEGE ADMISSION STRATEGIES

The major work in developing quantitative aids for the college admission problem has been the development of regression equations for predicting the college success, as determined by college GPA, of individual applicants. An example is shown below.[1]

Predicted Freshman Year G.P.A.

$$= -1.93 - 0.033* \text{(SAT: Verbal Test)}$$
$$+ 0.143* \text{(SAT: Math Test)}$$
$$+ 0.449* \text{Mean Value of Achievement Tests} + 1.187* \text{Adjusted High School Rank}$$

The correlation coefficient of the above equation is 0.627; the standard error is 0.519. This accuracy is representative of predictor equations in general.[2] Limited accuracy in predicting college success precludes the exclusive use of predictor equations in making individual accept/reject decisions. In addition, predictor equations do not address themselves to the whole college admission problem. They deal solely with the ability of only one individual to

A Simulation Model of the College Admission Process

do college work and neglect the problem of the college admission process.

Predictor equations can be used in conjunction with a cut-off score. When using cut-off scores, applicants, whose predicted G.P.A. is above a certain score, are accepted, and those whose predicted G.P.A. is below this score are rejected. A cut-off score can be set such that it yields the desired enrollment. This approach, however, does not adequately cope with the uncertainties associated with the parameters that are critical to the college admission process. In addition, it is important to be able to take into account the unique objectives of a particular institution when evaluating alternate admission policies.

For example, for a given institution, only a small penalty might be associated with enrolling 10–20 students more than the aim while a much larger penalty might be associated with a final enrollment 10–20 less than desired. The relative magnitude of these costs, or other costs, can greatly influence the selection of admission policy. Thus, a more comprehensive approach is proposed, where a decision theory format, which makes use of both predictive equations and cut-off scores, is used to account for the uncertainty associated with the parameters to the process. Under certain restrictive assumptions one can derive a closed form solution to this problem, but in order to provide complete flexibility a computer simulation of the process was agreed on.

In addition, the authors have always felt that to a large extent, the prophesied impact of computers on management decision making has failed to materialize and that this failure is largely due to insufficient attention to the integration of the experience, judgement, and imagination of the responsible manager with the mechanical processing power of the computer.[3] It must be remembered that the manager or admission officer, not the model builder, must remain in control of the decision making process. This problem thus provided an opportunity to not only improve the technical content of the solution procedure but also to improve the man-machine interface component.

A simulation of the college admission model was developed to address two problem areas:

- Due to the complicated and lengthy calculations in statistical decision theory, simulation becomes an effective method of evaluating many alternate college admission selection policies.
- For effective implementation of any operations research model, the decision maker must become intimately involved in using the model. A cause-effect simulation model showing the consequences of a given action can bring about this necessary involvement of and communication with the decision maker.

SIMULATION OF THE COLLEGE ADMISSION PROCESS

The simulator which was developed in modular form, consists of ten functional subprograms and nine general subroutines, all directed by a main or executive program. These subprograms define the college admission model. This modular approach was taken to permit isolated changes to be made with minimum disruptions to the remainder of the simulation system.[4] The basic time unit of this simulation was a month. This system runs for a period of five months with applicant selection policies being evaluated at the beginning and end of each month. Other time units can be used if desired. The basic functions of each of the subprograms and subroutines are described in the following section.

SIMULATION SUBPROGRAMS

Ten subprograms were developed, each of which describes a major part of the simulation of the college admission process. A flowchart of the system, showing the subprograms and their information flow, is seen in Figure 1.

PRIOR

This subprogram establishes the range and probability distribution for total applications, monthly rate of application arrival, acceptance/enrollment ratio, average applicant class quality and the standard deviation of applicant class quality. These prior distributions can be user input, if so desired.

SETAC

This program sets specific values for the five system parameters, mentioned in PRIOR, for each simulation run. Of course, neither the decision maker nor the subprograms that calculate admission policies have knowledge of the values set by this subprogram. Prior distributions of the system parameters, set by PRIOR, define the possible vlaues of the parameters established by SETAC.

CUTFST

The subprogram CUTFST uses the most recent information on system parameters to estimate the average number of applications that must be accepted to yield the desired enrollment and the cut-off score, in terms of predicted GPA, that will accept the correct number of applicants to yield the desired enrollment. This program also takes into account the uncertainty associated with the system parameters to calculate the standard error of these two. The standard error is then used to calculate the range of the number of acceptances required and the range of the cut-off score.

MINCUT

The subprogram MINCUT, a decision making program, calculates the single point selection

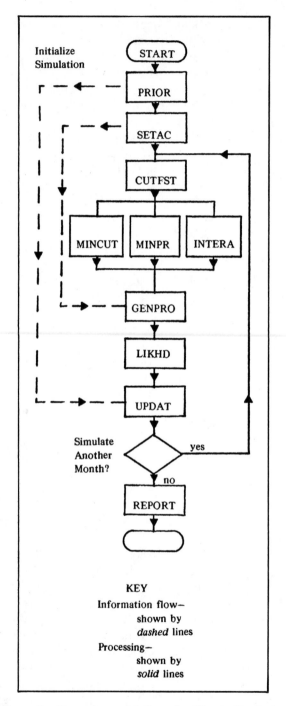

Figure 1. *Processing and Information Flow in Simulation Subprograms*

policy that minimizes the decision maker's objective function. This objective function consists of three costs:

- the cost of enrolling too many students;
- the cost of enrolling too few students;

- the cost of an enrolled student failing out of school due to inability to do adequate academic work.

The output from MINCUT is shown in Figure 2.

Figure 2. *Information Generated in the Subprogram Mincut*

The Following 3 Cases Illustrate the Calculation of the
Recommended Applicant Processing Policy

Acc/Rej Point	Number Accept	Average Enrollment	Enrollment Range
2.02	306.	185.	171–197
2.05	296.	178.	165–190
2.07	290.	175.	162–186

The Recommended Policy For March Processing:
    Accept Applicants: GPA Greater than   2.04
    Reject Applicants: GPA Less than   2.04
Total Applications Expected   401.
Total Applications Received   385.
    # Accepted   255.
    # Rejected   55.
    # No Action Taken   75.
Applications to be Received   15.
Applications Accepted   255.
    # Enroll As Freshman   56.
    # Turndown Offer   35.
    # No Response   164.
Effect of Recommended Policy
Total Applicants Accepted   296.
Total Applicants Rejected   104.
Resultant Enrollment   178.
Aim Enrollment   180.
Range of Possible Enrollments   165–191

Freshman Grades (Est) of Those Who Enroll	Number Students	Freshman Grades (Est) of Rejected Applicants If Had Been Accepted	Number Students
0.0–0.49	0.	0–0.49	8.
0.50–0.99	1.	0.50–0.99	13.
1.00–1.49	6.	1.00–1.49	22.
1.50–1.99	30.	1.50–1.99	30.
2.00–2.49	57.	2.00–2.49	20.
2.50–2.99	48.	2.50–2.99	6.
3.00–3.49	23.	3.00–3.49	1.
3.50–3.99	10.	3.50–3.99	0.

A Simulation Model of the College Admission Process

MINPR

The subprogram MINPR, a decision making program, calculates the two-point selection policy that minimizes the decision maker's objective function. This objective function consists of:

- the cost of enrolling too many students;
- the cost of enrolling too few students;
- the cost of exceeding the maximum applicant processing rate of the admission staff;
- the value of accepting applicants early such that the uncertainty of the acceptance/enrollment ratio is reduced.

INTERA

The subroutine INTERA is used when the simulation is operated in a conversational mode. This program permits the decision maker using this simulation to specify the selection policy to be used during any part of the processing year. This subroutine provides a cause-effect model for the decision maker.

The selection policy used by GENPRO is provided by one of two decision subprograms, MINCUT or MINPR or by the decision maker, through INTRA, if the simulation is being used in a conversational mode.

GENPRO

GENPRO is the basic subprogram in this simulation. For each time unit (in this analysis, a month) this subprogram:

- generates new applicants and their academic attributes according to predetermined arrival rates and an average and standard deviation of academic quality;
- accepts or rejects applicants based on an established selection policy;
- holds nonselected applicants in a queue for later processing;
- generates the response of accepted applicants, i.e., enrolling or not enrolling, according to a predetermined acceptance/enrollment ratio;
- generates the time of the above mentioned response;
- summarizes applicant processing to date.

The applicant arrival rate, total applications, applicant quality parameters and the acceptance/enrollment ratio are established by the subprogram SETAC.

LIKHD

The subprogram LIKHD takes the statistics generated from the monthly processing of applications of GENPRO and develops conditional probabilities or likelihoods for total applications, applicant class quality, and acceptance/enrollment ratio.

UPDAT

The subprogram UPDAT combines the conditional probabilities calculated in LIKHD with the prior probablities from PRIOR to calculate posterior probabilities for the system parameters previously mentioned.

REPORT

The subroutine REPORT summarizes pertinent data from each simulation run. An example of its output is shown in Figure 3.

EVALUATIONS BY THE SIMULATOR

The simulator facilitates the evaluation of various aspects of the model of college admissions process for given input data from a particular institution. Using this simulator the following assessments can be made:

(a) the value of having more precise estimates of total applications, the acceptance/enrollment ratio, and the applicant class quality.

For example, consider the acceptance/enrollment ratio average of 1.7. This implies that for every 100 students accepted, 59 students will

Figure 3. *Information Generated in the Subprogram Report*

Final Admissions Report	
Total Applications Received	360
Number Applicants Accepted	282
Number Applicants Rejected	78
Total Final Enrollment	190
Aim Enrollment	180

Cut-off Score That Would Have Yielded 180. Freshmen Was 2.02

Predicted GPA of Enrolled Applicants	Number Students
0.0–0.49	0
0.50–0.99	0
1.00–1.49	0
1.50–1.99	3
2.00–2.49	158
2.50–2.99	29
3.00–3.49	0
3.50–3.99	0

Actual GPA of Enrolled Applicants	Number Students
0.0–0.49	0
0.50–0.99	3
1.00–1.49	8
1.50–1.99	56
2.00–2.49	69
2.50–2.99	38
3.00–3.49	14
3.50–3.99	2

Applicant Processing Policy Summary

Month	Accept Applicants GPA Above	Reject Applicants GPA Below
November	2.14	0.93
December	2.11	1.65
January	2.08	1.83
February	2.06	1.88
March	1.99	1.99

A Simulation Model of the College Admission Process

enroll. This ratio historically ranges between 1.93 and 1.43 (standard deviation = 0.09). Therefore for every 100 students accepted, 50 to 70 students could enroll. This simulator determines the value of reducing the uncertainty associated with this ratio.

(b) the value of a more accurate predictor equation of college success. For example, consider the standard error of a given predictor equation to be 0.7. This implies that 95% of the time, an individual's actual G.P.A. will be ±1.40 Grade Points from this predicted G.P.A. This simulator determines the value of a more accurate predictor such as a predictor with a standard error of 0.5, which would result in an individual's actual G.P.A. begin [*sic*] within ±1.0 Grade Points from his predicted G.P.A.

(c) the effectiveness of a fixed, single point cut-off policy versus the effectiveness of a sliding two-point cut-off policy. In a fixed single point policy, all applicants whose predicted G.P.A. is above a certain point are accepted, whereas those whose predicted G.P.A. is below this point are rejected. The two point cut-off policy consists of upper and lower cut-off points. All applicants, whose predicted G.P.A. is above the upper point, are accepted; all applicants, whose predicted G.P.A. is below the lower point, are rejected. A decision is deferred on those applicants whose predicted G.P.A. lies between the two points. As additional information is received about the universe of applicants, the upper and lower cut-off points are updated and eventually converge.

(d) the sensitivity of alternate selection policies to various cost factors.

Using the simulator, two experiments were set up. The first established the value of reducing the uncertainty associated with the acceptance/enrollment ratio, and of increasing the accuracy of the predictor equation. The second experiment evaluated the two-point sliding cut-off policy versus the fixed, single point cut-off policy, and the sensitivity of these alternate policies to various cost factors.

In the first experiment a 2 × 2 factorial design was set up to establish the effect of acceptance/enrollment uncertainty and predictor equation accuracy on:

(a) the difference between the aim enrollment and the actual enrollment resulting from using a two-point sliding cut-off policy,
(b) the number of enrolled students who subsequently fail out of school,
(c) the total cost resulting from using a two-point sliding cut-off policy.

This cost is based on the difference between aim and actual enrollment plus a penalty associated with enrolled students who subsequently fail out.

The data from this experiment are shown in the table at the top of the facing page.

By reducing the variability of the acceptance/enrollment ratio from .09 to .06, the enrollment deviation was reduced from 9.5 to 5.0 (the average of tests A and B, and tests C and D). An analysis of variance indicated that this reduction in enrollment deviation was significant only at the 62.6% confidence level. The reduction in the acceptance/enrollment ratio reduced academic failures from 25 to 17 (the average of tests A and B, and tests C and D), and reduced the total cost of the system from $31,000 to $18,500. This decrease in costs represents the value associated with reducing the variability of the acceptance/enrollment ratio. The primary effect of predictor equation accuracy was to reduce academic failures from 28.75 to 12.75. Predictor equation accuracy had little effect on total cost.

In another experiment, the sensitivity to cost coefficients and prior information uncertainty of a fixed single point cut-off policy and a two-point sliding cut-off policy was evaluated using experimental design models. The two-point sliding cut-off policy was less dependent on prior information accuracy and less sensitive

Test	Standard Deviation Acceptance/ Enrollment Ratio	Predictor Equation Accuracy (Std. Error)	Aim-Actual Enrollment	Number of Failouts	Total Cost
A	.09	.50	13.5	15.5	$34,750
B	.09	.70	5.5	34.5	$27,250
C	.06	.50	5.5	11.0	$16,500
D	.06	.70	4.5	23.0	$20,500

to changes in cost coefficients. The accuracy of the two-point sliding cut-off policy was at least twice that of the fixed single-point policy.

SUMMARY

A systematic procedure for developing more accurate estimates of college admission parameters was established. This system quantitatively encodes subjective logic used by decision makers to combine historical data, statistically derived sample estimates from the current year, and subjective estimates of the decision maker.

This model allows quantitative incentives to be established by statistical decision theory as to the value of accurate estimation of system parameters. These techniques can provide guidelines for further research or policy changes on the basis of the value of more accurate information. Although predictor equation accuracy is important, there are other areas where more accurate information can have a very high value. For example, it was determined that one early response to an acceptance offer was worth approximately 1.5% of the marginal costs associated with too many or too few students. Perhaps financial rebates should be given to those accepted applicants who respond within two weeks of their acceptance. An example of further research to be done would be to determine if certain classification, e.g., in-state and out-of-state applicants, respond differently. Do these groups have different arrival rates or acceptance/enrollment ratios?

Also of importance was that this work was set in the framework of a cause-effect simulation model that allows a decision maker to interact more easily with this model. Easy man/model interaction is a prerequisite of model implementation.

ENDNOTES

1. Raj K. Minocha, "Development of Regression Equation for Prediction of Freshman Q.P.A. and Statistical Analyses of Students' Data," (unpublished Master's Thesis, University of Pittsburgh, 1968), p. 14.
2. Morris I. Stein, *Personality Measures in Admissions,* (New York: College Entrance Examination Board, 1963).
3. Curtis H. Jones, "At Last: Real Computer Power for Decision Makers," *Harvard Business Review,* Vol. 48, No. 5 (September/October, 1970), pp. 75–89.
4. Jacques Pezier, "Bayesian Methods in Decision Analyses Application to BOF Control" (unpublished Ph.D. dissertation, Thayer School of Engineering, Dartmouth College, 1971), pp. 15–31.

DISCUSSION QUESTIONS

1. Why is simulation such a useful tool in the admissions process?
2. How is regression commonly used in admissions decisions? Why isn't it more useful?
3. What are the results of a poor admissions policy?
4. What are the disadvantages of a modular approach to simulation programming?

Simulation for Fire Department Deployment Policy Analysis

David E. Monarchi
Thomas E. Hendrick
Donald R. Plane

16

BACKGROUND

In 1972, the mayor and the fire chief of Denver recognized the need to apply modern operations analysis to the Denver Fire Department. Several factors, which are detailed in [2], led to the formulation of a multi-disciplinary research team, organized by the Denver Urban Observatory. This team consisted of members of Denver's Fire Department Office of Budget and Management, and operations researchers from the University of Colorado. The team was led by Denver's Deputy Finance Director and the Director of the Denver Urban Observatory. The authors of this article acted as principal investigators. In addition, the research team was guided by a specially formed Policy Review Committee, consisting of the fire chief, several city officials, and a University dean. The research study was funded by HUD's Office of Policy Development and Research at a level of $140,000, of which $25,000 was an inkind contribution by the city and county of Denver.

The challenge given the research team was: Can the Fire Department provide approximately the same level of fire suppression service at a lower cost?

Reprinted by permission of *Decision Sciences*, Vol. 8, 1977, pp. 211–227.

Fire suppression activities account for about 90 percent of the Denver Fire Department's $13 million budget; of this 90 percent, most is allocated to fire fighters' labor costs. It currently costs Denver in excess of $250,000 *a year* to staff a fire engine or ladder truck[1] around the clock; in contrast, the vehicle itself may cost only $60,000 and the fire house has a one-time cost of $400,000. Because of this economic imbalance, the critical factor which accounts for most of the city's expenditures of fire protection and which impact most on the level of service is the number of fire companies (vehicles) and their location.

Static and Dynamic Analyses

Two approaches were used in the analysis of fire companies' locations. The first was a static analysis, which makes the assumption that every suppression vehicle is always available to respond to an incident. In the static analysis, two basic models were utilized. The first was a set-covering formulation designed to find the minimum number of companies and their locations that would satisfy a set of response time requirements. For Denver, the set-covering formulation contained 112 candidate locations for fire stations and 246 constraints. The research team developed and successfully utilized a hierarchical objective function for the set-covering problem. This objective function permits the simultaneous minimization of the number of the fire company locations and the maximization of the number of existing fire station locations within the minimum total number of fire stations [2] [3] [4] [5] [6].

The second static model, the Station Configuration Information Model (SCIM), is a

1. A pumper or engine is primarily responsible for putting water (or other means of extinguishment, as appropriate) on a fire. A ladder or truck is primarily responsible for rescue, and also serves as a "water tower" for directing a stream of water (provided by a pumper) down onto a fire. Typically, a city will have more pumpers than trucks.

descriptive device that demonstrates the consequences of any pumper/truck configuration specified by the user of the model. The configuration may be supplied judgmentally, or in combination with locations suggested by solutions to the set-covering problem. The consequences are shown using a variety of measures. For example, the SCIM provides estimates of average city-wide response times, average response time to different kinds of fire hazards, and frequency distributions of response times. It also shows the resulting service areas and the fire hazards within the service area of each fire company.

These two static models formed the basis for a tentative recommended configuration of fire companies, requiring five fewer companies than the existing configuration. According to static measures, the proposed configuration of companies provided an essentially unchanged level of fire suppression as measured by response time from fire house to fire incident. Details of the judgment, analysis and measurement of this proposed configuration may be found in [2] [3] [4] [5].

The second approach, and the focus of this paper, was a dynamic analysis of proposed and existing fire company configurations under different alarm rates. By dynamic, we refer to the realistic situation in which a vehicle may or may not be able to respond to an incident. In this situation, it may be necessary to provide a "cover" company to handle the incident. The specific method used for this dynamic analysis was a computer simulation model developed by the New York City-Rand Institute [1]. The primary purpose of using simulation was to explore the effects of changing alarm rate patterns upon the performance of the fire department for different fire company configurations when the "always available" assumption of the static approach is relaxed. Dynamic analysis allows the systematic study of alternative company configurations by allowing incidents of various kinds to occur throughout the city in such a way that

Simulation for Fire Department Deployment Policy Analysis

their pattern of occurrence, time required to respond, and the time to service the incident reflect, as closely as possible, the City of Denver's actual incident experience.

Fire Simulation Model

The dynamic analysis of company locations utilized three computer programs developed by the New York City-Rand Institute [1]. The first is an "incident generator," which creates a file that reflects what, where and when incidents occur and the equipment actually required to service them.

The second is a "simulator," which employs a mathematical model of the city's fire suppression system. The Model can reflect the system as it exists today or as it would exist with alternative company locations and/or dispatch policies. The simulator monitors equipment as it dispatches vehicles to incidents (which are defined in the incident generator), "services" incidents, and then returns the equipment to fire stations to await the next call. The process is repeated for a large number of events so that the analyst can observe how a given company configuration "behaves" while incidents occur throughout the city.

Finally, the third program, called "COMPARE," is utilized to compare (on an alarm for alarm basis) the behavior of the suppression system under alternative scenarios, such as different company locations dispatch policies.

A detailed description of the three programs is contained in [1].

Modification of the Simulation Programs—Each of the three programs was modified for use in this study. The incident generator was changed to provide a more appropriate mechanism for creating worktime distributions, and other parts, unnecessary for Denver, were deleted.

The simulator was changed in three ways. First, portions not applicable to modeling the activities the Denver Fire Department (such as

simulation of recovery times, accidents, and higher alarms[2]) were deleted. Second, the dispatching algorithm was changed to correspond to Denver's dispatch policy of sending the closest available units in terms of response time. Finally, difficulties caused by variations in the SIMSCRIPT compilers between IBM and Control Data Corporation computers required some program changes.

The "COMPARE" program was changed only to allow it to fit into the University of Colorado's CDC 6400 computer.

Data Requirements for the Incident Generator— The incident generator is a short SIMSCRIPT I.5 program that creates a file containing a sequence of alarms. For each alarm, information is generated on when it happens, where it happens, what equipment is required to work, and for how long. The incident generator develops a large set of events which closely replicate the kinds of emergencies which occur in Denver. In all of the dynamic experiments, the research team developed and used 1,000 incidents to test the effectiveness of alternative company configurations and dispatch policies. In order to determine the parameters used to create this sample of 1,000 incidents, the team analyzed the 18,000 incidents that actually occurred in Denver in 1972. First, a scheme for categorizing incidents was developed with the help of the Fire Department. The resulting incident codes, based largely on the "901" codes of the National Fire Protection Association, are contained in [3]. Each of the 18,000 incidents was assigned one of these codes along with other information relevant to the incident. The U.S. Census Bureau's ADMATCH program was then used to assign to each incident its (x, y) coordinates on a grid of the city, and the census block in which the incident occurred. This file became the empir-

---

2. Higher alarms, which are alarms that require more than the number of companies intially dispatched, comprise less than 0.1 percent of Denver's alarms.

ical backbone of the data base for determining the parameters for the incident generator.

The first major data requirement for simulation purposes was the determination of a set of discrete incident locations throughout the city. A uniform grid of incident areas was developed consisting of one-half mile square in most of the city, and one-fourth mile square in the downtown area. The downtown incident areas were rotated 45 degrees to match the angled streets in that area. A total of 458 incident areas resulted, and the centers of each became the "phantom boxes" for the incident generator and for the simulator. (The term "phantom boxes" is a fire department term denoting a specific intersection in the city.)

The second requirement was to specify the relative total frequency of alarms at each of the phantom boxes. This was accomplished by determining the proportion of alarms that occurred within the boundaries of each incident area.

The third data requirement was a specification of the different types of incidents that could occur in the simulation. For this purpose, the simulator required a definition of event types different from the incident codes. These codes define the *kind* of work performed at the scene of the incident; they are an objective description of the kind of emergency that led to a call to the fire department. For simulation purposes, however, two objectively similar incidents may be different both with respect to the time that elapses from the reporting of an incident until its extinguishment, and with respect to the number and types of equipment that perform work at the incident scene. For example, a single-family residence fire may require one pumper for five minutes (waste basket burning inside a residence); at the other extreme, it may require several pumpers and a truck for more than an hour (a working structural fire during high wind conditions). In the simulation, some of these single-family residence fires were grouped with other types of incidents that required one

pumper for five minutes (trash fires, weed fires, some automobile fires, etc.), and others were grouped with other types of "big" fires. The following terminology is used in distinguishing these aspects:

1. An Objective Incident type (O-type) is an emergency such as a building fire, rescue call, hazardous condition, or a false alarm.
2. A Simulation Incident type (S-type) is a grouping of all incidents that are alike in each of three attributes:
   (a) The number of each type of equipment (pumpers, trucks) required to do work at the incident;
   (b) The length of time each piece of equipment works (technically, a similarity among the probability distribution of work times rather than a similarity among actual work times);
   (c) The dispatch policy for that incident.

Figure 1 defines the 11 S-types used in this study.

The fourth data requirement for the incident generator was the specification of the frequency with which the various types of incidents occur at each phantom box in the city. The simulator requires that these incidents be classified by S-types; the data base had captured the incidents by O-types.

Figure 2 shows a simple example that illustrates the method used to convert the O-type for each of the 18,000 alarms in the data base into the S-type required by the simulator. Assume that a city has only three phantom alarm boxes and four objective incident types. Part (A) of Figure 2 shows the historical proportion of objective type incidents that occurred in the areas associated with each of the phantom boxes. For example, 50 percent of the incidents that occurred near Phantom Box No. 1 were building fires, 20 percent were vehicle fires, 20 percent were resuscitations, and 10 percent were animal rescues. Part (B) of Figure 2 shows the historical proportion of the O-type incidents that fell into

Figure 1. Classification of Incidents for the Simulation (S-Types)

S-Type	Equipment Required to Work	How Alarm Was Received
1	1 pumper	Phone
2	1 truck	Phone
3	1 truck	Box
4	1 pumper	Box
5	None (false alarm)	Box or phone
6	2 pumpers, 1 truck	Box or phone
7	1 pumper, 1 truck	Box or phone
8	2 pumpers, 1 truck	Box or phone
9	3 pumpers, 1 truck	Box or phone
10	3 pumpers, 2 trucks	Box or phone
11	4 pumpers, 2 trucks	Box or phone

Figure 2. An Example of the Conversion of O-Type Incidents into S-Type Incidents

(A)

Objective Type Incidents (O-Types)	Phantom Boxes		
	1	2	3
Building Fire	0.5	0.3	0.4
Vehicle Fire	0.2	0.5	0.2
Resuscitation	0.2	0.1	0.4
Animal Rescue	0.1	0.1	0.0
Total	1.0	1.0	1.0

(B)

Objective Type Incidents (O-Types)	Simulation Type Incidents (S-types) (Equipment Required to Work)			
	1 Pumper	1 Truck	2 Pumpers, 1 Truck	Total
Building Fire	0.1	0.8	0.1	1.0
Vehicle Fire	0.8	0.1	0.1	1.0
Resuscitation	0.9	0.1	0.0	1.0
Animal Rescue	0.2	0.8	0.0	1.0

(C)

Simulation Types (S-Types)	Phantom Boxes		
	1	2	3
1 Pumper	0.41	0.54	0.56
1 Truck	0.52	0.38	0.38
2 Pumpers, 1 Truck	0.07	0.08	0.06
Total	1.00	1.00	1.00

Simulation for Fire Department Deployment Policy Analysis

three hypothetical S-types. For example, the proportion of building fires that required only 1 pumper was 0.1; those that required 1 truck was 0.8; and finally, 0.1 of the building fires required 2 pumpers and 1 truck. Part (C) of the figure combines the data from parts (A) and (B) by matrix multiplication to obtain the frequency distribution of S-type incidents for each of the phantom boxes. For example, the proportion of time that 1 pumper will be required at Box 1 is 0.41, and is calculated as follows:

$$(.5 \times .1) + (.2 \times .8) + (.2 \times .9) + (.1 \times .2) = .41.$$

This proportion, 0.41, is conditional probability that one pumper is needed (the S-type), given that an incident has occurred at Box 1.

Using this approach, probability distributions over each of the 11 S-types were developed for all 458 phantom boxes. This process required collecting the data required to convert O-types into S-types (the type of data illustrated in part (B) of Figure 2). The required information was obtained from a stratified random sample of 1,099 incidents, categorized by O-types.

An analysis of the data resulted in grouping several O-types together because of their similarity in terms of the configuration of equipment that was required to work.

A special purpose computer program was written and utilized to:

(1) Associate each of the 18,000 incidents with one of the 458 phantom boxes.
(2) Compute the proportion of each O-type incident occurring within the incident area associated with each of the phantom boxes.
(3) Compute the proportion of alarms reported by telephone and by pull box for each phantom box.

The computations resulting from this program developed the probability distributions of the 11 S-types at each of the 458 phantom boxes.

Although each of the resulting 458 S-type distributions could have been used in the incident generator, it would have required a large amount of computer storage. Thus, a cluster analysis was performed to collapse them into a reduced number of distinct probability distributions. This procedure resulted in five clusters whose measures of similarity were strong. Two of the original five clusters were merged into the other three because they had so few members. The distribution of S-types across each of the three resulting groups [is] shown in Figure 3.

The final data requirements for the incident generator were estimates, for each S-type, of ser-

Figure 3. *S-Types Probability Distribution for Each Box Type*

		Probability		
S-Type	Description	Box Type #1	Box Type #2	Box Type #3
1	1P (Phone)	0.68802	0.33342	0.47791
2	1T (Phone)	0.01646	0.03637	0.05121
3	1T (Box)	0.02432	0.02792	0.03109
4	1P (Box)	0.01070	0.02519	0.02241
5	False Alarm	0.11819	0.41051	0.14487
6	2P, 1T (Non-Fire)	0.04664	0.07318	0.10575
7	1P, 1T	0.01839	0.01253	0.02725
8	2P, 1T (Fire)	0.04634	0.04240	0.08369
9	3P, 1T (Fire)	0.02370	0.02527	0.03827
10	3P, 2T (Structural Fire)	0.00580	0.00804	0.01192
11	4P, 2T (Structural Fire)	0.00144	0.00517	0.00518

vice time distributions for each piece of equipment working at the scene. The algorithm used to generate the work times for each piece of equipment for a given S-type is:

1. Generate the work time for the first-due pumper and/or the first-due ladder from its probability distribution.
2. The work times for other pieces of equipment required at the incident (if any) are obtained by multiplying the generated work time of the first-due pumper (ladder) by the ratio of the mean work time of the second-due (third-due, etc.) to the mean first-due time.

For example, an S-type 8 fire requires two pumpers. Assume a specific sample drawn from the probability distribution for the first pumper at an S-type 8 fire produces a work time of 10 minutes. Now assume that the mean work time for first-due pumpers for this type of incident has been estimated historically to be 6 minutes and the mean of the second-due pumper to be 2.4 minutes. The ratio is 0.4, so the work time assigned to the second-due pumper would be 4 minutes.

In all, six different incident files were produced by the incident generator for use in the simulation experiments. Each of these contained the same 1,000 incidents; they differed in their average inter-arrival times as defined by a Poisson process with different alarm rates. The selection of the six specific alarm rates is discussed later.

Data Requirements for the Simulator—The simulation model is a complex SIMSCRIPT I.5 program that reads a file of incidents created by the incident generator, dispatches equipment to "service" them, and tracks the behavior of the system throughout the run.

The data required by the simulator (in addition to that which it uses from the incident generator) can be divided into bookkeeping inputs and policy inputs. Only the more important bookkeeping and policy inputs will be mentioned here. For further data requirements, see [1] [2].

In utilizing the simulator, the city under examination can be divided into districts for use in aggregating the output data. Denver's seven chiefs' districts provided a useful aggregation scheme. Information on response times for first-, second-, third-, and fourth-arriving pumpers and on first- and second-arriving ladders was accumulated by the simulation program for each of the 11 different S-type incidents within each of the 7 districts. In addition, the program collected data on several combinations of these 77 classifications (*e.g.*, all incidents within a district, all districts for a specific type of incident, and all incidents for the city as a whole).

The policy options to be tested in the simulation are specified by providing the model with information on the dispatch policy to be used, the locations of every fire house, and the companies assigned to each location. The dispatching policy is specified by two sets of information. First, a "standard" dispatching policy for pull-box alarms is associated with each phantom box. For example, if Box 358 were assigned a standard dispatch of 2 pumpers and 1 ladder, any pull-box alarm received from that box in the simulation would be given that initial response. Second, the appropriate dispatch policy to alarms received by telephone must be specified. To duplicate Denver's actual dispatch policy in the simulation, a single vehicle dispatch to phone alarms of S-types 1 or 2 was specified. Dispatches to all other types of alarms were treated as if they were reported from a pull-box, even though a large proportion of them were reported by telephone, since the Department typically sends less than the full response to a telephone alarm only if it is of S-type 1 or 2.

The standard dispatching policy for pull-box alarms for each of the 458 phantom boxes was determined from the Denver Fire Department's Group Book. This book segregates the city into several hundred geographic zones and designates the specific number of pumpers and ladders to be dispatched to a typical alarm within any geographic zone. The research team determined the zone in which each of the 458 phantom boxes was situated and found the number of pumpers and the number of trucks that were to be initially dispatched. (The specific pumpers and trucks that are dispatched in the simulator are determined by their relative proximity in terms of response time and whether or not they are available to respond.)

Locations of fire stations and the assignment of companies to each of these stations for each of the simulation experiments was determined from the results of the static analysis described earlier and detailed in [2] [3] [4] [5]. The static analysis was able to reduce the original candidate sites to a set of 35 potential locations. All 35 locations were built into the simulation model, together with the flexibility to put both a pumper and a truck at each location and the ability to put two pumpers at the central station in downtown Denver. Then, depending upon the company configuration under consideration, the various pieces of equipment were selectively "activated" for each simulation run.

Validation of the Simulation Model—Much of the validity of the simulation model must be attributed to the degree of care exercised in gathering the data required for the simulation model. Several validity tests were made; the three that follow illustrate the validation approach.

(1) Average Response Time—The experiment to measure response times [2] found an average response time for 15,755 observations to be 121 seconds. The average response time from the simulation run that most closely approximates the time period in which these observations were taken (the 1973 average alarm rate of 2.5 alarms per hour) yielded an average response time of 116 seconds, or a difference of about 4 percent. This small difference is not important when

evaluating alternative fire company deployment policies and is probably not significant in any case.

(2) Actual Work Time Versus Simulated Work Time—For each company that existed in 1972, its actual proportion of department-wide pumper work time was compared to the proportion obtained from the simulation using the 1973 average alarm rate. The same comparison was made for trucks. Figure 4 presents a comparison of the actual and simulated work time percentages for selected pumper companies. It shows generally small differences between the actual and simulated results.

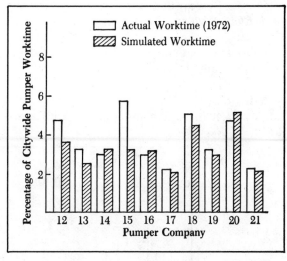

Figure 4. *Company Work-Time as a Percentage of Total City-Wide Worktime (Actual vs. Simulated)*

(3) Actual Incidents Versus Simulated Incidents—Figure 5 is similar to the previous histogram except it depicts the percent of department-wide pumper runs actually made by selected pumper companies in 1972 versus the percent of runs made in the simulation model using the average alarm rate of 1973. This histogram also shows that the simulation model rea-

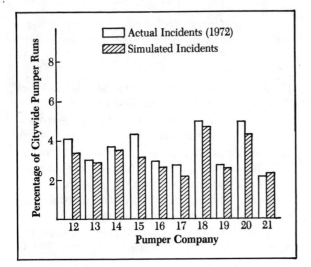

Figure 5. *Company Runs as a Percentage of Total City-Wide Runs (Actual vs. Simulated)*

sonably approximates the distribution of work for these companies.

In summary, the research team was able to satisfy itself that the simulator provided a rea-

sonable approximation to the behavior of the Denver Fire Department's fire suppression system.

The Simulation Experiments

A total of 17 simulation experiments were performed using various combinations of station locations and equipment configurations, alarm rates, and dispatch policies.

Denver's 1972 alarm data was analyzed and projections of future alarm rates were made. This analysis also showed that the highest rates of the year occurred between 5 p.m. to 10 p.m. during July. The variations in alarm rates by month and time of day are illustrated in Figure 6, which shows the time of day variations for July, the month with the highest alarm rate, and November, the month with the lowest alarm rate. The busiest period of the busiest month was used to obtain peak alarm rates for the simulation. To understand the behavior of the system during more typical periods, the average alarm rate (assuming that the alarm rate was

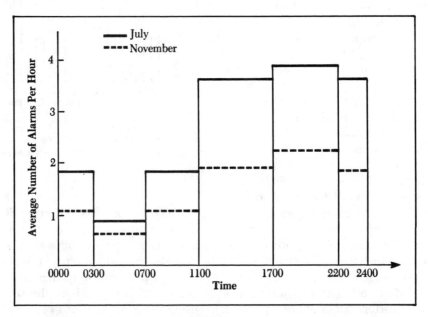

Figure 6. *Alarm Rate by Time of Day: July 1972 and November 1972*

Simulation for Fire Department Deployment Policy Analysis

constant throughout the day and throughout the year) was also used.

To account for a growth in alarm rates overtime, the historical annual growth rate of 13.5 percent was used. Projections were made for 1973, 1975 and 1978. Using these three years for both the peak and average alarm rates provided six different alarm rates for use in the simulation. These alarm rates range from 2.5 per hour (1973 average) to 9.65 per hour (1978 peak). The 1974 existing company configuration and the configuration proposed by the research team (which contained 5 fewer companies) were simulated for all six of these alarm rates. Other configurations, which were slight variations on the proposed configuration, were simulated at the 1973 peak alarm rate of 5.12 alarms per hour.

One further simulation experiment was performed to test the behavior of the suppression system under conditions of a reduced initial dispatch policy to all phantom boxes. Each box with an initial dispatch of "4 pumpers and 2 trucks" was reduced to a "3–pumper/2–truck" dispatch; all 3 and 2 dispatches were reduced to 3 and 1; and all 3 and 1 dispatches were reduced to 2 and 1. The results of this experiment indicated that the reduced dispatch was rarely insufficient, and that with the reduced dispatch policy, the first vehicle arrived slightly quicker, on the average. Such a policy is currently being considered at alarm headquarters and is likely to be implemented in the near future.

Results—The primary measure used in comparing the existing and proposed company configurations was the resulting average response time for the first fire suppression vehicle (pumper or ladder) to arrive at the scene of an incident. For the six alarm rates used in the simulation experiments, the first vehicle average response time for the proposed configuration and the existing configuration are shown in Figure 7. Note that for each alarm rate the average time is somewhat less for the existing configuration. The difference ranges from 7 seconds to 11 seconds, depending upon the alarm rate. This difference is in the opposite direction from the difference revealed by the static analysis [2]. In the static analysis, the existing configuration was slightly slower than the proposed configuration. Also, the average first unit response times as measured in the dynamic environment are slightly faster than the average first pumper response times for the static analysis. There are several reasons for these differences. First, alarms are assumed to occur at different locations in the two methods of measurement. The dynamic analysis used 458 phantom boxes, while the static analysis used 246 hazard locations. This accounts for part of the difference in the response times for static and dynamic analysis. A second factor is the difference in weighting factors in the two measurement schemes. In the static analysis, the alarm rate at each hazard location was not used to weight response times. Thus, the response time to every hazard is given equal weight in calcu-

Figure 7. *Simulation Results: Average Response Times for First Arriving Unit*

| | | Response Time (Minutes) | | |
Year	Alarm Rate Per Hour	Existing Configuration	Proposed Configuration	Difference (Seconds)
1973 Average	2.50	1.93	2.07	8
1975 Average	3.22	1.95	2.09	8
1978 Average	4.71	2.03	2.16	7
1973 Peak	5.12	2.04	2.19	9
1975 Peak	6.60	2.06	2.24	11
1978 Peak	9.65	2.14	2.33	11

lating the average. In the dynamic analysis, each phantom box is implicitly weighted by the alarm rate at that box. Hence, the higher density of alarms in areas of the city in which there is a higher density of companies would cause the simulation to produce a lower average response time. (Of course, response times in the static analysis can be weighted by alarm rates.)

Another important consideration in evaluating the predicted performance of a given configuration of fire companies is the occurrence of long response times. Figure 8 shows the number of responses, in a simulation of 1,000 incidents, in which the response time is greater than 5 minutes for the first vehicle. Note that for low alarm rates, the proposed configuration has fewer long responses. For high alarm rates, however, the proposed configuration has more long responses. The behavior at low alarm rates is explained by the better coverage achieved by better placement of the fire companies in the proposed configuration. But this configuration uses five fewer fire companies, and the effect of

this reduction of resources shows up at high alarm rates. For example, at the lowest alarm rate (2.50 alarms per hour), only 3 responses out of 1,000 (0.3 percent) are greater than 5 minutes for the proposed configuration, while 29 out of 1,000 (2.9 percent) are greater than 5 minutes at an alarm rate of 9.65 alarms per hour. For the existing configuration, 0.5 percent were greater than 5 minutes at the low alarm rate, but only 1.9 percent were greater than 5 minutes at the peak rate.

A final set of measures derived from the simulation program are the coverage statistics, some of which are shown in Figure 9. This figure shows that the percentage of phantom boxes that have either their first- or second-due unit of a particular type immediately available to respond is very close for the two configurations.

Comparison of Proposed Configuration With Existing Configuration—The static analysis showed that the average response time for first pumpers in the proposed configuration was superior to the corresponding average for existing configuration of locations. It showed a slight deterioration in response time for first truck. In Denver an average fire company is available to respond from its quarters about 95 percent of the time. Hence, the results of the static analysis provide a very good estimate of the level of fire protection provided to the citizens of Denver under any configuration of companies.

The primary purpose of the dynamic analysis was to ascertain whether there were hidden elements in the system that would cause problems when the non-availability of units that are working at incidents is considered. The simulation results showed that no such problems occur. Indeed, the number of long responses for the average alarm rates appear to be somewhat smaller for the proposed configuration. Of course, an extremely high alarm rate causes an increase in the number of long responses, but such peak periods occur very infrequently.

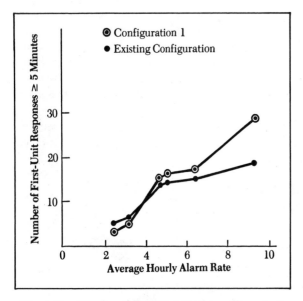

Figure 8. *Number of First Unit Responses Times ≥ 5 Minutes at Various Alarm Rates: Existing Configuration vs. Configuration 1 (Total Responses = 1000)*

Figure 9. *Coverage Statistics Simulation Results: Average Percentage of Phantom Boxes to Which First- or Second-Due Pumpers and Trucks Were Available to Respond*

Year	Alarm Rate Per Hour	Pumpers		Trucks	
		Existing Configu- ration	Proposed Configu- ration	Existing Configu- ration	Proposed Configu- ration
1973 Average	2.50	99.4	99.3	99.8	99.8
1975 Average	3.22	99.2	99.0	99.7	99.7
1978 Average	4.71	98.6	98.5	99.5	99.5
1973 Peak	5.13	98.3	98.1	99.4	99.2
1975 Peak	6.60	97.9	97.7	99.3	99.0
1978 Peak	9.65	96.8	96.1	98.6	98.2

In conclusion, the analysis showed that, using some of the static measures, the level of services is improved. The dynamic analysis failed to turn up any unanticipated problems. Hence, we concluded that the reduced number of companies could maintain approximately the existing level of suppression service.

Implementation: What Is Happening to These Recommendations?

In summary, using travel time as the measure of the level of fire suppression service, the research team utilized mathematical programming, simulation and heavy doses of judgment to produce a redesigned location of pumpers and trucks. This left the level of service essentially unchanged, with a reduction of five companies—from 44 suppression companies to 39 suppression companies. This reduction of five companies is being accomplished by closing obsolete stations and building new houses at better locations. In all, six new locations are recommended: two of these locations had already been budgeted and approved before the project began.

The project recommendations form a blueprint for fire department planning and capital budgeting for the next seven years. The plan was utilized heavily in the creation of the 1975 and 1976 fire department budgets. The 1975 budget was adopted by the Board of Councilmen

and its first stages were implemented. The Mayor's budget for 1976 reflected three station closings as recommended. However, the final outcome of this budget recommendation has not been determined due to strong opposition from the fireman's union. The Mayor's Office, Board of Councilmen, and the fire department are currently embroiled in this and related controversies.

This blueprint, if fully implemented in future budget decisions, will result in an accumulated net cost reduction of approximately $2.3 million over a seven-year period and a continuing annual cost avoidance of about $1.2 million, based on 1974 wage rates.

It is important to note, however, that this seven-year plan will not be blindly implemented; periodically, the plan will be reviewed to see if the recommendations are still appropriate in terms of the alarm rate experience, annexations and other changes in Denver's character. Such a review, performed in late 1975, revealed that the recommendations were still valid.

A final note concerns the use of the simulation in the implementation process. The original purpose of the dynamic analysis was to locate systemic problems which would not have revealed themselves in the static procedures. While the configuration of the Denver Fire Department was such that the simulation study essentially confirmed the static analysis assumptions, the simulation did serve a major role in this study through its use by the City of Denver as a tool to demonstrate the believability of this research's results. The fact that the City has been modeled in a dynamic environment provided a "more believable" method of presentation than was otherwise available through the straightforward set-covering techniques. This, of course, was in part due to the fact that the simulation effectively replicated the historical measures of 1972 so that the creditability associated with the predictions of the model was enhanced. This credibility was useful in "selling the results" of the study of the City and County of Denver.

REFERENCES

1. Carter, Grace. *Simulation Model of Fire Department Operations: Program Description,* New York: The New York City-Rand Institute, R—118/2—HUD/ NYC, December 1974.
2. Hendrick, Thomas E. and Donald R. Plane, *et al. Denver Fire Services Research Project Report; Feasibility Test of Applying Emergency Service Deployment and Facility Location Methods to Assist in Municipal Budget Decisions in the Fire Service,* Denver: Denver Urban Observatory, 1974.
3. Hendrick, Thomas E., Donald R. Plane, and David E. Monarchi, *et al., An Analysis of the Deployment of Fire-Fighting Resources in Denver, Colorado,* New York: The New York City-Rand Institute, R—1566/3—HUD, May 1975.
4. Monarchi, David E., Thomas E. Hendrick, and Donald R. Plane, "Simulation of the Denver Fire Department for Deployment Policy Analysis," Graduate School of Business, University of Colorado, Management Science Report Series, #75—24, November 1975.
5. Plane, Donald R. and Thomas E. Hendrick, *"Mathematical Programming and the Location of Fire Companies for the Denver Fire Department,"* Graduate School of Business, University of Colorado, Management Science Report Series, #74—9, (October 1974).
6. Plane, Donald R., David E. Monarchi, and Thomas E. Hendrick, "A Hierarchical Approach for Some Location Problems," Graduate School of Business, University of Colorado, Management Science Report Series, #75—25, November 1975.

DISCUSSION QUESTIONS

1. Why was an analysis of the Denver Fire Department necessary?

2. What are static analyses and how were they employed?

3. What is a dynamic analysis?

4. How was validation carried out on this model?

Network Analysis

Most realistic projects undertaken by businesses and non-profit organizations are large and complex. Constructing large manufacturing plants, projects undertaken by NASA, constructing a new building, installing pollution control devices, and many similar undertakings are projects that require careful planning and monitoring. The overall purpose of PERT and CPM is to plan and monitor sophisticated and complex projects.

Both PERT and CPM answer the same questions. These questions include when the entire project will be completed, what activities are critical activities, is a project on schedule, is the project on the specified budget, and are there enough resources to finish the project on time. In addition, such techniques as PERT/cost allow us to investigate the possibility of reducing project completion times while at the same time minimizing the cost and resources necessary for this reduction.

Project Control with Critical Path Scheduling

This article by Blevins and Pauler describes the fundamentals of project control using a construction illustration. The authors begin by discussing the similarities between CPM and PERT. PERT is a method primarily directed toward research and development projects, where a few of the activities have not been performed in the past. With CPM, it is assumed that there is more certainty concerning the project completion times. The initial analysis normally involves determining the necessary activities to complete a project, determining the predecessor activities, and estimating the time required to finish a particular activity.

One of the largest uses of critical path scheduling is in the construction industry. The authors describe the various activities involved in home building and develop a critical path for these activities, which include developing the foundation, framing, roofing, electrical, plumbing, appliance installation, painting, flooring, cleaning, and finishing. Using these activities and activity times, the authors develop slack times for activities and project network paths.

PERT and PERT/Cost for Audit, Planning, and Control

This article by Krogstad, Grudnitski, and Bryant discusses the use of PERT and PERT/cost for the planning and control of audits. Because of the increasing complexity and rising costs of audits, some type of scheduling and monitoring technique is needed. Furthermore, because of the need to accelerate audit completion dates under many circumstances and the fact that generally accepted auditing standards require that audit engagements be adequately planned, scheduling and control techniques are becoming increasingly popular for auditing.

This article discusses how PERT and PERT/cost can be used as a practical tool in solving everyday, auditing related problems. In this article, a hypothetical CPA firm is discussed in an auditing environment. The Barnes Company, a regional retailer of children's toys and garments, is the company undergoing the audit. With this example, the authors reveal how PERT and PERT/cost can be developed and successfully used. This article, furthermore, describes how time estimates can be obtained, the analysis and the determination of the critical path, and the concept and usefulness of slack times for activities.

Because PERT and PERT/cost can be difficult to implement by hand for large projects, the authors discuss numerous computer programs that can be purchased or leased to perform the required analysis. Computer programs selling for under $300 to computer programs with a price tag of approximately $24,000 are discussed in this article. In addition, the authors describe the importance of differential savings. Basically, these savings can be achieved through a more efficient audit and audit-sequencing system and from shifting administrative functions using the PERT/cost system.

Project Control with Critical Path Scheduling

David E. Blevins
Gerald L. Pauler

17

Critical path scheduling is a management tool which is useful for planning, scheduling, and controlling one-of-a-kind, usually very large, work projects. It was developed concurrently by government and industry in the decade of the 1950's. One of the most outstanding examples of the method's effectiveness in coordinating the activities of many people was its application to the Apollo space project.[1]

Critical path scheduling is most useful for construction projects, which almost invariably have a deadline with an associated penalty should the deadline not be met. It is to the benefit of the contractor to meet the deadline to avoid the penalty as well as to free resources for other projects. Unfortunately, however, many construction managers use intuition only, coupled, perhaps, with simple planning techniques, and the result is less than an optimal solution to the scheduling problems.

For small and moderate size projects, the critical path method can be applied to an advantage using pencil and paper techniques. For larger projects, there are readily available computer programs to simplify the calculations. The mathematical foundations on which the critical path method rests are quite sophisticated, but

Reprinted by permission from *Mississippi's Business,* Vol. 36, No. 4, February, 1978.

it is not necessary to master the underlying mathematics to be able to apply the *principles* of the method to project planning.[2] The result is better scheduling and progress tracking and, hence, greater work efficiency and cost savings for the contractor.

SCHEDULING MODELS

Two basically similar types of critical path scheduling are now in use: Critical Path Methods (CPM) and Program Evaluation Review Technique (PERT). PERT is a method primarily directed toward research and development projects, where some of the activities have not been performed before and which therefore include uncertainty as a part of the time estimate. Optimistic, pessimistic, and most likely time estimates of activity duration are made.[3] Then an expected activity duration is calculated based on these three time estimates. Once the expected activities are calculated for PERT, most of the remaining calculations are identical to those used in the CPM method. The exception is when the three time estimates using PERT are used to calculate probabilities of completing the events within the expected times.

CPM type models are useful where rather accurate forecasts for activity times may be made. The construction business is especially suited for this model, since activity times can often be accurately forecasted. It is well known, however, that even activities in the construction business are subject to uncertain delays. Still, the CPM technique is better suited to construction than to research and development activities.

INITIAL ANALYSIS

In devising a critical path analysis for any project, it is necessary to list three things:

1. Activities necessary to complete the project. (There must be a complete list of activities from the beginning to the end of the project.)
2. Predecessor(s) to each activity.
3. Estimated time required to complete each activity. When the planner has compiled these lists, a much better grasp of the project will enable the planner to construct a network graph and to calculate the Earliest Start Time (ES), Earliest Finish Time (EF), Latest Start Time (LS), and Latest Finish Time (LF) for each activity.

ILLUSTRATIVE EXAMPLE

A simplified list of activities and predecessors and of estimated activity times for constructing a house are shown in Table 1, Columns 1 through 4. Only the immediate predecessors of each activity are listed, with the understanding that if an activity is a necessary prerequisite for a second activity, then it is also a prerequisite for any third activity which has the second activity as a prerequisite. Columns 5 through 8 are results of calculations using the information in Columns 1 through 4. The procedures for making these calculations are discussed in the following section. The network diagram for this project is shown in Figure 1.

The question arises as to the degree of detail necessary in the activity list. It is usually easier to list general activities at first and from these construct an initial network diagram. Then it is possible to take the general activities and subnet them as necessary. Thus, the overall project can be kept easily in mind, while at the same time retaining control over each activity to any degree of accuracy desired.

SOLUTION PROCEDURES

The procedures for calculating the Earliest Start Time (ES), Earliest Finish Time (EF), Latest

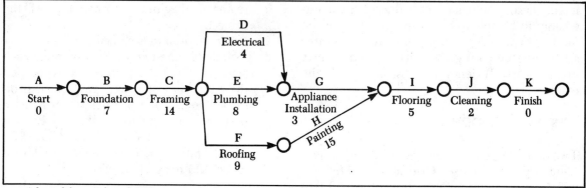

Adapted from Edward L. Summers, *An Introduction to Accounting For Decision Making and Control* (Homewood, Illinois: Richard D. Irwin, Inc., 1974), pp. 377–386.

Figure 1. *Simplified Network Diagram for Constructing a House*

Start Time (LS), and Latest Finish Time (LF) in Table 1 are as follows.

• ES of a particular activity = 0 if there is no predecessor activity; if there is a predecessor activity, then
ES = EF of the predecessor activity (or latest EF if more than one predessor activity is required).

For example, in Table 1, ES of activity B = EF of activity A which equals 0.
ES of activity H = EF of activity F which equals 30.
ES of activity G = EF of activity E which equals 29 because it is the *latest* EF of the *two* predecessor activities, D and E.

• EF of a particular Activity = ES of this activity plus Estimated Time required to complete this activity.

For example, in Table 1 EF of activity E = 21 + 8 = 29.

The calculations of ES and EF can be completed by progressing from top to bottom of columns 5 and 6 of Table 1, or from left to right in Figure 1. Then by progressing from bottom to top in columns 7 and 8 in Table 1, or from right to left in Figure 1, LS and LF values can be calculated.

• Set LF of "Finish" = EF of "Finish."
• LS for a particular activity = LF *minus* Estimated Time required to complete this activity.
• LF of any other particular activity = the *earliest* LS of the activities for which the subject activity is a predecessor.

For example, in Table 1 J is a predecessor to K. Hence, LF of J = LS of K = 52. LF of C = LS of F = 21, because this is the *earliest* LS of the three activities, D, E, and F, for which C is a predecessor.

SLACK TIME ACTIVITIES

The *Slack Time* for any activity is equal to its Latest Start Time (LS) minus its Earliest Start Time (ES) or its Latest Finish Time (LF) minus its Earliest Finish Time (EF). Either calculation will yield the same Slack Time value if there are no errors in the calculations of the ES, EF, LS, and LF Times. The Slack Time of an activity is

Table I. *Simplified Scheduling Table for Constructing a House*

Activity No.	Activity Description	Predecessor Activity	Estimated Time (Days)	Earliest Start (ES)	Earliest Finish (EF)	Latest Start (LS)	Latest Finish (LF)	Slack*
A**	Start	None	0	0	0	0	0	0
B**	Foundation	A	7	0	7	0	7	0
C**	Framing, Roof Underlay	B	14	7	21	7	21	0
D	Electrical	C	4	21	25	38	42	17
E	Plumbing, Insulation, Plasterboard	C	8	21	29	34	42	13
F**	Roofing, Siding	C	9	21	30	21	30	0
G	Appliance Installation	D,E	3	29	32	42	45	13
H**	Painting	F	15	30	45	30	45	0
I**	Flooring	G,H	5	45	50	45	50	0
J**	Cleaning	I	2	50	52	50	52	0
K**	Finish	J	0	52	52	52	52	0

*Slack Time = Latest Start minus Earliest Start or Latest Finish minus Earliest Finish
**Critical Activities

the number of time units (e.g., days, weeks, etc.) which this activity may be delayed without delaying the expected completion time of the entire project. Those activities having zero Slack Time (i.e., activities A, B, C, F, H, I, J, and K in Table 1) are called Critical Activities for just this reason. That is, according to our calculations, these activities cannot consume more than the estimated time required for their completion without delaying the completion of the project.

PROJECT NETWORK PATHS

In the simple network shown in Figure 1, it is easy to see that there are only three possible paths:

1. A-B-C-D-G-I-J-K requiring 35 days,
2. A-B-C-E-G-I-J-K requiring 39 days,
3. A-B-C-F-H-I-J-K requiring 52 days. This is the critical path, the longest path in the network.

For larger, more complex projects, it is difficult to draw a network depicting all the activities and their relationships. Listing the required activities, their estimated time, and their prerequisite activities is comparatively easy, however, and these three items are all that are needed to calculate an ES, EF, LS, and LF for each required activity. These values then furnish the manager with the data needed to develop an optimum schedule for the project. The reader is cautioned that should any activity require more *or* less than the estimated time for its completion, recalculating ES, EF, LS, and LF for subsequent activities is advisable, since the previously ascertained critical activities may have changed.

The manager may, of course, decide to move some resources from noncritical activities to critical activities in order to shorten the time for completing the project. Such manipulations are frequently possible. Of course, the ES, EF, LS, and LF calculations must be repeated after doing so to insure that *new* critical activities have not appeared as a result. For example, Activity H in Table 1 is presently a critical activity. If Activity H can be shortened 8 days, one can expect the project to be completed within 44 days. If, however, Activity F can also be shortened 8 days, one could *not* expect the project to be completed within 36 days, because Path 2 is expected to take 39 days. Naturally, any shortening of the time to complete activities common to all paths (i.e., A, B, C, I, J, and K) will not change the originally ascertained critical path, but its length (i.e., time duration) would change.

PROJECT CONTROL

After the critical path study is completed, the most useful application is in controlling the project. The planning that has gone into the analysis gives an insight into the project and enables the construction manager to quickly see any difficulties or delays that might lengthen or adversely affect completion of the project. The project director using such tools has much more readily available information on which activities need to be rushed and whether overtime is necessary in order to economically complete the project.

CONCLUSION

Critical path analysis provides a method of planning, controlling, and scheduling projects. Manual methods provide solutions if a computer is not available. Computer methods are available which require no programming knowledge other than that necessary to compile and correctly format the necessary input data. The time savings of the computer method over the manual method are considerable when the project is large and complex.

ENDNOTES

1. A. Kaufman, and G. Desbaqeille, *The Critical Path Method* (New York: Gordon and Breach, 1969).
2. Martin K. Starr, *Production Management* (Englewood Cliffs, N.J.: Prentice-Hall, Inc., 1972).
3. R. B. Chase and N. J. Aquilano, *Production and Operations Management* (Homewood, Illinois: Richard D. Irwin, Inc., 1977).

DISCUSSION QUESTIONS

1. Why is project control with critical path scheduling important in the construction industry?

2. In performing critical path analysis, what are the first steps that need to be performed?

3. Describe a fundamental difference between PERT and CPM.

4. What would happen if the roofing activity were delayed by two weeks in this particular problem?

5. What would be the consequence of delaying the electrical activity by one week?

6. The latest activity start time for the electrical activity is 38. What does this number mean?

PERT and PERT/Cost for Audit Planning and Control

Jack L. Krogstad
Gary Grudnitski
David W. Bryant

18

Increasingly complex audits, rising audit costs and accelerated audit completion dates all place emphasis on audit planning and control. Generally accepted auditing standards require that audit engagements be adequately planned and that assistants be properly supervised. In this article, PERT (program evaluation and review technique) and PERT/Cost are advanced as useful tools for planning and controlling an audit; the ready availability of computer packages enhances the potential of PERT and PERT/Cost for audit applications. The article focuses on how these tools can be of practical value to auditors in scheduling audit work, in allocating personnel resources, in predicting engagement completion time, in estimating audit costs, in anticipating work bottlenecks and in guiding audit acceleration. A simplified, hypothetical audit engagement is employed to demonstrate the principal features and advantages associated with the application of PERT and PERT/Cost in auditing.

PERT

PERT is an activity-network model designed for planning, coordinating and controlling complex projects with many interrelated tasks. Historically, the most extensive use of PERT has been in one-time projects (for example, Defense Department research and development projects, large construction projects), but PERT has recently been successfully applied to a broader range of projects. One example is its use in the preparation of consolidated financial statements.[1]

PERT is especially effective when applied to projects with many distinct tasks, with complex interrelationships between tasks and to projects where personnel scheduling and time constraints are of importance. It is also very useful where workload pressure is heavy, where teamwork is required and where great amounts of data are to be collected, sorted and combined again.[2] Applications that satisfy the following criteria are especially suitable to PERT modeling:

1. "There is a definite objective that can be achieved at a given point in time. . . .
2. "There is a completion date requirement for the objective event.
3. "There are many identifiable activities and events that must be completed in proper sequence before the objective event can be achieved.
4. "Time estimates can be made for the events and activities in the network.
5. "Resources can be shifted from one activity to another in order to affect the completion date of the activities in the network."[3] Independent public audit engagements satisfy all of these criteria. Burgher,[4] Cirtin[5] and Davis[6] report applications of PERT to actual audit programs. Cattanach and Hanbery,[7] Sully[8] and Waldron[9] encourage the use of PERT in planning and controlling audits. The following simplified, hypothetical audit engagement is integrated into this article to illustrate how PERT and PERT/Cost can be of value to auditors.

A Hypothetical Audit

XYZ, a CPA firm, has audited Barnes, Inc., for the last three years. Barnes, Inc., is a regional retailer of children's toys and games. Each of the three previous audits resulted in unqualified opinions. Barnes's yearend is December 31, and XYZ has agreed to provide the audit report on March 1, 1977, ten days before the annual board of directors meeting. During the slow month of August 1976, Boyd and Cain, manager and senior-in-charge, respectively, of the Barnes engagement, developed the audit plan shown in figure 1, page 265. Billing rates are indicated in parentheses below the various professional levels. Combining these rates with the budgeted hours leads to budgeted costs for the audit areas.

Boyd recalls that last year there was a 25 percent budget overrun. He attributes one-third of the overrun to unforeseen circumstances and the remaining two-thirds to poor planning. He estimates that poor planning resulted in approximately 130 hours and $3,400 in audit fees that were not billed to Barnes. In an effort to avoid another costly overrun, Boyd wisely decides to devote more time to audit planning. Thus, he spends an additional 17 hours planning this year's audit, including computer setup and analysis time, using PERT/Cost.

The Network

The network is the backbone of PERT. It provides an easily understood diagrammatic representation of the sequence of activities to be completed. Diagramming simple networks can proceed by trial and error. More complex projects require the completion of a work segregation structure, prior to actual network construction. Figure 2 illustrates the segregation of work for the Barnes audit.

After the component areas are identified, the audit is ready for diagramming. Each audit area is analyzed as a separate work package in

Figure 1. *Audit plan*

Audit areas	Time budget (in hours)				Total budgeted hours	Budgeted cost	Duration hours*
	Staff ($20)	Senior ($30)	Manager ($40)	Partner ($50)			
Planning 1976 audit		8	20		28	$ 1,040	20
Preliminary discussions with Barnes		1	2		3	110	2
Review internal control		8	2		10	320	8
Compliance tests		5			5	150	5
Yearend procedures	20	3	1		24	530	13
Field work:							
General audit procedures	7			8	15	540	11
Audit cash	31	7		3	41	980	19
Audit receivables	10	8	2		20	520	10
Observation of inventory	16	12	8	2	38	1,100	25
Inventory pricing	154	33	12	6	205	4,850	145
Audit other current assets	27	4			31	660	11
Audit fixed assets	29	9		4	42	1,050	22
Audit liabilities	102	28	15	8	153	3,880	93
Audit capital stock and R/E				1	1	50	1
Audit sales	10	5	1		16	390	6
Audit COGS	42	7	4	2	55	1,310	25
Audit other revenues and expenses	17	7	1		25	590	10
Lawyer's letter			1		1	40	1
Management's letter			1		1	40	1
Subsequent review	12	8	6	4	30	920	18
Prepare financial statements		12	3		15	480	15
Prepare tax returns			12		12	480	12
Partner/manager review			4	4	8	360	6
Total hours	477	165	95	42	779	$20,390	479

*Duration hours refers to the "net" time it takes to complete an audit area. Duration hours are less than total budgeted hours where audit areas permit simultaneous auditing by two or more audit personnel. Thus, to some extent, duration hours are variable depending upon the number of audit personnel available for an engagement and their assignment to various audit areas.

which the detailed audit activities are specified in chronological order. Figure 3 illustrates the liabilities work package for the Barnes audit. Each numbered circle (node) in the network, called an event, represents a distinct accomplishment of an audit activity. Sequencing activities (or events) requires determination of activities (events) logically preceding, concurrent to and succeeding the activity (event) under consideration. The arrows (lines) indicate the flow of progress through the network. The numeric subscript below each arrow indicates the hours budgeted for respective audit activities. The darkened line shows the critical path through

PERT and PERT/Cost for Audit Planning and Control

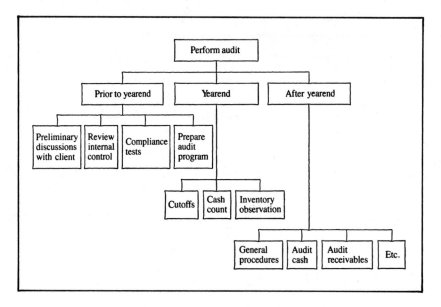

Figure 2. *Work Structure*

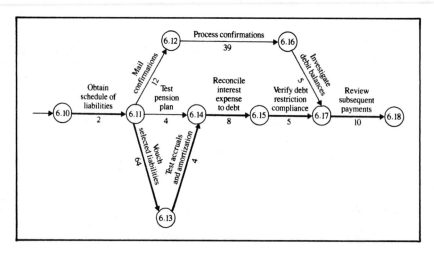

Figure 3. *Liabilities Work Package*

the network. The significance of the critical path is clarified later.

The final step in diagramming the Barnes engagement is accomplished by linking the various work packages together in chronological order. Figure 4 shows the engagement network or overall audit plan for the Barnes audit. It should be noted that subscripts below work packages correspond to duration hours (see Figure 1). The relationship between budgeted hours and duration hours is clarified further by reference to Figure 3. Some of the activities will be

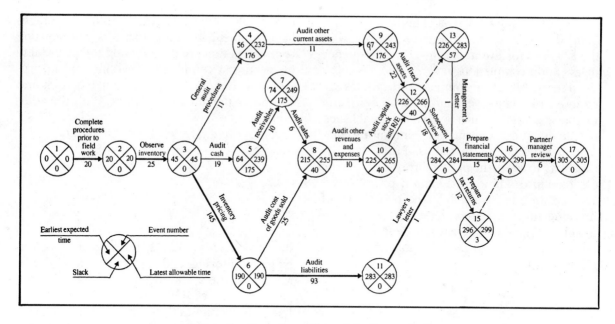

Figure 4. *Engagement Network for Barnes Audit*

performed simultaneously by different audit personnel. For example, while one staff auditor vouches selected liabilities, a second member of the audit team may be processing confirmations. Thus, only the critical path duration (93 hours) is carried forward to the engagement network (Figure 4), since 93 hours represents the "net" time required to complete the liabilities work package with the number of audit personnel assigned to this area.

The engagement network may be as detailed as desired. A relatively detailed network may be used in assembling time estimates and in controlling audit progress while a summary version may be provided the engagement partner. The summary version illustrated in Figure 4 depicts each work package as a simple engagement activity. Broken lines indicate activities which require zero time and no expenditure of resources. These "dummy" activities are used for clarity when two or more activities exist between any pair of predecessor and successor events.

Time Estimates and Critical Path

The most important element in PERT applications is accurate time estimates for activities. Good estimates enhance the effectiveness of PERT as a planning and controlling device. Fortunately, auditing's time budget orientation, coupled with large amounts of prior history on comparable audit activities, usually provides the auditor with reasonably good time estimates. Typically, auditors are familiar with the condition of a client's books, the effectiveness of internal control, the actual work times from previous audits and the likely problem areas of the current engagement.[10]

Once estimated times are determined for all activities in the network, the critical path is found by adding the estimated times of the activities along each alternative path. The critical path is the longest path through the network.[11] It is indicated in the Barnes engagement network by the darkened line in figure 4 (events 1, 2, 3, 6, 11, 14, 16 and 17). All audits have a critical path, but auditors seldom recognize it as such without the aid of network analysis. The term "critical path" denotes a sense of urgency. Any delay in the activities (or events) in the critical sequence delays audit completion.

Frequently, audit completion deadlines are imposed by clients, regulators or others. Even in the absence of such externally established deadlines, auditors normally communicate completion expectations to clients. PERT has the capability to assess the probability of meeting the completion deadline as the audit progresses.[12] If, according to firm policy, the probability of finishing the audit after the deadline becomes too high, then the firm may decide to add more personnel to shorten the duration time of the critical path.

Slack Time

Another method an auditor may use in analyzing an audit network is based upon calculation of slack time both for various audit activities and for alternative paths through a network. The less slack time the more critical an activity or path, and vice versa. Slack is computed by subtracting the earliest expected time from the latest allowable time. The earliest expected time is the earliest time that an activity can be expected to start, because of its relationship to preceding activities. The latest allowable time is the latest time that an activity may begin and not delay the completion date of the audit. Slack is determinable only in relation to an entire path through the audit network and is shown in Figure 4 in the lower portion of each event node. Activities along the critical path have a maximum slack of zero. All noncritical activities have positive slack. Resource availability is identified in the Barnes engagement by slack times for activities leading up to events 4, 5, 7, 8, 9, 10, 12, 13, 14 (as an activity on noncritical paths) and 15.

The PERT network model can assist an auditor in sequencing audit detail work (including work requested from client personnel), in effi-

ciently allocating personnel resources, in highlighting potential audit bottlenecks, in estimating completion time, in determining the probability of meeting a completion deadline and in providing a framework for relevant feedback and control as the audit progresses. With the addition of the cost variable, however, PERT becomes even more useful to an auditor.

PERT/COST

PERT/Cost adds to PERT the capability for planning, monitoring and controlling audit costs. Moreover, the addition of the cost component permits analyses involving time/cost tradeoffs. For example, an auditor can analyze the time/cost efficiency of various audit personnel in each audit work package and can estimate the impact on audit costs of varying the duration of the audit or any of its constituent activities.

Valid cost estimates are essential if full benefit is to be derived from PERT/Cost. Several approaches are available for developing cost estimates.[13] However they are determined, cost estimates probably are best associated with work packages (see Figure 3). The estimated total audit cost then is found by totaling the costs of the individual work packages. This approach leads to realistic audit cost estimates and permits continuous reassessment of estimated total cost as an audit progresses. Actual costs for individual work packages can be broken down by professional level (that is, staff, senior, manager and partner) and compared routinely with estimated costs, and reports can be generated that highlight deviations. The ready availability of pertinent cost information, which corresponds with engagement activities and personnel allocation, facilitates effective front-end audit planning and timely audit control decisions. The Barnes audit illustrates the value of PERT/Cost for front-end audit planning.

Front-end Audit Planning

Boyd used the PERT/Cost model to analyze alternative personnel allocations for each audit work package. For example, last year's inventory pricing required 192 hours of staff time, 30 hours of senior time, 8 hours of manager time and 6 hours of partner time. Multiplying hours by the billing rates of the four professional levels shows that this personnel scheduling plan resulted in a total cost of $5,360.[14] This year, Boyd estimated the relative efficiency per dollar of cost for each professional level in each work package. With the aid of a computer, time/cost analysis quickly revealed that Boyd's time and Cain's time would be more time/cost efficient than a portion of staff time in the inventory pricing work package.

The specific effect of PERT/Cost planning in the inventory pricing area was to substitute 4 hours of manager time ($40 per hour) and 3 hours of senior time ($30 per hour) for 38 hours of staff time ($20 per hour). Here the manager's and senior's general competence and familiarity with Barnes's inventory enabled them to apply overall tests of reasonableness to a major segment of inventory in lieu of staff performance of more time-consuming detail price vouching. Total cost for the inventory pricing work thereby was reduced to $4,850 (see budgeted cost in figure 1).[15] The resulting $510 saving illustrates how PERT/Cost's ability to incorporate personnel time/cost tradeoffs can reduce overall audit cost.

Accelerating the Audit

All auditors, at one time or another, are faced with the need to accelerate or expedite an audit. If auditors lack an effective expediting plan and are only vaguely conscious of expediting costs, their tendency is to hurry audit procedures currently being performed so that they can rush on to other audit steps. Additional personnel may be assigned to the audit without a clear understanding of the impact such assignments will have on audit duration and cost. In a situation requiring audit acceleration, PERT/Cost is particularly valuable in guiding an auditor to the specific activities that should be expedited to achieve the desired acceleration at minimum additional cost.

Personnel assigned to expedite noncritical activities do not accelerate audit completion. PERT/Cost first directs attention to activities along the critical path. Next, the order in which critical activities should be expedited is determined. The objective of PERT/Cost in this instance is to accomplish the greatest time reduction for the least additional cost. Acceleration times and costs are estimated. Acceleration time is the minimum practical duration time to which an engagement work package can be reduced. Acceleration cost is the total cost associated with this minimum practical duration time of the work package. Acceleration times and costs are then related to normal times and costs for each work package as follows:[16]

$$\text{Cost per hour} = \frac{\text{Acceleration cost} - \text{normal cost}}{\text{Normal time} - \text{acceleration time}}$$

The cost per hour determines the order in which critical activities are shortened. The duration of the critical activity with the smallest cost per hour is shortened first. Other activities, in order of their progressively higher costs per hour, are shortened until the overall duration of the audit conforms to the accelerated completion deadline. The Barnes audit provides an illustration of the acceleration procedure.

Assume that the Barnes audit has progressed 106 duration hours along the critical path. The audit is on schedule and is within the cost budget as a result of Boyd's use of PERT/Cost. A need for acceleration arises when Boyd is informed by Barnes's controller that merger negotiations have been initiated with a toy man-

Figure 5. Acceleration of Barnes Engagement

Work package	Normal Time	Normal Cost	Acceleration Time	Acceleration Cost	Cost per hour	Order of acceleration — First Time	Order of acceleration — First Cost	Order of acceleration — Second Time	Order of acceleration — Second Cost
Inventory pricing	84	$2,813	56	$4,521	61			−10	$610
Audit liabilities	93	3,880	63	4,720	28	−30	$840		
Lawyer's letter	1	40	1	9,999	—				
Preparation of financial statements	15	480	15	9,999	—				
Partner/manager review	6	360	6	9,999	—				

ufacturer. The controller urgently requests delivery of the audit report one week (40 hours) earlier than originally agreed. Boyd assures Barnes's controller that he will attempt to comply with the acceleration request.

Figure 5, this page, shows how Boyd accelerated the Barnes audit with minimum additional cost. PERT/Cost directs attention to the critical activities. These are listed in sequence in the first column. Since the audit has progressed 106 duration hours along the critical path, the duration time (normal time) remaining for the inventory pricing activity is 84 hours, and the corresponding normal cost still to be incurred is assumed as 58 percent (84/145) of estimated total cost for this work package (see Figure 1), or $2,813.

Since this is an extremely busy period for XYZ, no idle auditing personnel is available in the firm for assignment to the Barnes engagement. Thus work package durations (not budgeted hours) can be reduced only by application of personnel at overtime rates, by increased use of more experienced professionals (i.e., seniors, managers and partners) and similar cost-inflating alternatives. Such considerations lead to the estimated acceleration times and costs for inventory pricing and auditing liabilities in Figure 5. Arbitrarily high acceleration costs ($9,999) are assigned to lawyer's letter, preparation of financial statements and partner/manager review to

indicate that these work packages cannot be expedited.

The work package with the smallest cost per hour is auditing liabilities. The 40-hour acceleration plan first reduces the duration of this work package by 30 hours at an additional cost of $840. Reference to figure 3 shows one reason for the small cost per hour in the liabilities area. The activity "vouch selected liabilities" leading to event 6.13 is critical within the work package and very time-consuming. Further, this audit activity can be accomplished effectively with relatively lower-paid, staff level professionals because of the nature of the audit activity and because such personnel can be efficiently integrated into the Barnes audit within a few days. Accelerating inventory pricing is relatively less cost efficient because of the high cost of immediate, temporary personnel reassignments and the greater tendency to utilize higher-level professionals in emergency situations than is required by the nature of the audit activity. Accordingly, the expediting plan includes utilization of additional staff at overtime rates in vouching liabilities so as to reduce the duration of this activity from 64 hours to 34 hours. This shortens the duration both of the liabilities work package and of the critical path for the Barnes engagement by 30 hours. The remaining 10-hour decrease is achieved by expediting inventory pricing (10 hours for $610). Hence, Boyd achieves the desired acceleration for a total additional cost of $1,450. Had Boyd made the mistake of fully expediting inventory pricing, acceleration would have resulted in additional costs of $2,044 (28 hours × $61 plus 12 hours × $28). By focusing only on critical work packages and by accelerating on the basis of cost per hour, PERT/Cost has held expediting costs to a minimum.

Implementation Guidelines

The following guidelines provide the auditor direction in initiating PERT/Cost for audit planning and control:

1. The single most important planning document is a work segregation structure, since it provides the framework for developing the PERT/Cost network. All basic work packages of the audit engagement should be identified and clearly labeled.
2. The work packages should be arranged in chronological order, from earliest to latest starting date. Component activities within each work package should be identified, where possible, and sequenced. Each activity should be numbered and should bear a description that is of sufficient detail to be meaningful to the PERT/Cost user.
3. Time estimates should be assigned to each activity. It is desirable to subdivide activities having estimated time durations of more than five days.
4. The audit planner now is ready to finalize personnel needs for the engagement in terms of numbers of professionals and skill levels. Skill levels may be categorized into partner, manager, senior and staff. Frequently, more than one skill level is recognized in senior and staff categories. As a general rule, skill level categorization should reflect all the different billing rates. For large audit engagements, a matrix showing personnel involved in each work package may be of value.

5. The work package networks now can be shaped by determining the set of predecessor-successor relationships. These relationships are of two types: predecessor activities that must be finished before a successor activity can be started, and predecessor activities that must be finished before a successor activity can be completed.
6. The audit engagement network is formed by linking the work packages together in chronological (sequential) order. Two considerations are of importance in this step: (a) the degree of concurrent execution of two or more work packages is not only a function of the predecessor-successor relationships among work packages, but also is a function of the audit personnel available and (b) the network should be made as meaningful as possible to the auditors who ultimately will carry out the work. For example, where work packages have no strict predecessor-successor relationships with other work packages, they should be arranged in their order of appearance in the financial statements.
7. A first-pass critical path analysis should be performed. Based on the outcome of this first-pass analysis, the audit planner may wish to change activity sequences, to shift personnel among activities or work packages, to change the composition or number of persons assigned to the audit or to make no changes in the engagement network.
8. Depending on the decision in step no. 7, individual auditors should be assigned to specific activities, beginning with the earliest activity and proceeding through the network. Care should be taken to achieve a balanced workload for all audit personnel.

PERT/Cost Software

PERT/Cost analysis may be done manually. However, computers are of great advantage when engagements are large and complex. A firm may wish to tailor PERT/Cost computer software to its specific requirements by using in-house computer development personnel. Alternatively, it may be more practical to obtain a generalized PERT/Cost package from a software vendor.

Vendor-supplied PERT/Cost software varies widely in terms of capability and cost. At one end of the spectrum, the FOCUS system, marketed by Westinghouse and carrying a price tag of $24,000, accommodates 12,000 activities, accumulates costs by time period or cost center, handles up to 8 personnel levels per activity and provides up to 30 optional reports. At the other end of the spectrum is VPERT, a minicomputer-based PERT system marketed by Varian Data Machines. It sells for $300. PERT/Cost software packages with capabilities between these extremes are available on a monthly lease basis, on a charge per activity rate and on a time-sharing basis.[17]

Typical of the PERT/Cost software systems at the lower end of the cost spectrum is IBM's Project Management System IV. System IV can be leased from IBM at $100 to $300 per month, depending on the options selected. Moreover, the fee for management training in the application of PERT/Cost and other control techniques is $532 per person. This is a one-time charge for a limited number of people in the firm. Most other setup and operation costs are variable.

For example, based on an audit engagement that is budgeted at $20,000, involves 500 professional hours, spans 12 weeks and contains 25 work packages and 125 activities, the approximate differential costs to setup and operate the PERT/Cost system are estimated in figure 6, this page.

Differential Savings

What differential savings result from PERT/Cost implementation? Basically, savings can be divided into two categories: (1) savings that result in more efficient audit sequencing and personnel allocation and (2) savings that result from shifting administrative functions to the PERT/Cost system.

It has been illustrated that activity sequencing, personnel allocation, audit control and engagement acceleration can be accomplished efficiently with PERT/Cost. The capacity of a computer-based system to utilize numerous personnel and cost inputs, incorporate time/cost trade-offs and simulate various allocation strategies, far exceeds human abilities. Differential savings will vary with different audit situations

Figure 6. *Differential Costs*

Setup costs		Operating costs	
1 Preparation of predecessor-successor activity sequence (4 hours at $50 per hour)	$200	1 PERT/Cost software package rental, pro-rated over five audit engagements* (12 weeks at $40 × .2)	$ 96
2 Professional training in the use of PERT/Cost (4 hours at $40 per hour)	160	2 Machine time (12 hours at $50 per hour)	600
3 Conversion by clerk of audit activities to PERT/Cost source data form (8 hours at $5 per hour)	40	3 Data preparation for update of engagement progress (24 hours at $5 per hour)	120
Total estimated setup costs	$400	Total estimated operating costs	$816

*It is assumed that the CPA firm uses the PERT/Cost system for five audit engagements during the same 12-week period.

and are not precisely predictable. However, it is realistic to expect that PERT/Cost will provide substantial cost savings on most audits and facilitate quality control.

PERT/Cost also can be expected to reduce administrative costs substantially within a public accounting firm. Usually three professional levels (senior, manager and partner) have administrative responsibilities on each audit. Some routine clerical and feedback tasks are necessary to enable each professional to discharge his or her responsibilities. For example, actual times normally are recorded by each auditor working on the engagement for every audit step performed. Periodically, these times are manually totaled and compared with budgeted times, and significant deviations are reported to higher administrative levels. PERT/Cost requires that actual times be recorded and encoded only once (for example, on a punched card). All calculations, comparisons and exception reporting then is performed by the system. Relevant control information is available to all administrative levels within minutes. Suppose, for example, that a senior devotes just two hours a week to these administrative functions. Over a 12-week audit engagement, this administrative function alone can add $600 to $800 in audit fees to the client's bill.

On a much larger scale, consider the accounting firm which has a number of audits simultaneously in progress. This situation presents an administrative task of much greater complexity. A PERT/Cost system, however, by treating each audit as a work package, can accomplish corresponding firmwide administrative savings. For those administrative functions that PERT/Cost can perform, experts suggest that a conservative rule-of-thumb is that a 50-percent cost reduction should be experienced. Thus, a firm might estimate the dollar value of the time absorbed by such administrative functions, and compare one-half of that amount with the differential cost of implementing and operating a PERT/Cost system. This savings alone may be substantial.

CONCLUSION

PERT and PERT/Cost are established managerial tools. Analysis of these tools in an auditing context strongly suggests that their use can lead to improved audit planning and control. Many CPA firms are equipped with computer facilities and capable systems personnel. Systems consultants and PERT and PERT/Cost software packages are readily available to all firms. The potential benefits presented in this article should stimulate experimentation with these tools. Perhaps PERT and PERT/Cost can be applied initially to small audits or to individually significant work packages. As familiarity with the tools increases, applications to larger, more complex audits can follow.

ENDNOTES

1. Dan A. Bawly and Joseph M. Dotan; "Using PERT in Accounting Reports," *Management Services,* July–August 1970, pp. 29–36.
2. Ibid.
3. Gordon B. Davis, "The Application of Network Techniques (PERT/CPM) to the Planning and Control of an Audit," *Journal of Accounting Research,* Spring 1963, p. 97.
4. P. H. Burgher, "PERT and the Auditor," *Accounting Review,* January 1964, pp. 103–20. *Review,* January 1964, pp. 103–20.
5. A. Cirtin, "Network Analysis—Audit Planning Tool," *CPA Journal,* May 1976, pp. 34–36.
6. Davis, pp. 98–100.
7. R. L. Cattanach and G. W. Hanbery, "Audit Planning: An Application of Network Analysis," *Accounting Review,* July 1973, pp. 609–11.
8. J. M. Sully, "Critical Path Analysis," *Accountant,* May 1975, pp. 608–10.
9. R. S. Waldron, "PERT as an Audit Tool," *Accountancy* (England), January 1967, pp. 8–10.
10. A technique combining three time estimates recognizes the uncertainty of a single estimate and gives PERT predictive capability. This approach solicits (1) the most optimistic, (2) the most likely

(modal) and (3) the most pessimistic time estimates. A weighted average of the three estimates yields an *expected time*. The formula to compute expected time (E) is:

$$E = \frac{o + 4m + p}{6}$$

Where o = the most optimistic time,
m = the most likely time and
p = the most pessimistic time.

11. The critical path is not fixed in relation to the network. It may shift to an alternative sequence of events due to an acceleration of the original critical path or a sufficient delay in any noncritical activity. For example, assume the audit of other revenues and expenses in the Barnes engagement discloses irregularities. After consultation with Barnes's audit committee, XYZ expands its audit in this work package to 60 hours. Now a subcritical path through the engagement network (events 1, 2, 3, 6, 8, 10, 12, 14, 16 and 17) becomes critical.

12. This requires use of the three-way time estimate approach which allows for calculation of the variance for each activity. The variance (σ^2) can be approximate with the formula $\sigma^2 = \left(\frac{p-o}{6}\right)^2$ where p = the most pessimistic time and o = the most optimistic time. An alternative is to develop the complete network using single time estimates and then recompute only the critical path using three-way estimates. This allows for probabilistic assessment of completion time without incurring the time and cost involved in making three-way estimates for all audit activities in the network. The probability of completing the audit on schedule is determined by the number of standard deviations (R) between the completion deadline (D) and the expected completion time (E). The formula for making this calculation is:

$$R = \frac{D - E}{\sqrt{\Sigma\sigma^2}}$$

Where: $\sqrt{\Sigma\sigma^2}$ = the square root of the sum of the variances of the activities on the critical path.

For example, assume that on December 30, 1976, Boyd determines that the expected completion time required on the Barnes engagement is 58 eight-hour days (464 hours). The variances associated with the activities on the critical path sum to 256 hours. Since the completion deadline for the audit is March 1, 1977 (60 eight-hour days hence), the probability of the audit being completed on schedule is determined as follows:

$$R = \frac{480 - 464}{\sqrt{256}} = \frac{16}{16} = 1 \text{ standard deviation}$$

Based upon the statistical properties of the normal distribution, there is an 84 percent probability that the Barnes engagement will be finished by March 1 (50 percent probability it will be finished in 58 days plus 34 percent probability it will be completed between the 58th day and March 1).

13. Don T. DeCoster, "PERT/Cost: The Challenge," in *Information for Decision Making: Quantitative and Behavioral Dimensions*, ed. Alfred Rappaport (Englewood Cliffs, N.J.: Prentice-Hall, 1970), pp. 253–57.

14. Billing rates for the four professional levels (indicated in parentheses in figure 1) are taken as surrogates for relevant costs of personnel. Breakdown of estimated audit costs into variable and fixed (direct and indirect) components greatly increases the usefulness of PERT/Cost which focuses primary attention on variable (direct) costs.

15. Cost estimates should reflect the relative scarcity of personnel at the various professional levels if optimal allocation on a firm-wide basis is to be approached.

16. George J. Nenzel, "The Critical Activities Network," *Journal of Systems Management.* August 1971, p. 41.

17. See *ICP Software Directory*, July 1975, pp. 549–62, published by International Computer Programs, Inc., 1119 Keystone Way, Carmel, Indiana 46032, for descriptions and costs of a wide variety of PERT and PERT/Cost software packages. PERT software systems are also available from time-sharing organizations with no substantial capital outlays required for computer equipment.

DISCUSSION QUESTIONS

1. What are some of the conditions that make a technique such as PERT useful for planning and controlling?

2. Would the techniques discussed in this article be applicable to other situations?

3. What do the authors mean by "accelerating the audit"?

4. Is it possible to determine the probability of project completion when three time estimates are not made for each activity?

5. What are some of the software packages available to perform this type of planning and control?

Markov Analysis

The overall objective of Markov Analysis is to investigate events or probabilities by analyzing current events and probabilities. Markov Analysis assumes that the system we are looking at starts at some initial state or condition. Furthermore, Markov Analysis assumes that the factors that cause the system to change over time remain the same. When expressed in probabilities, these factors are normally embodied in a matrix of transition probabilities. Markov Analysis can also be used to predict equilibrium conditions in the long run.

Student Flow in a University Department: Results of a Markov Analysis

Bessent and Bessent, in their article on student flow in a university department, describe the use of Markov Analysis in an academic setting. The purpose of their paper is to reveal the modeling of student flow in order to establish more effective admissions policy at the University of Texas at Austin.

As a result of the Markov Analysis, a number of interesting results were obtained. For example, students who withdraw are likely to remain unenrolled for the next semester. The probability of graduation for a student who has been advanced to candidacy is about 0.18. Using steady state analysis, it was determined that in the long run approximately 51 students would be in the dissertation stage. This and similar analysis provided a model for limiting enrollment as a function of the number of faculty members, the number of new programs implemented, and other factors that have an impact on faculty load and involvement with students during the dissertation process. In this setting, Markov Analysis was used to predict how students would progress through a graduate program and what impact this would have on faculty loads. This information was then used to control enrollments in the graduate program to avoid faculty overloads.

Student Flow in a University Department: Results of a Markov Analysis

E. Wailand Bessent
Authella M. Bessent

19

In university departments which strive to maintain high quality graduate programs, the availability of qualified professors to supervise dissertation production is a scarce resource which can be overextended easily before the problem is detected. The problem arises because of the lag between the time students are admitted and the time they are advanced to candidacy, which is the first point requiring the formal appointment of a dissertation supervisor.

The purpose of this paper is to present an easily implemented procedure for modeling the student flow system so that admission policy can be set to maintain control of faculty load and number of graduates at desired levels. While the procedure—a Markov analysis—is not a new one, the application is in an area and of a size which has received little attention from Management Science.

Markov modeling has been used extensively in macro-analysis of social systems for such purposes as manpower planning, studies of voting behavior, social mobility, and marketing. An excellent brief review of applications and a concise introduction to Markov concepts is found

Reprinted by permission of E. Wailand Bessent and Authella M. Bessent, "Student Flow in a University Department: Results of a Markov Analysis," *Interfaces*, Vol. 10, No. 2, April, 1980, Copyright 1980 The Institute of Management Sciences.

in McNamara [1974]. Reviews of applications in other fields suggestive of similar applications in educational systems may be found in the special issue of *Operations Research* [May-June, 1972].

Reports of microanalytic studies are uncommon although they are beginning to appear. For example, a recent report by Meredith [1973] of a geriatric ward of a state hospital is similar to the present study. Applications in educational systems are even more rare in the literature and, when found, deal with large systems such as the study of teacher mobility in San Diego schools reported by Greenburg and McCall [1973].

The present study is unique in that it reports a small scale application used for an actual policy decision at the university department level. Successful implementation was enhanced by having a department member participating in the OR team who presented the findings and made the recommendation. The second team member, an OR specialist, constructed the model and analyzed the data.

CONTEXT OF THE PROBLEM

Over the years, the Department of Educational Administration at The University of Texas at Austin has admitted students for doctoral studies without any policy for the number to be admitted into various programs in any given time period. Informal limitations in some programs are based on the number of students who can be successfully taught in entry level courses, but overall, the enrollment has been primarily a function of success in recruiting and/or availability of stipends for support of students. An examination of enrollment by years shows a generally stable condition, suggesting that the market is reasonably efficient in that the natural operation of factors affecting enrollment has been a satisfactory basis for planning departmental resource requirements. In short, no admission limitation policy has been required.

In recent times, some changes have taken place that might make future needs for faculty positions somewhat more uncertain. Two new programs were initiated and a major foundation grant was received in the last three years. In addition, changes in the public school work force appear to be affecting recruiting of students in ways that may change historical student flow from that stream into continuing doctoral programs.

Because of these and other factors, it was decided that a study of student flow through the program was needed so that some basis would exist to determine how admissions related to available faculty resources and what adjustments might be required if admissions increased. (The department had experienced a history of full placement of graduates at appropriate job levels and there had been a recent no-growth policy for College of Education faculty. Consequently, the number of graduates was constrained by faculty resources rather than by the job market.)

The Problem
The study was designed to answer the following questions:

1. At any given time, what is the probability that students who have been previously admitted will be enrolled, but not advanced to candidacy, withdrawn for one or more semesters, or advanced to candidacy and pursuing dissertations?
2. What is the average length of time students will spend in the program phases listed in (1)?
3. How many students, on the average, will be enrolled for dissertation study given the number previously admitted?

THE MODEL

Finite Markov chains have the needed computational properties in that knowledge of the probability of progressing from one state to another in one semester allows one to calculate estimates which will help answer the questions given above [Budnick, Mohena, and Vollman, 1977]. The required conditions for an appropriate application of a finite Markov chain are:

1. A finite number of discrete states. A student may be enrolled, withdrawn, advanced to candidacy, or not advanced. Various transition chains through these four states fully describe the student flow process for the present purpose.
2. The probability of progressing from one state to another in one time period (transition probabilities) is independent of all prior states except the current state (Markov property).
3. The transition probabilities remain fixed over time (stationarity). University requirements for granting a Ph.D. have changed relatively little in the span of a decade.
4. If transition matrices for different persons are to be combined, then these persons must be homogeneous with respect to the system modeled. Though this assumption was not fully met, all students must satisfy the same admission, advancement, and completion criteria and this was accepted as sufficient homogeneity.

The program states were modeled as a Markov chain with five transient states (a state which one may leave at any transition) and one absorbing state (one which, once entered, is never left). The absorbing state included was graduation; another possible absorbing state—forced withdrawal—was not included after an examination of the data indicated a low incidence which would have given near zero probability for that state. Likewise some possible transient states were excluded as a simplifying measure for the model. The most questionable of these deletions was the exclusion of states representing different periods of time that one has been

enrolled. Over time, the probability of advancement or graduation begins to diminish. Thus predictions for the near future are more accurate than those for longer periods of time.

The model, like all simplifications of complex processes, requires certain assumptions. In the present instance, the Markov chain requires an accurate assignment of each student to one of the defined states at each semester. The states and the Markov chain are shown in Figure 1. Transition probabilities shown on the arrows will be discussed at a later point. Let us consider the states, some of the ambiguities of assignment and how they were resolved.

(S1) When is a student enrolled in a doctoral program? Most students are admitted to doctoral study when they initially enroll, but some students are in non-degree programs which they may later continue by using their prior study as the core program for a doctorate. This makes it difficult to determine at what point certification study (not in model) becomes doctoral study (S1 in model). This problem was resolved by including any student who later continued course work whether or not he advanced to candidacy.

(S2F) When is a student advanced to candidacy? There are several steps involved in this process but since registration for the dissertation course required completion of all these steps and was available data, this was used to assign a student to S2F—the first semester of advancement to candidacy.

(S20) Students in S20 were those enrolled for the second and subsequent semesters of advancement to candidacy. They were considered to be in a separate state from students in their first semester of advancement (S2F) because at least two semesters of registration for the dissertation were required before graduation, giving a zero probability of graduating (S5) from the first semester of dissertation registration (S2F).

(S3 and 4) Is a student who has not re-enrolled still in the system or has he exited? It was observed that students who were not en-

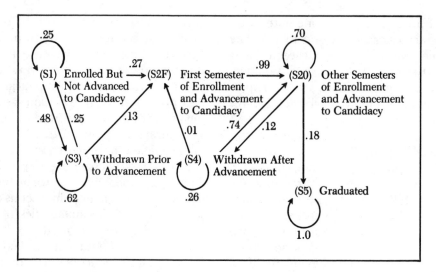

Figure 1. *Student Flow Model from Entry to Graduation*

rolled in a given semester might (and usually did) re-enroll at some subsequent time in the period studied and hence remained in the process. The practical consequence of this was that, once enrolled, a student was counted in the system unless he graduated.

(S5) Graduation was defined as the semester in which a student was awarded his degree. For many students, this was really an additional semester after he had completed all requirements but too late for graduation that semester. In that event, he registered *in absentia,* but available data did not distinguish this from regular registration, hence it was disregarded.

THE DATA

The years from fall semester 1969 to the fall semester 1978 were chosen for data. Grade sheets for every semester and summer session were examined and casual students and students from other departments were eliminated from the list.

Working from the list, a transition matrix was calculated for each successive semester or summer session by tabulating each student with respect to the state he was in the previous semester or summer session and the state he was in the subsequent semester.

Twenty periods were studied in all and a transition matrix was calculated for each year by taking the average number in each state for summer session, fall, and spring. Inspection of the transition probabilities indicated a satisfactory degree of stationarity with respect to time units and a mean of all ten years was used as the expected value of transitions among all states.

Some errors of coding undoubtedly exist since work was done by different sets of student volunteers during two different semesters. The transition matrices were prepared by the authors and were carefully checked.

Results
The transition probabilities for the student flow (shown in Figure 1) may be interpreted as the probability that a student from a given state will be in a given state at the next time period. For

example, it was found that students who have not advanced to candidacy have a 0.25 probability of remaining enrolled but not advanced in the following semester, a 0.27 probability of advancing to candidacy, and a 0.48 probability of not being enrolled in the following semester [Kemeny and Snell, 1960].

The transition probabilities revealed that (1) the continuation rate is low for students not advanced to candidacy and once withdrawn, they are likely to remain unenrolled for the next semester; (2) students who have advanced to candidacy are more likely to remain enrolled and if withdrawn, are more likely to re-enroll in the next time period; and (3) the probability of graduation in a given semester for students who have advanced to candidacy is about 0.18.

Average Time in Program States

The transition probabilities were used to calculate the mean number of times that a student in the system will be in a given state. These mean stay times indicate the average number of semesters (or summer sessions) the student will be in a given state for different starting points. The recurrence may not be continuous, but is cumulative over the period of time in the system. Calculated stay times showed: (1) a student may be expected to enroll for 2.3 semesters (or summer sessions) and will be unenrolled for 3 semesters before advancing to candidacy, (2) a student will be enrolled for dissertation about 6.6 semesters before graduating and the stay time is the same whether or not he has withdrawn previously, (3) students who withdraw prior to advancement are withdrawn an average of 4.65 semesters and the mean withdrawal time after advancement is 0.92 semesters, (4) students who withdraw after advancement are withdrawn an average of 2.26 semesters, and (4) about 12.8 semesters or 4.3 calendar years elapse from entry to graduation and stay time is longer (13.7 semester) for those starting from nonenrollment prior to advancement.

Mean Number of Changes of State

The number of times that a student may be expected to be in a given state before graduation was calculated, but it is not clear from that information whether there is a large transiency with students entering and withdrawing frequently after short periods of enrollment or whether students tend to remain continuously enrolled. The transiency factor can be assessed by calculating the number of state changes and by comparing results to stay times in corresponding states. It was found that students do not frequently leave and re-enter states during their degree programs even when the stay time is long. For example, although students may be withdrawn three semesters prior to advancement to candidacy, they tend to withdraw only one time.

Steady State Probabilities and Dissertation Load Estimates

If one assumes the continued experience summarized in the transition probabilities, we can think of a system that has reached a steady state and cell probabilities can be used to calculate long-run expectations. Put more simply, the proportions of the student group in each state at any given time can be estimated [if it] is reasonable to assume that inputs and outputs are balanced.

The required simplifying assumption that those completing are replaced one-for-one by students entering seems tenable in that the resulting steady state probabilities match observed experience reasonably well. Steady state probabilities indicated that the largest proportion of students (0.51) were in the states requiring dissertation supervision (S2F and S2O). This finding was consistent with the stay time estimates presented earlier.

About a third (0.31) of all students might be unenrolled at any given time. Most of these (0.24) were not advanced to candidacy.

POLICY IMPLICATIONS

It was pointed out earlier that the problem arose because of concern in a university department that the number of admissions to doctoral study was creating a future problem of faculty overload when students arrived at the point of requiring dissertation supervision. In dealing with such a problem in a period of austerity when new faculty cannot be added to absorb the imbalance, the department has no throttle for control—only a brake. There is no humane or feasible way to accelerate students' progress through a doctoral program without serious damage to program quality. Hence, the most accessible control is to limit enrollment through admission policy.

Four most likely circumstances would cause such a policy to be invoked: (1) an increase in the average number of qualified students applying for admission to existing programs, (2) the implementation of new programs enrolling additional students, (3) a loss of faculty positions to other departments with high growth rates, and (4) exogenous factors such as changes in the economy that would force students to extend their programs by extended periods of parallel employment.

In any of these events the department requires (1) a decision-making process that monitors the system to detect changes before serious imbalances occur, (2) an algorithm for calculating the needed adjustment, and (3) a decision rule to determine when the process is in acceptable balance. The Markov chain analysis provides a basis for monitoring and detecting system changes.

First, as a monitoring device, the stay times and steady state probabilities provide information on the long-run expectations for proportions of admitted students in various states of the process the length of time before an imbalance has its effect. In the calculations just presented, for example, we see that on the average 0.51 of the enrollment is in dissertation pro-

duction, which begins an average of five semesters after a student is admitted and lasts an average of seven semesters.

We can estimate, therefore, that a sustained average increase of only two additional students per semester will increase average dissertation loads by one in nine semesters after the increase begins (assuming 10 faculty members). The number of dissertations per faculty member continues to increase for three additional semesters (12 semesters before leveling off—total average increase of 1.6 per faculty member in all). This is a rather sensitive response in the small system studied, but the lead time is sufficient to detect and control effects. With a current mean of five dissertations, the system would be at capacity (assuming six as a desirable average) with only the small change of two in mean number of admissions. With this small margin it is recommended that close monitoring of admission trend and recalculating transition probabilities, stay times, and steady state probabilities annually be part of the departmental policy.

Secondly, two alternative computing algorithms to give estimates of needed adjustments were suggested:

Alternative 1. Under no change in number of faculty positions, status quo can be maintained by estimating the number of admissions required to replace those expected to graduate since the process is already in a steady state. As was illustrated, an average sustained increase in admissions without a balancing increase in graduates would overload the present faculty in eight semesters.

Alternative 2. Under a decrease or increase in faculty positions and/or a sustained increase or decrease in numbers of qualified applicants, the timing and number of allowable admissions can be estimated. Let $\bar{d}$ be the mean number of dissertations at time of change, $\bar{c}$ be sustained change in mean number of admissions, and F_i be the number of FTE faculty available for dissertation supervision in semester i.

Table 1. *Estimates of Effect and Enrollment Changes*

Number of Semesters after Change	Average Number of Dissertations per FTE Faculty (ADF)	Assuming Five New Fellow- ships/Year
1-4	$\bar{d}/F_1$	50/10 = 5 (dissertations per faculty member)
5	$(\bar{d}+\bar{c})/F_5$	$(50+5/3)/10=5.2$
6	$(\bar{d}+2\bar{c})/F_6$	$(50+10/3)/10=5.3$
—	•	•
—	•	•
—	•	•
h	$[\bar{d}+(n-4)\bar{c}]/F_n$	$[50+5(n-4)/3]/10=$ ADF
—	•	•
—	•	•
—	•	•
12[a]	$(\bar{d}+8\bar{c})/F_n$	$(50+40/3)/10=6.3$

[a] After 12 semesters, entries begin to exit and ADF remains constant assuming the conditions employed in the example.

Employing the table in the system studied, for example, would begin with $\bar{d} = 50$ and $F_0 = 10$, hence $\bar{d}/F_0 = 5$. If a new program is initiated providing for five new fellowships a semester and with no change in FTE faculty, the result would begin to be observed in the fifth semester with the increases in dissertation shown in the table above.

Finally, the procedure provides a specification of the decision rules the department should adopt as part of the policy: (1) the maximum average number of dissertations per full-time equivalent faculty member; (2) in case of new programs, the FTE faculty positions required before the program can be accepted; and (3) in cases of loss of faculty positions, the lead time required to avoid serious imbalance of dissertation load.

To conclude, it should be emphasized that, since the above suggestions are based on a probabilistic model, the suggested policy is not to be interpreted as producing deterministic outcomes. The policy should not be used to seek an immediate correction or a precise adjustment in expected outcomes. The validity of the model should be verified and adjusted by comparing annual observed outcomes with projected outcomes.

ENDNOTES

McNamara, James F., 1974, "Markov Chain Theory and Technological Forecasting," Chap. 14 in *Futurism in Education*, Hencley, Stephen P. and James R. Yates (eds.), McCutchan Publishing Corporation, Berkeley, CA.

A number of applications of Markov models are reviewed in *Operations Research*, 1972, Vol. 20, No. 3, May-June.

Meredith, Jack, 1973, "A Markovian Analysis of a Geriatric Ward," *Management Science*, Vol. 19, No. 6, February, pp. 604–612.

Greenburg, David and McCall, John, 1973, *Analysis of the Educational Personnel System*, Part I: Teacher Mobility in San Diego (R-1071-HEW), Rand Corporation, Santa Monica, Calif.

A concise introduction to Markov chains is found in Budnick, Mohena, and Vollmann, 1977, *Principles of Operations Research for Management*, Richard D. Irwin, Inc., Homewood, Ill.

All calculating formulas except steady state probabilities can be found in Kemeny, John D. and J. Laurie Snell, 1960, *Finite Markov Chains*, D. Van Nostrand Co., New York: Chapter 6, pp. 43–58. Steady state formulas employed are on p. 72.

DISCUSSION QUESTIONS

1. What are some of the major problems investigated in this article?

2. What are some of the assumptions made in applying Markov analysis to this particular problem?

3. What states were used in predicting student flow from entry to graduation?

4. Would this type of analysis be appropriate for settings other than dissertations in a department of education?

5. What benefits were obtained by using Markov anlaysis in predicting student flow patterns?

Implementation

A recent study conducted by Thomas and DaCosta determined that more than 80 percent of the firms responding to their questionnaire used quantitative analysis. Approximately 40 percent of these users of quantitative analysis didn't start applying these techniques until the late 1960s. This indicates that quantitative analysis is still a relatively new approach to many firms and organizations.

Implementing quantitative analysis results is the final step of the quantitative analysis approach. This approach includes defining the problem, developing a model, acquiring input data, developing a solution, testing the solution, analyzing the results, and implementing the results. If any one of the steps above implementation is incorrectly or not completely performed, implementing the results can be either difficult or impossible.

In the past, major reasons for problems encountered in implementation include a lack of commitment of users, resistance to change, and a lack of user understanding concerning the models and quantitative analysis techniques used. Other difficulties with implementation include a lack of data access, poor communication, solutions outdated because of changes, and shortages of funds, workers, and computer access time. Realizing these traditional problems and barriers to successful implementation can help managers and decision makers in successfully implementing quantitative techniques.

Implementation of Quantitative Techniques: A Managerial Perspective

This first article by Freeman and Mulkowsky presents both the problems and potential solutions to implementing quantitative techniques. The orientation of the article is to describe in easy-to-understand terms some of the traditional problems that have blocked the successful implementation of quantitative analysis approaches. Then, the authors discuss some of the managerial techniques that can be used to enhance the successful implementation of a quantitative technique.

One of the largest barriers to successfully implementing quantitative analysis techniques is the lack of involvement of the operational staff. This is true for both external consultants and internal employees that are used to perform quantitative analysis. Another problem dealt with is that analysts who develop quantitative analysis solutions are often unaware of the organizational politics. Other potential barriers include limitations inherent in the techniques, poor communication, and inadequate presentation of the results and the conclusions that can be drawn from quantitative analysis.

One of the biggest needs in more completely implementing quantitative analysis techniques is to broaden the roles and horizons of the technical analyst who is involved with developing the quantitative analysis solutions. This procedure starts with clarifying the role of the technical analyst and then directly involving the analyst with the operational staff and other managers and decision makers who will be the ultimate users of quantitative analysis results. Such cooperative efforts should then allow superior understanding and improved communication between managers and analysts.

Fantasies, Fundamentals, and a Framework in Corporate OR
This article by McArthur pinpoints many of the misconceptions and problems of implementing quantitative analysis or operations research (OR) techniques. The author starts off by discussing many of the misconceptions that OR or quantitative analysis people have. Some of these misconceptions are that OR people fit in like "one of the gang," everyone will cooperate in carrying out a quantitative analysis study, and when I feed the data into the computer program, I'm near the end. Then McArthur describes some of the common mis-

conceptions that managers have. These include that the manager knows what the problem is, that the OR analyst is really a computer person, and that it will take very little time before the OR analyst will show results.

There are a number of ways that a quantitative analysis person can determine or measure the impact of his or her analysis on the decision-making problem. A number of questions can be asked, such as what level in the organization does the quantitative analysis function report, and how much does management participate in the quantitative analysis project? There are also a number of guidelines for failure and there are a number of guidelines that can tell you whether or not the project has been successful.

One of the most important factors in successfully implementing quantitative analysis techniques is closing the gap between managers and the quantitative analysis personnel. One of the best approaches, as discussed by Professor Woolsey, is to become one of them. In addition, quantitative analysis people must show that they are sensible people, they must accept responsibility, they must become more effective in applying quantitative techniques to business problems, and they may decide to move into line management positions. A number of rules to implement a quantitative analysis technique successfully include working *with* the business, not *for* it, working on important problems, keeping it short, getting the job done, presenting the results simply and positively, helping implement the results, and working as individual consultants as well as members of a team.

Implementation of Quantitative Techniques: A Managerial Perspective

Michael Freeman
Gary Mulkowsky

20

When Operations Research/Management Science first introduced the concept of using quantitative techniques to solve problems faced by managers, it was hailed by many as a harbinger of revolution in executive decision making. Words like "scientific," "rational," "analytic" and so on abounded. And there is no question that management sciences and information sciences, together with contributions from related fields, have had a considerable impact on the decision-making process. It has become increasingly apparent, however, that quantitative techniques are not as widely used as was originally hoped.

One of the major contributions of OR/MS has been in the area of problem definition. The OR/MS approach helps to clarify problems, separate symptoms from sources, and to take a wider view so that alternative solutions can be developed and an "optimum" one chosen. Increasingly, however, it has been the experience of practicing managers that the technical analyst, rather than aiding in problem definition, tends to define "the problem" in terms of the techniques available. Often the only techniques considered are those that the analyst is familiar with, a dangerous bias foreseen 15 years ago by

Russell L. Ackoff and Patrick Rivett when they wrote (*A Manager's Guide to Operations Research*, Wiley, 1963) that:

> . . . they (the OR people) should appreciate the primacy of the problem rather than of the technique. The task of OR is to develop techniques for existing problems. The task is not, repeat *not*, to search for problems to fit existing techniques.

In a much cited case, they give the example of the manager of a large office building whose tenants complained about having to wait too long for an elevator. The manager hired a firm of consulting engineers, who saw the problem as one of slow elevators and applied the appropriate techniques and produced a set of alternative solutions for speeding up the elevator service. But the manager, dissatisfied with the engineers' proposals because they were either too costly or failed to yield enough reduction in waiting time, mentioned the problem to a psychologist. The psychologist perceived the problem as one of boredom, not slow elevators, and suggested placing mirrors on the elevator banks to provide a diversion for those waiting. The complaints stopped.

This analyst tendency to find the "right" solution to the "wrong" problem usually results in the solution's not being implemented. Another common outcome is the manager's avoidance of such techniques in the future.

An obvious, though neglected, solution to this dilemma is for the manager and the technical analyst to spend sufficient time with each other examining and discussing the situation with mutual respect. The analyst must understand the decision-making process well enough to get what has been described as "an adequate solution to a major problem (rather) than an elegant solution to a trivial one." The analyst must recognize that it is the manager's responsibility to define the problem and that the manager's judgment in this area is probably superior to his own.

On the other hand, the manager should consider receptively the analyst's recommendations, recognizing that "objectivity" and technical skills are being provided in search of insights and alternatives. Familiarity with the proposed techniques will aid the manager to evaluate their applicability, advantages, and limitations. But most important, straightforward communication about the problem and about the manager's own preconceptions and judgments must be shared. With this managerial orientation and technical interface, we can avoid what E. S. Savas calls "the triumph of technique over purpose."

OPERATIONAL STAFF

Typically, the analyst has only limited involvement with operational staff, tending to isolate, rather than involve, himself as he goes about the business of problem solving. This not only occurs in the case of external consultants but is also frequently true where the organization's own employees are used for the analysis.

This is not only counter-productive, it is also contrary to one of the basic principles of OR/MS, that of systems orientation; that is, "the activity of any part of an organization has some effect on the activity of every other part. Therefore, in order to evaluate any decision or action in an organization, it is necessary to identify all the significant interactions and to evaluate their *combined* impact on the performance of the organization as a whole, not merely on the part originally involved." The analyst cannot do this working in isolation. As Ackoff and Rivett point out: "OR is *action* research, its objective is not to turn out reports but to improve operations. This cannot be done without becoming directly involved in the operations."

Another key reason for involving operational staff is that they invariably have information that is important to the analyst. But organizational communications channels often inhibit information flow to top-level management.

A dramatic, though not unusual, illustration of this problem is the case of a management analyst who was directed to design a new set of procedures for a municipal agency in order to comply with revised state regulations. The analyst did not interact with the agency's operational staff, except for a brief information-collecting interview at the beginning of the project. While the project was under way, the staff learned, through the interagency grapevine, that the state was shortly going to rescind the regulations. Because of what they perceived to be the analyst's indifference to their involvement, they did not pass this information on, but "filed it" until a formal meeting where the analyst presented a completed project to top management. The information, that forthcoming regulations would render the existing ones obsolete, sent the analyst back to the drawing boards with considerable frustration.

The positive experiences of management consultants in getting their recommendations implemented, even under highly charged political conditions, have some common characteristics. A problem-solving approach with active involvement of relevant staff from problem definition to implementation results in both "better" solutions and smoother implementation.

It has been widely noted that the product of quantitative analysis almost always results in a recommendation for change. Further, it is axiomatic in management that the more the people affected by a change are involved in planning that change, the greater the chances of successful implementation. Yet we often lose sight of this relationship.

ORGANIZATIONAL POLITICS

Analysts all too often ignore the dynamics of organizational relationships and do so to their disadvantage, as the following case illustrates:

A vice-president of a major banking corporation assembled a high-powered group of internal and external consultants, who were charged with making recommendations on a particular type of insurance that the bank had historically purchased from an outside insurance company. The group produced an impeccable report, using all the latest quantitative techniques. They proved that, without doubt, the bank would be better off writing its own insurance. What they did not know was that several influential members of the bank's board of directors were connected through family ties with the insurance company from which the bank was—and still is—buying their insurance. The report gathers dust.

Analysts typically perceive themselves "above" organizational politics—and rightfully so in terms of model development, construction, and quantification. Most analysts have neither the inclination nor the means to involve themselves in such "unrelated" political matters. When the analyst believes an "optimal" solution cannot be implemented because of reasons outside his domain, suboptimal alternative approaches that are increasingly feasible must be sought. That is, the objective of feasible implementation must outweigh the quest for unrealizable optimality. What's unfortunate about this "incremental suboptimality" approach is that information, whether it be defined within the political or managerial domain, never receives consideration by the analyst.

LIMITATIONS INHERENT IN THE TECHNIQUES

Recognition of the limitations inherent in quantitative techniques is a major reason why managers are reluctant to use them more extensively. One researcher sent his students out to find real-world situations where queueing theory could be applied. Invariably, there was one reason or another why the theory was inapplicable. Examination of the literature and reported empirical evidence leads him to question whether this relatively simple, straightforward technique, with its apparent face validity for a wide variety of applications, is of any significant utility in the "real" world.

Most quantitative techniques were initially designed for use at the operational level in production-oriented situations. Their use in these situations appears to have been successful, but their applicability at higher levels in the organization is suspect. Increasingly, attempts at applying these techniques within strategic planning and policymaking levels, and in service-oriented circumstances have resulted in confusion and conflict. In these situations, the most important variables very often defy quantification. In *The Effective Executive*, Peter Drucker described two dramatic examples:

> In the development of thalidomide, in Europe they relied on statistics. By the time the statistics showed substantial abnormalities, the damage had been done. In the United States, on the other hand, the damage was prevented because one physician noticed a qualitative change—a skin tingling caused by the drug. He followed his instincts, investigated it, and was able to alert public officials to the potential dangers. The Edsel was launched after a great deal of statistical analysis of all the quantitative data that could be obtained. Its much-publicized failure was due to the failure to consider the determining qualitative variable—change in consumer tastes and preferences.

In recognition of such limitations, researchers have sought derivative systems that combine both quantitative and qualitative factors. Though these approaches would seem to offer considerable promise, we could end up with Anthony Downs's "horse-and-rabbit stew" where:

> The tiny rabbit is minutely examined and exhaustively analyzed with sophisticated tech-

niques before it is placed in the stew—but then we go out and get any old random horse and throw him in. Thus it often seems that we are doing an exhaustive analysis of certain variables which are capable of being so analyzed, then making wild guesses about relatively incommensurable variables which are in fact more important in determining the outcome. We are making stew with a scientifically-prepared rabbit and a randomly chosen horse. The quality of such a stew is bound to be rather indeterminant.

Another approach to alleviating the limitations of the quantitative techniques is to evolve more complex techniques to deal with increasingly complex problems. But as we develop more complex techniques, we narrow the scope of application. We are building a sophisticated solution to a smaller and smaller problem. An obvious additional burden associated with this increased complexity is that we increase the likelihood the manager will not understand it!

The quantitative techniques have a further limitation, particularly serious at the strategic planning and policymaking level. They are basically incapable of generating totally new alternatives; they represent reactive rather than projective thinking and do not generate creative, innovative approaches. They stagnate and become almost introspective. With these deficiencies in mind, we should pursue alternatives, as Robert Graham suggests: We might look at opportunities instead of problems. We ought to develop techniques for providing an "opportunity solution" that would "pick the best opportunity from the set of all feasible opportunities."

One could also view the problem as inadequate management input. It is the manager's knowledge, or at least should be, that bridges the gap between the inner workings of the model and the world where it will be applied. Ultimately model outputs must be converted into real-world solutions.

PRESENTATION

Citing the manager's "failure to understand" simply begs the question. A greater part of the problem lies in model presentation and in communication of results. Simply put, quantitative techniques must be in language that a manager can understand.

Managers need more analysts with the attitude expressed by Robert Graham in *Interfaces* (August, 1976) where he realistically describes the crucial project objective:

> We wanted the results to be believed and used, not just gazed upon in bewilderment. The requirements, then, were a bit tricky. The model had to be powerful enough to reflect what might actually happen in the future and simple enough so that managers could understand exactly how the model operated.

On their part, the managers require sufficient knowledge to question model assumptions, understand the data and the principles of data manipulation, and to evaluate the outcomes. Managers and analysts making such mutual efforts could then narrow the "subculture gap" between them and reinforce the system in which they both operate. Communication, comprehension, and the implementation would, hopefully, follow easily.

THE BIGGEST NEED

What managers need most is a broadening of the role and horizons of the technical analyst. The analyst cannot remain organizationally isolated, operating out of unchanging models and paradigms, but must phase in the dynamic nature of short-term problem solving, long-term policy alternative assessment, and managerial judgment. But how to accomplish this?

One must start with role clarity: model structuring and quantification for the analyst and the input of judgment by the manager when quantification is not possible. Involvement in output or solution implementation is essential. This role dichotomy, with its related responsibilities, creates a mutually dependent, yet differentiated approach. Each party can still be secure in his own as well as each other's role perceptions. Managerial personnel will then become part of the process of model construction through their expressed judgmental inputs. Analysts will become increasingly aware of constraints upon management, as well as the qualitative limitations on whatever solutions they may propose.

Such cooperative efforts will then serve to enhance manager/analyst understanding and thus provide a more relevant basis for implementation. In effect, role redefinition and communication, rather than "forced" specialization, provides more useful alternatives and more probable implementation than previously achieved.

DISCUSSION QUESTIONS

1. In this article, the authors emphasized the importance of involvement with the operational staff. Where during the quantitative analysis approach should this involvement take place?

2. Why is it important to understand organizational politics and dynamics in implementing a quantitative analysis technique?

3. Why is problem definition such an important step as related to the implementation of quantitative analysis techniques?

4. What is one of the biggest needs for better implementation of quantitative analysis techniques?

5. Pick one of the cases or problems you have solved in quantitative analysis and describe in detail how you would go about implementing the results of your solution.

Fantasies, Fundamentals, and a Framework in Corporate O.R.

D. S. McArthur

21

I've been doing OR work in industry for over 25 years now. It's fun. But it can be frustrating. Frustrations come from an inability to see the reality around us. There is a gap between what we think and what management knows. Some fantasies of OR people (especially when they are just starting their careers) are listed below:

1. I have completed my education and am now ready to apply it.
2. OR work consists of applying mathematical techniques.
3. Management may not know a lot about OR but they know enough so that I will have a few problems to work on.
4. I'll listen to the manager's problem and proceed to solve it for him.
5. Managers behave rationally and their decisions are well thought out.
6. Managers in one area of the company know what goes on in the other areas.
7. I'll teach the manager what I'm doing so that we'll be able to talk in OR terms.
8. I'll set up models that will help solve the

Reprinted by permission of D. S. McArthur, "Fantasies, Fundamentals, and a Framework in Corporate O.R.," *Interfaces*, Vol. 10, No. 4, August, 1980, Copyright 1980 The Institute of Management Sciences.

problem; someone else will pull all the details together.

9. The greater the detail of my model, the more I can explain the situation I'm studying.
10. I don't need to know how much about computers; someone else will do the programming.
11. The key to a computer program is rapid, accurate calculations.
12. When I feed the data into the computer program, I'm near the end of the project.
13. Everyone will cooperate in carrying out such a study.
14. If someone answers my request for data, I can assume that he knows exactly what I meant and that the data is accurate.
15. OR people fit in like "one of the gang" in the company.

Not one of these statements is true. These myths make it difficult for decision scientists to communicate with decision makers. There's a gap between us. But the gap is not entirely a result of the fantasies of the OR man. Some fantasies are also held by management such as:

1. I know what my problem is.
2. I'll turn my problem over to OR to work on while I go to other things I must do.
3. OR analysts are mathematicians.
4. OR analysts are computer people.
5. The computer output of the model:
   a. must be right because it came from the computer, or
   b. shows something which is impossible, so go away with your model and quit bothering me.
6. All OR projects must show tangible savings.
7. OR can help me by forecasting the future for almost anything.
8. OR uses data accumulated by MIS.
9. OR just needs time to grind out the answers to my problem.
10. As soon as the model has its "inevitable"

computer program working, the job is done and OR can turn to another project.

11. How can someone with little experience in my area of responsibility help me?
12. It will take very little time before the OR analyst, fresh from school, will show results. On the other hand if I hire an accountant, salesman, management trainee, etc., I expect that it will take time for him to get his feet on the ground.

We OR people will not be effective in business until we have closed this gap between the decision scientists and the decision makers. A good way to start closing the gap is by measuring it. The width of the gap can be determined by observing the impact that decision-scientists are having on decision-makers.

MEASURING THE IMPACT OF DECISION SCIENCES ON DECISION MAKING

How can we tell how well we're doing? There are several measures; they come from answers to questions such as:

1. At what level in the organization does the OR/MS function report?
2. How much does management participate in OR/MS work?
3. What is the financial impact of the problems worked on? Do they have to do with developing two sigma limits on laboratory tests, or do they have to do with the future of the company?
4. Are our recommendations implemented?

Honest answers to these questions give a pretty good indication of the impact OR is having.

In your and my operations there are more direct ways of knowing how we are doing. The evidence is there:

Evidence of Failure

1. The boss tells you.
2. Budget problems appear.
3. Business managers avoid you.
4. You don't get invited to meetings.
5. People refer to you as "Doctor _____ ."
6. Top management haven't heard of you.
7. You have no work to do.
8. The department is cut in half in the next overhead reduction drive.

Evidence of Success

1. Budget problems go away.
2. Business managers want to talk to you.
3. You are invited to meetings.
4. You are referred to as "Joe."
5. You get help and cooperation on project work.
6. Project recommendations are implemented.
7. Managers write letters to your boss saying "That was a great job."
8. You get special bonuses.
9. Independent surveys show that your organization is looked upon as helpful, cooperative and as of great value to the company.
10. The president listens to what you have to say.
11. You're awfully busy.

Where the evidence comes out wrong, we need to think about closing the communications gap.

BECOMING ONE OF "THEM"

Professor Woolsey reported on problems that the decision scientist faces in applying science to "real life" decisions in business (*Interfaces*, November, 1974). He poses a problem that practitioners have, and gives his answer in his fresh, humorous, lucid style:

Problem: "When we try to get the data, we get lied to, or things fall on us."
Tactic: Becomes one of "them."

I believe that he has put his finger on the answer here. The way to implement Operations Research in business is to become one of "them."

The real problems are not mathematical, they are behavioral; they are problems in the relationship between the decision scientist and the decision maker. There is a tendency for us decision scientists to look down our noses at the "stupid" management when they won't use a beautiful tool such as our latest model. We have trouble understanding how they can overlook its "brilliance." Of course, on the other side of the fence, management tends to have little respect for us if we can't help them with real problems. And we have fallen flat on our faces too often, because of the communications gap between us.

HOW CAN THE GAP BE CLOSED

I have seven suggestions.

1. The way to apply decision science to management decisions is to *become management*. The successful practitioner must think like management, talk like management, and have the same concerns as management. He must look upon himself as "management" rather than as a "decision scientist."

Management wants the truth as much as we do. Although they don't understand the techniques we use, they do respect the truth. We "become" management in our mind's eye, i.e., we associate ourselves with the management's objectives and desires and become concerned about those things, rather than about developing a paper for the next professional meeting.

2. We must *"sell ourselves as sensible people."* As long as we perceive of ourselves as "scientists" rather than as "managers," we'll be thought of

as scientists. We won't be accepted as management until we think of ourselves as management. Becoming one of "them" will lead to mutual respect: the scientist begins to see the "real-life" problems which the manager is facing, and the manager begins to see the scientist as something more useful than an "oddball."

3. The decision scientist must develop a rapport with management which permits the free exchange of ideas at the eyeball-to-eyeball level. Without this kind of acceptance from management, we can't really be useful. We'll find ourselves doing Mickey Mouse projects instead of advising the president as to how he should change the organization.

4. We must *accept responsibility*. Where decision scientists are effective in business, they step into some strange roles. For example, we find that we serve as coordinators between line managements in different businesses.

A good many of our problems cross business lines, and even division lines. There is no one, short of the owner himself, with line responsibility over the whole problem. For example, our Texturing Yarn Business supplies textured yarns to the Knitted Outerwear Business. Knitted Outerwear is not only in a different business, but it's in a different division, reporting to a different president. Quality problems in the finished fabric may go back to the textured yarn. We must then step in and serve as "management" in solving the problem, where no line manager exists. The decision scientist must accept responsibility for how the job is done and for the results obtained.

5. The Management Scientist must be *hard-nosed*. He represents management in the scientific arena and can't afford to let wishy-washy decisions pass without interrogation. He must not be sloppy in his conclusions, nor permit others to be sloppy in theirs, where the decision is significant in terms of the company's profits. He may even have to be nasty. He must probe the decisions that are being made, suggest how they might be firmed up, within the time frame allowed, to increase the probability of success. In short, he must do precisely what the company top mangement would like him to do; help management increase the probability of correct decisions. It's not our duty to be nice for fear we'll lose some consulting business.

6. We may even *move into line management*. Of course, this is the most direct way to become management. In Milliken we have moved many people from the Corporate Operations Research Department into our businesses. Several of our "graduates" have been promoted to line management jobs. These men make use of the decision sciences technology in reaching decisions. For example, one of them makes effective use of the business planning model, a complex econometric model we have developed which simulates the operation of a business over the period of a year, in great detail. It shows the implications of decisions which might be made regarding the product lines selected and the market forecasts. It shows what profits will be generated and how much manufacturing capacity will be required. The OR graduates make excellent clients since they have a clear understanding of what we can do, and what we can't do.

7. Finally, to close the gap between the decision makers and the decision scientists we professionals must *become more effective in applying OR techniques* to business problems. We have developed, through experience, a set of seven operating rules which help us to be more effective. They are:

A) *Work* with *the business, not* for *it*

We find that we can be most useful by working *with* the business manager in solving problems. Occasionally a business manager will say, "Don, would you look into this problem," but upon inquiring, we discover that he doesn't have any time to work on it himself, and moreover none of his people do either! We interpret that to mean that it has a low priority. Since we typically have more to do than we can handle, these problems come last on the list. In other situations, the manager desperately needs an answer, he is already working hard on the problem and has two people working on it with him. We can be a lot more useful if we work *with* him on this kind of problem, than *for* him on some other problem.

B) *Work on the important problems*
There are more projects around than we can handle. The first look at each project must be to estimate its potential contribution to company profits. If its maximum potential is a savings of $1000 per year . . . don't do it; it will cost more than it's worth. If it might net $100,000 per year, do it! Each project should pay for itself within a year after the results are implemented.

It's sometimes difficult to estimate the potential dollar return on a project, but there are other ways of determining how important it is to the company. For example:

- *Who's asking for it?* Top management can estimate the potential value of a project involving intangibles (such as planning) better than the lower levels. If top management is asking for it, it's important!
- *How much effort is the business itself willing to put on it?* If the project is really important to the business, the manager will be willing to allocate manpower to it.

C) *Keep it short*
Projects that take more than three months get lost. The management changes, the problem disappears, or interest dies. We come in too late with too little. An approximate answer in three to six weeks is of more value than a more exact answer in a year. If it's a long project, divide it into phases. Make each phase a separate, clean-cut project that can be reported upon in three to six weeks.

D) *Get the job done*
Each project has a starting point; it should also have an end point. It's important that the

end be clearly indicated, either by a written report or an oral report to the management involved. The manager should know the purpose of the study, the results obtained, what we recommend doing about it, and how much it is worth to the business to do it.

E) *Present the results simply and positively*
Management is willing to accept us as technically competent. We don't have to "prove" that we have approached the study properly in each report. They don't have time (or interest) in knowing in detail what we did, or exactly what "ingenious" methods we used to solve the problem. They want to know our answer, and what we would recommend doing about it. We must present the results simply and make our recommendations clearly.

The results should be reported in a positive, not a negative vein. If further action is needed, the report should indicate what it is. Management isn't interested in what we couldn't do, or what didn't work. They want to know what did work, and what action we would recommend taking. Accentuate the positive.

F) *Help implement the results*
The manager, even after hearing and understanding the results of the study, may not know precisely what he should do to implement it. We must help him implement it.

G) *Work as individual consultants—but members of a team*
We have found it most effective to work as individual consultants, each with a group of businesses as our particular clients. This enables us to establish a good working rapport with the managers. It leads to more involvement in the studies. It enables us to work *with* the business, rather than *for* it. Splitting our areas of responsibility by type of specialization (statistical design of experiments, linear programming, simulation, etc.) doesn't work. We must sell ourselves as people, not specialists.

On the other hand, we also work as a team. Where one of us has more know-how in an area than the others, we seek help from him. We help each other. This increases our effectiveness as a group over operating solely as individuals.

We have found that these seven operating rules help us serve our company more effectively. We have a good "image" in management circles. We have become one of "them."

DISCUSSION QUESTIONS

1. What are some of the misconceptions that managers typically have?

2. What are some of the misconceptions that quantitative analysis people have?

3. How do you know when a particular quantitative analysis technique fails?

4. How do you know when a quantitative analysis technique has been successful?

5. How can you be more effective in applying quantitative analysis techniques to business problems?

6. Locate and conduct an interview with a business manager who has attempted to apply quantitative analysis techniques. During the interview find out some of the problems that were encountered during implementation and then write a report that discusses these problems and how you think they can be solved.

APPENDIX

Tables

The Standardized Normal Distribution Function

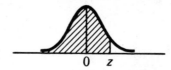

Area: Under the Normal Curve

Z	.00	.01	.02	.03	.04	.05	.06	.07	.08	.09
0.0	.50000	.50399	.50798	.51197	.51595	.51994	.52392	.52790	.53188	.53586
0.1	.53983	.54380	.54776	.55172	.55567	.55962	.56356	.56749	.57142	.57535
0.2	.57926	.58317	.58706	.59095	.59483	.59871	.60257	.60642	.61026	.61409
0.3	.61791	.62172	.62552	.62930	.63307	.63683	.64058	.64431	.64803	.65173
0.4	.65542	.65910	.66276	.66640	.67003	.67364	.67724	.68082	.68439	.68793
0.5	.69146	.69497	.69847	.70194	.70540	.70884	.71226	.71566	.71904	.72240
0.6	.72575	.72907	.73237	.73536	.73891	.74215	.74537	.74857	.75175	.75490
0.7	.75804	.76115	.76424	.76730	.77035	.77337	.77637	.77935	.78230	.78524
0.8	.78814	.79103	.79389	.79673	.79955	.80234	.80511	.80785	.81057	.81327
0.9	.81594	.81859	.82121	.82381	.82639	.82894	.83147	.83398	.83646	.83891
1.0	.84134	.84375	.84614	.84849	.85083	.85314	.85543	.85769	.85993	.86214
1.1	.86433	.86650	.86864	.87076	.87286	.87493	.87698	.87900	.88100	.88298
1.2	.88493	.88686	.88877	.89065	.89251	.89435	.89617	.89796	.89973	.90147
1.3	.90320	.90490	.90658	.90824	.90988	.91149	.91309	.91466	.91621	.91774
1.4	.91924	.92073	.92220	.92364	.92507	.92647	.92785	.92922	.93056	.93189
1.5	.93319	.93448	.93574	.93699	.93822	.93943	.94062	.94179	.94295	.94408
1.6	.94520	.94630	.94738	.94845	.94950	.95053	.95154	.95254	.95352	.95449
1.7	.95543	.95637	.95728	.95818	.95907	.95994	.96080	.96164	.96246	.96327
1.8	.96407	.96485	.96562	.96638	.96712	.96784	.96856	.96926	.96995	.97062
1.9	.97128	.97193	.97257	.97320	.97381	.97441	.97500	.97558	.97615	.97670
2.0	.97725	.97784	.97831	.97882	.97932	.97982	.98030	.98077	.98124	.98169
2.1	.98214	.98257	.98300	.98341	.98382	.98422	.98461	.98500	.98537	.98574
2.2	.98610	.98645	.98679	.98713	.98745	.98778	.98809	.98840	.98870	.98899
2.3	.98928	.98956	.98983	.99010	.99036	.99061	.99086	.99111	.99134	.99158
2.4	.99180	.99202	.99224	.99245	.99266	.99286	.99305	.99324	.99343	.99361
2.5	.99379	.99396	.99413	.99430	.99446	.99461	.99477	.99492	.99506	.99520
2.6	.99534	.99547	.99560	.99573	.99585	.99598	.99609	.99621	.99632	.99643
2.7	.99653	.99664	.99674	.99683	.99693	.99702	.99711	.99720	.99728	.99736
2.8	.99744	.99752	.99760	.99767	.99774	.99781	.99788	.99795	.99801	.99807
2.9	.99813	.99819	.99825	.99831	.99836	.99841	.99846	.99851	.99856	.99861
3.0	.99865	.99869	.99874	.99878	.99882	.99886	.99899	.99893	.99896	.99900
3.1	.99903	.99906	.99910	.99913	.99916	.99918	.99921	.99924	.99926	.99929
3.2	.99931	.99934	.99936	.99938	.99940	.99942	.99944	.99946	.99948	.99950
3.3	.99952	.99953	.99955	.99957	.99958	.99960	.99961	.99962	.99964	.99965
3.4	.99966	.99968	.99969	.99970	.99971	.99972	.99973	.99974	.99975	.99976
3.5	.99977	.99978	.99978	.99979	.99980	.99981	.99981	.99982	.99983	.99983
3.6	.99984	.99985	.99985	.99986	.99986	.99987	.99987	.99988	.99988	.99989
3.7	.99989	.99990	.99990	.99990	.99991	.99991	.99992	.99992	.99992	.99992
3.8	.99993	.99993	.99993	.99994	.99994	.99994	.99994	.99995	.99995	.99995
3.9	.99995	.99995	.99996	.99996	.99996	.99906	.99996	.99996	.99997	.99997

From *Quantitative Approaches to Management*, Fourth Edition, by Richard I. Levin and Charles A. Kirkpatrick. Copyright © 1978, 1975, 1971, 1965 by McGraw-Hill, Inc. Used with permission of McGraw-Hill Book Company.

Table of Random Numbers

52	06	50	88	53	30	10	47	99	37	66	91	35	32	00	84	57	07
37	63	28	02	74	35	24	03	29	60	74	85	90	73	59	55	17	60
82	57	68	28	05	94	03	11	27	79	90	87	92	41	09	25	36	77
69	02	36	49	71	99	32	10	75	21	95	90	94	38	97	71	72	49
98	94	90	36	06	78	23	67	89	85	29	21	25	73	69	34	85	76
96	52	62	87	49	56	59	23	78	71	72	90	57	01	98	57	31	95
33	69	27	21	11	60	95	89	68	48	17	89	34	09	93	50	44	51
50	33	50	95	13	44	34	62	64	39	55	29	30	64	49	44	30	16
88	32	18	50	62	57	34	56	62	31	15	40	90	34	51	95	26	14
90	30	36	24	69	82	51	74	30	35	36	85	01	55	92	64	09	85
50	48	61	18	85	23	08	54	17	12	80	69	24	84	92	16	49	59
27	88	21	62	69	64	48	31	12	73	02	68	00	16	16	46	13	85
45	14	46	32	13	49	66	62	74	41	86	98	92	98	84	54	33	40
81	02	01	78	82	74	97	37	45	31	94	99	42	49	27	64	89	42
66	83	14	74	27	76	03	33	11	97	59	81	72	00	64	61	13	52
74	05	81	82	93	09	96	33	52	78	13	06	28	30	94	23	37	39
30	34	87	01	74	11	46	82	59	94	25	34	32	23	17	01	58	73
59	55	72	33	62	13	74	68	22	44	42	09	32	46	71	79	45	89
67	09	80	98	99	25	77	50	03	32	36	63	65	75	94	19	95	88
60	77	46	63	71	69	44	22	03	85	14	48	69	13	30	50	33	24
60	08	19	29	36	72	30	27	50	64	85	72	75	29	87	05	75	01
80	45	86	99	02	34	87	08	86	84	49	76	24	08	01	86	29	11
53	84	49	63	26	65	72	84	85	63	26	02	75	26	92	62	40	67
69	84	12	94	51	36	17	02	15	29	16	52	56	43	26	22	08	62
37	77	13	10	02	18	31	19	32	85	31	94	81	43	31	58	33	51

Excerpted from page 7, *A Million Random Digits with 1,000,000 Normal Deviates,* The Free Press, 1955, with permission of the Rand Corporation.